Piaget and conceptual development

To Peter, Susan and Nicholas

Piaget and conceptual development

with

A cross-cultural study of
number and quantity

D. M. G. Hyde

Visiting Professor,
The American University, Cairo

formerly head of Education Department,
Southlands College of Education, Surrey

Holt, Rinehart and Winston
London * New York * Sydney * Toronto

Acknowledgments

In trying to make a selection of literature relevant to the aims of this book, I have been faced with the same problem experienced by the students whom it is meant to serve: that of the ever-increasing volume of literature by and about Piaget. My indebtedness extends therefore to authors and researchers in many parts of the world. I am particularly grateful to the following authors and editors whose recent publications not only helped me to clarify my thinking with reference to this book, but whose excellent bibliographies led me to many journal references which I might have overlooked. My thanks are combined with a recommendation to students to consult these texts for further study.

Baldwin, A. L. (1967). *Theories of Child Development.* New York: Wiley.

Bruner, J. S., R. R. Olver and P. M. Greenfield, Eds. (1966). *Studies in Cognitive Growth.* New York: Wiley.

Butcher, H. J., Ed. (1968). *Educational Research in Britain.* London: University of London Press. (Particularly the contribution by E. A. Lunzer.)

Flavell, J. H. (1963). *The Developmental Psychology of Jean Piaget.* New York: Van Nostrand.

Maier, H. W. (1966). *Three Theories of Child Development.* New York: Harper and Row.

Sigel, I. E., and F. H. Hooper (1968). *Logical Thinking in Children.* New York: Holt, Rinehart and Winston.

Vernon, P. E. (1969). *Intelligence and Cultural Environment.* London: Methuen.

Wallace, J. G. (1965). *Concept Growth and the Education of the Child.* Slough, Bucks.: National Foundation for Educational Research.

Among the researchers overseas who have been kind enough to correspond about current research and send copies of their investigation reports, I should like especially to thank M. de Lemos of the Australian National University, Jean-Claude Lasry of Montreal University, E. Hendriks of the University of Southern Rhodesia, Gottfried Kleinsmidt, Researcher of Teachers Training College, Karlsruhe-Bergwald, West Germany, Millie Almy, Teachers College, Columbia University, New York, P. R. de Lacey, The University of New England, Australia, and Pierre R. Dasen of the Australian National University whose energy and enthusiasm has enabled researchers in cognitive development along Piaget lines to receive abstracts of each other's investigations. I am also most grateful to Jacqueline J. Goodnow who sent me a copy of her essay on 'Problems in research on culture and thought' taken from *Studies in Cognitive Development* (1969) edited by Elkind and Flavell, Oxford University Press.

My investigation in Aden, South Arabia, (now The Republic of South Yemen) was carried out as part of the requirements for a Ph.D. degree of London University. My thanks are therefore also due to friends in Aden, including Heads of schools, Arab Education Officers, parents and children who made it possible for the research to be carried out, and to the Directors of Education for the use of school buildings. I am particularly indebted to Sayyid Zain Hazmi for his help with Arabic. While in Aden, out of reach of university libraries and bookshops, I appreciated very much the kindness of correspondents in England, particularly the late Nathan Isaacs, who lent manuscripts and kept me informed about current research on Piaget's theories, and K. Lovell of Leeds who invited me to meet other researchers when on leave. I must also express my thanks and gratitude to members of the Department of Psychology, University College London: to my supervisor, A. R. Jonckheere, who also drew my attention when an undergraduate to Piaget's work, to Professor Roger W. Russell, J. Whitfield, Gertrude Keir, Charlotte Banks, Ken Miller and others for help and encouragement.

During the last ten years many researchers have written to me about my unpublished thesis, the result, I think of the interest of K. Lovell who drew attention to it in his lectures and writings. From his comments and many others in the literature I realize that I missed many significant interpretations of my own data, which have since been followed up by other investigators who have concentrated on fewer tests or special aspects. I thank them for keeping alive my interest during a period when the responsibilities of heavy jobs have made writing and further research a joy to be postponed. I hope that they and others, especially in Australia and the Philippines, who requested publication will still find some interest in having access to the full data.

Finally, and most important, my thanks are due to Piaget himself, whose original studies provide endless fascinating material for research investigation, and to Inhelder, whose account of her tests on children's concepts of the conservation of substance, weight and volume described in *Le Diagnostic du Raisonnement chez les Débiles mentaux* (1943) were a revelation of research possibilities in the field of child development. In a personal communication Piaget wrote in 1955: 'Je suis extrêmement intéressé par votre projet de reprendre sur les enfants des differents milieux d'Aden les recherches concernant le nombre. C'est un travail extrêmement utile et qui sera fructueux à tous points de vue. Vous avez particulièrement bien fait de choisir les épreuves sur le nombre, car c'est dans ce domaine qu'on peut espérer trouver les résultats les plus généraux indépendamment du milieu social.' No greater encouragement could a lone investigator hope to have!

I should also like to acknowledge my further debt to K. Lovell, who read the manuscript very thoroughly and made several useful suggestions, and to the editors of Messrs Holt, Rinehart and Winston Ltd., who have given me valuable help in the last stages of preparing the manuscript and have solved many of the problems arising from my residence abroad. My former secretary, Mrs Ward, must not be forgotten, for, without her assistance, the manuscript would not have reached the publishers by the appointed date.

Thanks are also due to J. S. Bruner and to John Wiley and Sons Inc. for permission to reproduce figures 3 and 4 from Bruner, J. S., R. R. Olver and P. M. Greenfield, Eds. (1966). *Studies in Cognitive Growth*, and to the University of London Press for permission to quote from Piaget, J. (1969). *Six Psychological Studies*, which was originally published in the French by Denoël Gonthier © 1964.

Contents

List of tables

In the Aden investigation, tests were given in the order of the original experiments described in Piaget's work, The Child's Conception of Number (1952). *In this book, there has been a regrouping in two cases to facilitate comparison between tests which are related. The Parallel Glass Test appears in chapter 7 with the Water Tests, and the Bath, Towel and Doll Test appears in chapter 10 with the Bath and Doll Test. Tables have therefore been renumbered to correspond with their position in the text; tests, however, are still numbered in the order in which they were originally given. This makes possible the use of table A9, pages 220–221 and indicates Piaget's own scheme.*

Part I
Conceptual Development—
Piaget in context

CHAPTER ONE

Introduction and aims

Jean Piaget has been described as a zoologist by training and an epistemologist by vocation. It could be added that he is a psychologist by accident, since it was not interest in behaviour that inspired his many studies, but discontent with the speculative treatment by philosophers of the problems of knowledge. He hoped that it would be possible to devise a 'genetic' theory of knowledge by studying it as a function of its growth and development in the child. What was initiated as an adjunct to a philosophical study became a life's work.

At first, concentrating on the problem of logic in the child, Piaget tried by the direct method of question and answer to discover in what ways a child's reasoning differs from that of an adult. The results of those early studies were embodied in his books *The Language and Thought of the Child* (1952a) and *Judgment and Reasoning in the Child* (1951). Pursuing his original aim, he then studied the child's concepts of the world and causality. By 1932 he had extended his interest from basic scientific concepts to moral judgments, and was investigating, for example, the conditions under which small boys cheated when playing marbles.

By this time, Piaget felt ready to formulate a theory of child development. His book *The Origin of Intelligence in the Child* (1953) traced the sensori-motor development of the child in early infancy, on which his theories of the growth of reasoning are founded. Meanwhile, many psychologists, such as Hazlitt (1930) and Isaacs (1930), had criticized not only Piaget's identification of thought with language in the child, but also his reliance on verbal techniques in studying concept formation. He discovered gradually that it was necessary for him to study actions themselves in order to follow the reasons which prompted them. His work on the concept of number, the techniques of which are discussed in a later chapter, marks an important stage in his method. Setting up objects with which the child could make experiments, he systematically studied the child's reasoning in arriving at his solutions. In his later work on concept formation, which deals with mathematical and physical concepts, such as time, speed, space, volume, he continues to follow behavioural techniques rather than relying on verbal methods.

During recent years Piaget, Inhelder and co-workers have engaged in studies and writings designed to supplement or clarify their earlier work. The range and extent of the Genevan activities can be gauged by a perusal of Flavell's bibliography (1963). One is reminded of the existence of a large body of Genevan literature on the development and characteristics of perception which is available only in the French language. Most well known in this country are studies of optical illusions. Most interesting is the fact that, in his studies of perception, Piaget uses the rigorous procedures and statistical analyses the lack of which have formed the main criticism of his investigations of concept formation. It is obvious that the choice of a 'clinical' approach to the study of children's thinking (described later in the book) is quite deliberate. He has, however, set in motion large-scale replications of his earlier studies, which meet the criticism that he generalized from results on small numbers of children. More recently his growing conviction of the importance of comparative studies for the purpose of separating the effects of biological factors from social and cultural influences on development has been expressed not only in his important article on the subject (1966) but in his interest in social and cross-cultural studies by Goodnow (1962), Almy et al. (1966), Mohseni (1966), Price-Williams (1961) and others.

However, in spite of his life-long work with children and his widely acknowledged contributions to psychology, Piaget's orientation is philosophical rather than psychological. Elkind (in Piaget, 1969) has taken the view that 'it would be hard to overemphasize the importance of regarding Piaget as a genetic epistemologist rather than as a psychologist.' His work to establish a Centre of Genetic Epistemology in Geneva confirms Elkind's view. He fits the results of his experimental work into a developmental scheme which, on the one hand, relates to biological growth and on the other accords with his own particular system of logic. He has been widely criticized on both counts. Discussions on his theories of developmental stages will be found throughout this book. Evidence not only of the existence of his 'stages' but of factors which challenge his theories as a whole continue to be made. While psychologists produce glossaries to help students to understand his difficult terminology and philosophers quarrel with their logical content, educators see Piaget as a worthy successor to great shapers of educational thought such as Montessori and Froebel. Even if what Bunt (1950) calls his psycho-logic system were discredited and his biological theory of development found to be untenable, his contribution to child psychology and his influence on education would be outstanding. He has succeeded in externalizing the processes of concept formation in a manner unknown to his predecessors in the same field. While Hull (1920), Kuo (1923), Heidbreder (1946–1949) and others had studied the processes of concept attainment in subjects already capable of adult reasoning, Piaget was the first to analyse the formation itself of the basic concepts which become the frames of reference for all future adult thinking.

Much of the impetus for experiment in cognitive function and growth and for a new approach to educational method and content has been generated by Piaget, Inhelder and the Genevan school over a period of more than forty years. So great has been the output that the task of verifying, modifying and extending Piaget's ideas has resulted in a proliferation of studies all over the world. Objective and comprehensive appraisals of the practical results of his tests in relation to his basic theories of development have been attempted by Flavell (1963), Bruner et al (1966) and others. His multi-disciplinary approach makes the task of evaluation formidable even for the experts. So fascinating are his individual studies of concept formation that it is easy for even the experienced investigator to lose sight of Piaget's central theme of invariable sequence in mental development. How much more difficult is it then for the student of psychology or education and the busy teacher, conscious of the importance of relating theory to practice, to select wisely from the wealth of literature and to see the significance of what he reads. In general, one can say that the problem of selection is a growing one for lecturers, students and teachers alike.

It is hoped that this book will help to meet the needs of undergraduate students of education and the social sciences who are not yet ready for the weighty anthologies of research and explanatory texts published in recent years. Its contents fall into two sections. In the first chapters an attempt is made to help the student to see Piaget's work on child development and concept formation in perspective, so brief accounts of other work in these areas are included. It is not a digest: Piaget's work (Piaget, 1952b) on the development of the concepts of number and quantity is used as an example of the application of his theories of development to an important field of knowledge. The aim is to encourage students to read Piaget for themselves and to consult at least some of the authorities mentioned in the text and bibliographies. It is also hoped that teachers, some of whom are bewildered by the ever-changing fashions of mathematical teaching in the primary school, will be helped to understand some of the broad principles behind those changes.

The rest of the book concerns the author's Aden investigation, produced in its original form but with expanded discussions, covering some of the main investigations since 1959. During the last ten years, research in education and allied fields, once the prerogative of the post-graduate student, has, through the influence of such bodies as the National Foundation for Educational Research in England and in Australia, the Scottish Research Council and the Schools Council, become of vital interest to the primary school teacher trying to adapt to yet another 'new mathematics' scheme or 'creative' method of teaching. The Piaget-type tests in this book have been presented in a way that it is hoped will not only encourage students and teachers to try out experiments for themselves but give them some training in a simple experimental procedure.

Post-graduate correspondents and research workers who up till now have requested microfilms through university libraries will now have easier access to the data.

References

Almy, Millie, E. Chittenden and P. Miller. (1966). *Young Children's Thinking: Studies of some Aspects of Piaget's Theory*. New York: Teachers College Press, Columbia University.

Bruner, J. S., R. R. Olver and P. M. Greenfield, Eds. (1966). *Studies in Cognitive Growth*. New York: Wiley.

Bunt, L. N. H. (1950). *The Development of the Ideas of Number and Quantity According to Piaget*. Groningen: Djakarta.

Flavell, J. H. (1963). *The Developmental Psychology of Jean Piaget*. New York: Van Nostrand.

Goodnow, J. J. (1962). A test for milieu effects with some of Piaget's tests. *Psychol. Monogr.*, **76**, Whole No. 555.

Hazlitt, V. (1930). Children's thinking. *Br. J. Psychol.*, **20**, 354–361.

Heidbreder, E. The attainment of concepts. A series of articles in: *J. gen. Psychol.*, **35**, 173–223 (1946); *J. Psychol.*, **24**, 93–138 (1947); **25**, 299–329 (1948); **26**, 45–69, 193–216 (1948); **27**, 3–39, 263–309 (1949).

Hull, C. L. (1920). Quantitative aspects of the evolution of concepts. *Psychol. Monogr.*, **28**, Whole No. 123.

Isaacs, Susan. (1930). *Intellectual Growth in Young Children*. London: Routledge and Kegan Paul.

Kuo, Z. Y. (1923). *J. exp. Psychol.*, **6**, 247–293.

Mohseni, N. (1966). La comparaison des réactions aux épreuves d'intelligence en Iran et en Europe. Thèse d'université: University of Paris.

Piaget, J. (1951). *Judgment and Reasoning in the Child*. London: Routledge and Kegan Paul.

Piaget, J. (1952a). *The Language and Thought of the Child*. London: Routledge and Kegan Paul.

Piaget, J. (1952b). *The Child's Conception of Number*. London: Routledge and Kegan Paul.

Piaget, J. (1953). *The Origin of Intelligence in the Child*. London: Routledge and Kegan Paul.

Piaget, J. (1969). *Six Psychological Studies*. (Ed. David Elkind). London: University of London Press.

Piaget, J., and B. Inhelder. (1941). *Le Développement des Quantités chez l'Enfant*. Neuchâtel: Delachaux et Niestlé.

Price-Williams, D. R. A. (1961). A study concerning concepts of quantities among primitive children. *Acta Psychol.*, **18**, 293–305. (Reprinted in Price-Williams, 1969.)

CHAPTER TWO

Piaget's theories in relation to other theories of development

Introduction

Theories lacking in scientific rigour about the behaviour and development of children are largely socially determined and very closely linked with child-rearing practices. They are much influenced by what society regards as the ideal end-product of child development, that is, a man or woman who conforms to social norms. The child has not always, as in Western society today, been regarded as a person in his own right. Traditionally in many societies he has been viewed as man in miniature, whose successful development as a worthy member of his group depends on how effectively he can be conditioned to adult standards, that is, 'knocked into shape'. This attitude has resulted historically in the harsh punishment of children for not thinking and behaving like adults, a practice which has lingered in some of our schools. In some societies, including our own, this attitude towards children has resulted from or been reinforced by religious beliefs. The doctrine of original sin, necessitating beating out and cleansing processes, has been responsible for much childhood misery. The banning of the child from adult company in Victorian society, where, at best, he was expected to be seen and not heard, implied that his immaturity was a condition of shame. He had nothing of value to contribute to social discourse, his role being to observe and emulate the behaviour of his elders and, above all, to show instant obedience.

 In contrast to what I have somewhat crudely termed the 'original sin' attitude towards children is the view expressed by the philosopher Rousseau and the poets, notably Blake and Wordsworth, that the babe is born innocent, but becomes corrupted through his contact with adult society. Divorced from the pure influences of 'nature', his growth to manhood will be marked by progressive moral deterioration. In Britain such thinking accorded with the humanitarian spirit which inspired efforts to protect children from some of the worst evils of the Industrial Revolution. Exploitation of adult labour led inevitably to the exploitation of child labour. Industrial slavery among adults could lead to riots and the eventual formation of trade unions, but for the helpless children, shouldering adult burdens at a tender age and deprived of all the basic requirements for healthy physical, mental, moral and emotional development, the only hope was their eventual removal from the factory to the school environment. While writers such as Charles Dickens drew attention to the corruptive influences of an industrial society, pioneers of education for the masses saw the acquisition of knowledge as the answer to all social and individual problems. These two factors, environment and education, play an important part in all discussions of child development.

Somewhere between the miniature man, born in sin, and nature's innocent child exist Tommy and Jane who both delight and sadden their parents, infuriate and inspire their teachers and provide, by their norms of behaviour and their individual differences, unlimited material for scientific study.

Methods of studying children

Long before developmental psychology became a science the exploits of animal pets and children were the subject of anecdotes by their admiring owners or parents. Even psychologists are subject to the human weakness of relating details of their children's behaviour especially if it highlights their intelligence or superiority over other children. However, they have the advantage of being trained observers and the supreme convenience of access to their subjects without let or hindrance, day and night. Much valuable information about child development has been gained by the systematic study of their children by psychologists such as Watson (1930), Valentine (1946, 1956) and Piaget. The father and mother psychologists do not confine their studies to observation: they can manipulate the environment, for example, subjecting their infants to conditioning experiments, rearing them with chimpanzees or attaching them to a variety of machines to record their responses.

Observation of children has not been confined to children in the home. Susan Isaacs, a very keen and perceptive observer, studied a group in the school situation at Malting House and embodied her findings in her volumes (1930) on the social, emotional and intellectual development of children. Her sample was small, but her insight makes her books still acceptable reading for students of child development. Piaget's sample was also small when he observed the language behaviour of children in a Genevan kindergarten, but, unlike Isaacs, he was concentrating on only one aspect of behaviour which could be incorporated into his overall theories of child development. Other developmental studies have used various techniques to determine to what extent the development of behaviour can be said to follow a set of laws. Those which have most relevance to Piaget's theories or techniques can be grouped as follows:

Normative studies

Studies in the fields of comparative and child psychology have been carried out to trace the course of development from prenatal stages to maturity. They aim at achieving a behavioural framework corresponding to physical maturation. The most relevant to Piaget's work are the studies of infants and young children. The term 'maturation' which, in the strictest sense, can only apply to the growth of physical structures, was extended by Gesell and his co-workers (1946) at the Yale University Clinic to describe behaviour itself. His extensive surveys of the motor and sensory development of the infant were made under controlled conditions using a one-way screen. His work has been supplemented by that of others including Bühler (1930), Goodenough and Maurer (1942), Shirley (1951) and McGraw (1951).

Investigations have included both the cross-sectional and the longitudinal type. In the former, large numbers of children of the same chronological age are examined to ascertain the norm or average performance for that age, while, in the latter, individual children are observed and tested over long periods of time. From the cross-sectional type of study came the concept of 'mental age' used by Binet (see Terman and Merrill, 1937) and other compilers of standardized intelligence tests. (It was then extended by the educational psychologists for classifying performance in attainment tests of reading and arithmetic.) The longitudinal studies are more ambitious, aiming not merely at establishing norms for isolated sections of behaviour, but at tracing the total pattern, in which particular facets can be studied in perspective. Piaget's investigations, until recently, have been of the cross-sectional type, since he has applied tests to children in different chronological age groups and generalized on the results, without, incidentally, applying the usual standardization techniques. Yet he is not primarily interested in how many children, at a given age, can pass his tests, but in how any particular child arrives at his answers. It seems that the importance of longitudinal studies for Piaget's theories cannot be overemphasized. Scientists in other disciplines have stressed the dependence of behavioural maturation on other factors besides structural development. If, as a result of longitudinal studies, Piaget finds that, for most children, his sequential pattern of mental development is lawful, not only will his 'stages' be confirmed, but deviations can form the basis of studies of environmental aspects of development, to which he is currently paying more attention.

Besides sequence, normative studies have produced evidence of something akin to the turning points in Piaget's 'stages' of development. From the comparative psychologists comes a growing body of evidence of the existence of critical periods of development during which the organism is ripe for certain types of behaviour, such as pecking of chicks, swimming of tadpoles, mice catching by cats, etc. Techniques include restrictive measures to prove that the activity is the result of maturation rather than learning. Classical experiments include those of Spalding (1890) with chicks, Yerks and Bloomfield with kittens and Carmichael (1926, 1927, 1928) with frogs and salamanders. In each case the experimental group was prevented from exercising a function until it appeared in the control group, and in each case the performance of the two groups approximated. It is obviously difficult to use such techniques with human babies, but cross-cultural studies of infant-rearing practices have confirmed the results. Dennis (1935, 1938), for instance, found that the cradle-binding of infants by Hopi and Navarre Indians did not produce in them a fundamentally different development from that of American babies who enjoy much more freedom. These studies relate to physical maturation, but the principle of critical periods of development has been extended by Bowlby (1953), who maintains that the relationship formed between a child and his mother or mother-substitute during his first two years of life not only shapes all his future emotional relationships, but, if undeveloped through separation or deprivation, cannot be formed at a later period. Bowlby's original work comparing the institutional child with the child in the normal home situation lacked many important details which he and others have since investigated. It appears that from the first seven months it is most important that one person returns again and again to the baby. After this period he is emotionally tied to those who take care of him and is very vulnerable to separation up to about the age of three and a half years. Skard in Oslo (1968, personal communication) has investigated the implications for children of working mothers. The problem is complicated since an evaluation cannot be made simply from the needs of the child, other considerations being the type of arrangement made in the absence of the mother, the age of the child and how the husband and family feel about the wife working. Many investigations comparing children of working with those of non-working mothers have shown little difference. Skard concludes that for some women it is best to go out to work and for others to stay at home, as long as there is a permanent arrangement; that children develop best if the mother is happy, whether at work or not, and that the most important factor is the developmental stage of the child and the provision for his changing needs from one age to another.

Skard's studies are complemented by those reported by Yarrow (1961) who found that the character of the mother–child relationship preceding separation affected the subsequent reaction of the child, a reaction modified by the adequacy of the substitute mothering after separation. He quotes Spitz and Wolf (1946) who found that infants separated from 'poor mothers' did not develop severe depressive reactions and concluded that 'the better the mother–child relationship preceding separation, the more severe the immediate reactions'. They also concluded that infants provided with a satisfactory substitute mother did not develop the depressive syndrome. Bowlby confirmed this himself (Robertson and Bowlby, 1952). No satisfactory conclusions have yet been reached on the long-term effects of separation and the question of irreversible damage. Yarrow suggests that more research is needed to identify the specific conditions under which irreversible damage occurs to the nervous system, and those which might make possible the reversal of intellectual or personality damage.

The overall conclusion at present is that maturity does not imply perfection of the activity in question, but a readiness to respond if the conditions allow, the activity not being so much a sudden emergence as a fruition of organic development supported by environmental opportunity. Piaget's description of the genesis of his 'stages' of growth is described in detail later in this chapter and is consistent with the above conclusion. He thinks of mental structures developing until a point is reached at which a new type of reasoning emerges, a type that marks a distinct stage in mental growth, consolidating what has gone before and at the same time forming the basis of future development.

There is no satisfactory evidence that recovery is impossible in the case of mental retardation due to lack of suitable environmental stimulation at a critical period. In fact, studies by Vernon (1965) relating to the increase in IQ after the appropriate treatment of backward children suggests the contrary. In several investigations concerning the effects of coaching and practice on intelligence tests for grammar school selection, he found that a single previous practice test raised the average IQ by about five points, and that further practice showed diminishing returns but reached a total of about ten points. After about five tests there was no further improvement, IQ's fluctuated and began to decline. When practice was combined with coaching the average maximum rise was 12–15 points. None of the subjects had ever seen a group of intelligence tests before; had they been familiar with the tests, Vernon believed that the effects might have been only half as great. All the present schemes for compensatory education for deprived children express confidence in the effects of environmental change even at the adolescent stage. In the Aden investigation, there is evidence for thinking that Piaget's tests, even the simplest of them (and, by inference, his 'stages' at any given period of a child's life), depend much more on environmental factors than is immediately obvious. Unfortunately political circumstances have not favoured a retest which might have thrown light on this subject.

Experimental manipulation of environment

Besides studying norms of development, investigators have been interested in the source of deviations. For obvious reasons the factor of heredity cannot be manipulated in human as in animal subjects, but the environmental factor has been studied from many angles. From the point of view of Piaget's investigations, the most relevant are concerned with the effects of practice on performance. Main techniques include the following:

Restrictive practices of the type already mentioned. Dennis (1935, 1938) for example, studied motor retardation of twin girls subjected to a minimum of social and motor stimulation during their first fourteen months. This treatment did not, in his opinion, affect their behavioural development.

Co-twin control. This method, introduced by Gesell and Ilg (1946) and Thomson (1958), has been used mainly in connection with motor development. In one study, one of identical twins was given a daily practice in stair-climbing and cube-building for six weeks, after which her twin was given similar training for two weeks. The results have been interpreted both as a support for maturational theories and as evidence of the effect of practice on skill. In another study, McGraw (1951) tried to determine at what age children would begin to show improvement, from practice influences, in motor performance. Between the ages of 21 days and 22 months, one twin was kept in his cot, while the other was being exercised in a group of activities. Records of development were kept for comparison between the twins themselves and a control group of children. The results showed that basic activities were less affected by practice than those important for survival.

(The above studies are concerned with motor development but are included as important examples of experimental techniques used in developmental studies.)

EFFECTS OF PRACTICE AND COACHING ON TEST PERFORMANCE

Numerous studies have been made to ascertain how far skill is related to practice, the main variables being length of practice and methods employed. The following are typical:

Hilgard (1932) trained a group of children for 12 weeks to use buttons, cut with scissors and climb a ladder. Subsequently, a further group, trained for one week, reached the same standard in these activities, a result that was attributed to maturational factors. Many critics of the investigation have pointed out that practice on related skills might be equally responsible for the results.

Gates and Taylor (1925) tested memory span for digits in two groups of children, one of whom was given intensive practice over a period of five months. It was found that the practised group gained initially, but lost its advantage a few months after practice had been discontinued.

Vernon and Husen (1951) and many others have studied the effects of coaching on intelligence test performance. It has been found that skill is increased by practice, but only within certain limits.

The results of all the above and similar type studies can be summarized in the comments of McGraw (1951), who observed that

> Behaviour patterns which have received a high degree of fixity and are controlled at the infracortical level are subject to no appreciable alteration through mere repetition of the activity during the postnatal development of the subject. . . . Activities of ontogenetic origin can be greatly accelerated through exercise of the performance, but the degree to which they can be modified is dependent upon the state of maturation or plasticity of the behaviour pattern at the time the factor of exercise is introduced.

The main difficulty in all such studies is the impossibility of assessing the influence of incidental activities on results, as the Subject cannot be kept in a vacuum during the period of investigation. Frequently results attributed to maturation can also be interpreted in terms of learning and experience. Piaget's investigations have not included systematic studies of the effects of coaching or practice, but the similarities between his tests and the opportunities for learning during the course of the investigation, make a maturational interpretation of his results equally subject to criticism. Describing tests on conservation, Inhelder stresses the fact that if, for example, the child who is at the 'global' stage is allowed to verify his judgment of weight by the use of scales, he will adhere to his judgment of inequality, denying the evidence of his own eyes. Would he persist in his judgment if allowed further trials? The main safeguard in Piaget's tests is the insistence on the child justifying his answers. Nevertheless, many children who start by giving a perceptual judgment not only correct it during the course of the testing, but give a sound reason for doing so. In the seriation tests, children have remarked on the similarity of the process, and many who failed to seriate spontaneously have completed the series successfully after help with the first three sticks, cards, houses, etc. Piaget's theory of 'stages' would be greatly strengthened if it could be demonstrated that coaching and practice in his tests would not significantly affect the results. In recent years a number of investigations have been made by researchers into the effects of training programmes on the results of Piaget's tests. Accounts of some of these can be found in the discussions following descriptions of the Aden tests. The theoretical issues are discussed in more detail in the section on Bruner at the end of this chapter. The two main facts which emerge from these studies are that results are not clear cut as they depend on the type and content of the training procedure, and that their significance for Piaget's theories cannot be assessed without further research into the scope and duration of improvement and the amount of transfer to other tasks.

Control is also needed in longitudinal studies, although it is necessarily limited. An unsolved problem is a challenge to a child, and even if, because of a promise, he does not go to the lengths of consulting parents, teachers and friends about the solution, he is likely to be alert towards any similar problem in his environment. Inhelder quotes Marco's changes in behaviour when confronted with the same experiments after six months. Before assessing the value of the results in the second test, one would need to know a great deal about the intervening period.

Theory construction

The scientist is always seeking law and order in the world around him. On the basis of his knowledge, observations and experience he makes hypotheses which he tests and retests, varying both the method and content of his experiments. Gradually he builds up a framework of theory, that is, related assumptions in the area under study against which all the results of his own and other people's investigations can be tested. The data on which he bases his theory could be used in another context, to support a different theory. If facts are available, why are theories necessary? They are useful insofar as they can be used to make predictions which are testable.

Psychological science aims at making predictions about behaviour. The psychologist does not merely want to describe behaviour, but to explain at various levels what takes place and predict what will happen if the circumstances change. For many years theory construction concentrated on the learning processes, well-known contributors including Hull, Tolman, Lewin, Guthrie and Skinner. (For a broad survey of their work see Hilgard, 1956.) The same behaviour is interpreted by each theorist according to a pattern. The model which he chooses for expressing his assumptions is often 'borrowed' from another science. For psychologists mathematics is a favourite model but physiology, biology, logic and other sciences are also used. Understanding the theory can therefore involve a knowledge of the science on which the model has been based. The transference of the related concepts to the field of psychology makes for inexactitude in terminology and difficulty in making comparisons between theories.

A fruitful theory is one in which the process of making hypotheses, testing, predicting, testing, making further hypotheses, etc., is continuous. It is more efficient if the area of study is narrowed so that as many variables as possible may be controlled. The aim is to find an explanation to fit all the facts, so the fewer the facts, the more precise the explanation and the more reliable the prediction. Theories of child development are inadequate, lacking precision, not fully tested and generally relating to only one aspect of child growth. This is not surprising when one considers that they aim at a framework within which all behaviour can be explained from birth to maturity. As Maier (1966) points out, 'a theory that can account for any conceivable behaviour is untestable.' Theories evolved up till now usually have a historical origin, stemming from theories of behaviour represented by certain schools of psychology. Many of their apparent contradictions arise from the varied backgrounds and experience of the pioneers of developmental theory. Both Baldwin (1967) and Maier have attempted to find the common elements in theories of child development, to clarify concepts and terminology and to lay the foundation for an integrated theory. This book does not purport to duplicate the work of these authors, whose own works should be read for details, but to indicate the importance of Piaget's contribution, seen in the context of other theories.

The behaviourist approach to child development

Between the World Wars there was a movement among psychologists to establish psychology as a scientific rather than a philosophical discipline. This involved turning away from 'mentalistic' and introspective studies which were speculative, individual and not amenable to statistical evaluation. Concentration was on studies of overt behaviour and its variations under conditions manipulated by the experimenter. Subjects ranged from the amoeba to man, covering as many living creatures as could be brought into the experimental situation. Out of this new activity grew theories of behaviour and systematic thinking about the aims, concepts and methods of psychology. The approach was objective: theory was firmly based on evidence. Since nothing could be accepted which had not been confirmed by testing, progress was slow, but it was believed that such an approach would ultimately lead to a comprehensive theory of behaviour.

The central tenet was that behaviour is learned, so learning theory received most attention. Behaviourists such as Watson (1930), Guthrie,

Hull, Tolman and Skinner (see Hilgard, 1956) all regarded behaviour as the response of an organism to a stimulus in the environment although they differed in their experimental approach to an S–R situation. All exploited Pavlov's experiments (1964 ed.) on the conditioning of animals as the mechanism for explaining how stimuli and responses come to be linked. One of the most important laws of behaviour was *The Law of Effect* which states that learning, both positive and negative, takes place as the result of the pleasant or unpleasant effects of an action. A rewarded response is reinforced whereas an unrewarded or punished response becomes extinguished, hence the importance of punishment and reward in the learning situation.

The developmental psychologist who derives his theories from behaviourism sees the child exposed to all the stimuli in his environment, in other words, continuously faced with a multiple-choice situation. He can be conditioned to make the kind of responses acceptable to the society in which he lives. Watson and the Russian psychologists, Luria and Yodovich (1959) and Vygotsky (1962) are among those basing their theories on Pavlov's model, while social-learning theorists like Sears (in Maier, 1966) regard social conditioning, that is, socialization, as the crucial process in child development. Piaget, in contrast, stresses the active part played by the child in his own development.

The Gestalt approach to child development

Tolman had already modified the mechanistic approach described above by emphasizing the purposive character of behaviour, but the conceptual framework was too limited for psychologists influenced by the Gestalt view of behaviour. Briefly, this is the view that experience cannot be explained in terms of discrete elements and the association between them: the context in which it takes place is important. The 'whole' is much more than the sum of its parts. The organization of such 'wholes' or 'configurations' is most apparent in perceptual experience. Discrete dots become organized into patterns, geometric forms such as squares and triangles are easily recognizable and a broken circle is still recognized as a circle. The experiments of the Gestaltists have contributed much to our knowledge of perception, learning and remembering.

Lewin (1935) has built up a theory of child development which uses concepts derived from Gestalt psychology. He sees the child as living in a psychological environment within a framework of 'life space'. The patterns of behaviour within the life space become more complex and interdependent as the child grows older. Tension arises as his areas of interest compete for dominance, and frustration when his goals are blocked. Maturity implies a raising of the level of organization and the balancing of the needs of one region against another within the life space. Lewin's mathematical model for representing psychological concepts is as individual to him as Piaget's psycho-logic. However, some of his concepts have proved fruitful in studies of children in groups, one of the most notable of these studies being Lewin, Lippitt and White (1939).

Psychoanalytic theories of child development

These theories are modifications and extensions of the explanations of behaviour and development arrived at by Freud, Jung (1939) and Adler (1930). This discussion concentrates on Freud (1900, 1922), whose influence has been most far reaching (see Stafford-Clark, 1965).

Medical psychology can be traced back to humanitarian efforts to improve the lot of inmates of asylums in Europe, believed, until about two hundred years ago to be possessed of evil spirits. By the time that Freud began his studies of hypnotism many advances were being made in the treatment of patients with mental disorders. Freud built up a system for the analysis and treatment of patients which convinced him that such disorders could be explained in psychological terms. His theory was extended to form a systematic psychology which would explain the whole of behaviour.

The great difference between the method of Freud and those of other developmental psychologists is that whereas they studied children first hand, he developed his theories of growth by delving into the childhood memories of his patients and himself. Also, instead of deriving norms of behaviour from a cross-section of the 'normal' public, he concentrated on a section of the population which needed psychiatric help. The result was many valuable insights into deviant behaviour, which are now accepted as valuable in the study of normal development, but not a generally acceptable overall theory.

The main difference between psychoanalytic and other theories of development is the importance attached to unconscious factors, particularly the part played by basic instinctive drives. Freud was interested in covert, rather than overt behaviour, in motivation behind a response rather than the response itself, so that for many years his contributions to psychology were completely rejected by the behaviourists. Briefly, the Freudian theory is that a child's development is dominated by three psychological structures, the Id, the Ego and the Superego.

The Id

This consists of everything psychological inherited and present at birth, including instincts, that is, unlearned behaviour. It is the source of psychic energy, providing power for the other structures (or systems). It derives its energy from bodily processes consisting of reflex action which is inborn and automatic, e.g. sneezing, and 'primary processes', which discharge tension by means of imagery (dreams and all kinds of imaginative experience). Its main function is to avoid pain and obtain pleasure.

The Ego

This system is firmly rooted in reality: it prevents the discharge of tension until a need, such as hunger, is really satisfied and tests experience to make sure that it is true. It exists because the needs of the organism can only be satisfied by the objective world of reality. Its function is to organize action, to control instinctive behaviour, to maintain life and to see that the species is reproduced.

The Superego

This structure covers the functions and characteristics of what is generally known as the 'conscience'. It inhibits the impulses of the Id, responds to rewards and punishments, provides moralistic goals in the place of realistic ones and generally guides behaviour according to the pattern laid down by the parents in early years.

The pattern of child development is determined by the balance maintained between the Id, the Ego and the Superego, each of which dominates the individual at different stages, although all are functioning simultaneously in the adult. Because of its mediating function, the Ego is the most important: failure to fulfil its role results in mental and behavioural disorders.

Freud describes the following stages in the child's development. Because his theories are dominated by the part played by sex, he includes sex differences in his analysis, unlike Piaget. Like Piaget, he considers that the first years of life are decisive for future development, so they receive his fullest attention.

Oral stage (0–1 year)

During this period of life, the mouth is the principle region of dynamic activity. Eating is the main source of pleasure, so the baby tries to put everything within reach into his mouth. Later this activity includes biting and chewing which Freud likens to the pleasure of acquiring knowledge and possessions. Fixation at this stage can result in the development of a gullible personality who swallows everything he is told. Pleasure in biting is the basis of aggression, which can be expressed later as sarcasm and argumentativeness. Because of the child's helplessness, this stage is also marked by feelings of dependency on the mother, which, if persistent, may result in an unconscious desire to return to the womb. In fact, a whole network of attitudes, interests and traits of an individual is founded in this period.

Anal stage (1–2 years)

Also many traits of character have their roots in the anal stage during which attention is focused on the process of elimination and the relief experienced. Toilet training is the first real experience that the child has of an external regulation of an instinctual impulse. He has to learn to postpone the pleasure of relieving anal tensions. The kind of training he receives will have far-reaching effects upon value systems in later life. If his mother greets his performance with praise she may be establishing a foundation for his creativity and productivity in later life. Harsh training, which gives the impression that the mother can be made anxious by refusal to cooperate, may result in a withholding action to 'punish' her. This may produce the trait of stinginess, for example, or lead to cruelty and destructiveness.

Phallic stage (3–5 years)

This period corresponds roughly to what Piaget calls the stage of 'pre-operational thought' described below. It is characterized by the development of sexual and aggressive feelings associated with the genital organs. The child becomes aware of the pleasures of masturbation. His attitudes towards his own and the opposite sex will largely be determined by the way he handles his feelings of love and hatred towards his parents during this period. Freud sees an important difference in the sexes at this stage, the boy and girl oscillating between feelings of rivalry and feelings of admiration and the desire for identification with the parent of the same sex. As, according to Freud, every person is bisexual, the girl's feelings towards the mother and the boy's towards the father are ambivalent. Resolutions of the conflicts involved in this situation are responsible for sexual relationships and attitudes in later life.

Latency period (6–adolescence)

Freud has less to say about this period in which the child becomes less interested in fantasy and his own body and more interested in the real world. His affections, previously centred on his parents are extended to schoolmates and his activities are characterized by a passion for exploring his environment and collecting information of all kinds. It is a period of relative stability.

Genital period (adolescence to adulthood)

During this period the child comes to realize that the pleasure received from the stimulation and manipulation of his own body can be supplemented and enhanced by contact with others. Through the processes of socialization his love is already less concentrated on himself so his attitudes and feelings are more outwardly orientated. With maturity he is prepared both physically and psychologically for the biological function of reproduction.

Freud, like Piaget, uses 'stages' and chronological ages to mark the course of child development, but both emphasize that they are describing a continuous process during which any of the characteristics of a particular stage may appear in a different context in a later stage.

Because of its origins and methods, psychoanalysis developed separately from the main stream of psychology. One of the most important unifiers of psychological science has been the acceptance of the contribution made by psychoanalytic theories. A major contribution was that of Sears (in Maier, 1966), whose early work on infant sexuality paved the way for making Feudian theory 'respectable' in the eyes of the empiricist. Modern psychologists apply Freud's theories in their studies of children with behavioural difficulties and clinicians adapt his methods of analysis to suit the age and interests of their subjects. Erikson (1965), whose developmental psychology is described by Maier (1966) in detail, relies on the psychoanalytic model but takes account of socio-cultural factors. In his studies of infancy Piaget develops 'schema' relating to the symbolic processes which can be compared to Freud's systems. Piaget, like Freud, believes in the importance of early experience to later development, but his main interest is in the cognitive rather than the emotional aspect of the personality.

Genetic theories of development

Introduction

This section is almost exclusively devoted to the theories of Piaget, although some reference will be made to Bruner, whose approach to cognitive growth is termed 'genetic' by Inhelder. According to Wohlwill (in Sigel and Hooper, 1968), Bruner has failed to consider the developmental aspects of thinking, but it seems appropriate here to compare his system of 'levels' with that of Piaget's 'stages' in order to note some of the differences. Both Piaget and Bruner are concerned with mental development, but, whereas Piaget traces the growth of development, Bruner (in Bruner et al., 1956) does so only by implication when he differentiates between strategies of thinking.

Piaget's theories

Piaget's approach to child development is interdisciplinary. His biological background has supplied many of the concepts he uses: he thinks of a child as an organism developing in an environment. In the course of development it adapts itself to the environment, assimilating what is needed for its growth and changing its own behaviour (accommodating) in the process. Piaget calls the part of the thought process that is responsible for the adaptation a *schema*.* As the process of adaptation is continuous from birth, the individual will continuously be producing schemas to deal with the situation. However, from birth to maturity the schemas will develop and undergo changes. The term covers not only simple responses to stimuli in the environment, such as the baby's response when an object is dangled in front of it, but complicated responses such as perceiving the mother, which involves not only seeing her, but recognizing her as the person who supplies all physical needs and comforts. As the child develops, simple schemas, based on sensori-motor experience, become internalized and organized into thought structures. As any schema may become a part of an unlimited number of patterns of thought, the whole system is very complex and mobile, providing both continuity and overlapping of Piaget's 'stages' described below.

Another interest of Piaget's—logic—becomes evident when he begins to describe more fully the internalization of the child's actions and schemas, making possible the development of language and other symbolic processes. He believes that the integration of all these mental activities is logical, that is, it follows a definite system, subject to its own laws. In Piaget's writings, he refers to pre-logical and logical stages to describe the differences in the child's thinking before and after full integration has taken place. All the mental acts involved were, in Piaget's earlier books, termed *operations*, so we found references to pre-logical operations and logical operations. More recently Piaget and Inhelder (1969) refer to pre-operatory and operatory levels of thought. The former covers the period of sensori-motor development: it is a practical level culminating in what Piaget and Inhelder call a 'kind of logic of action'. During this period the child is mainly concerned with adapting himself to his environment and establishing personal relationships. His world extends from his own body to objects

---

* In classificatory tasks, the term 'schema' is applied when the grouped elements form a structure which is capable of generalization and transfer. At first the child recognizes common features but only gradually, by means of what Inhelder and Piaget (1964) call 'adjustment governed by hindsight together with a limited degree of foresight', is co-ordination of the different criteria into a single system possible. Inhelder and Piaget consider that, with coordination, the child achieves 'the adequate schema which characterizes operational thinking'. Flexibility enables him not only to anticipate his classification of elements (at an earlier period described in Geneva as 'graphic collections'), but also to manipulate them in the light of experience.

1. operations + cog. dev.

pre-operat. of thinking

within an ever-expanding universe. His thinking is occupied with mapping his surroundings and classifying the objects within sight. After about 18 months he becomes capable of symbolic function, which comprises symbolic gestures and language and the formation of mental images which represent real objects. Piaget and Inhelder (1969) have now adopted the linguistic term 'semiotic function' to cover these activities. The term 'operation' is now confined to internalized actions which are grouped into coherent reversible systems of thought functioning at two main levels: the 'concrete' level preceding an understanding of conservation, and the level of 'formal' thinking. The growth that takes place is known as *cognitive development* which is a long and complicated process, described in brief outline in the section on stages of development and illustrated in the detailed account of the Aden investigation.

Piaget's other deep psychological interest is in *perception*, about which he *2* has written much that has not yet been translated into English. (For an important text recently available see Piaget, 1969b.) Perception, which, as Lovell (1969) points out, is variously defined, can be broadly viewed as the sensation of seeing, hearing, feeling, etc., plus an individual's interpretation based on experience. This is a very important aspect of child development, intimately linked with learning and attention. However, Piaget treats its development separately, because although he acknowledges the close relationship between cognitive and perceptual development, his research points so far to a separate development. The same can be said for other aspects of child development; physical, emotional, and social development, for example, are all taking place at the same time, but each has a characteristic growth pattern. Piaget's work on perception is discussed in chapter 3.

Perhaps Piaget's greatest interest is in *genetic epistemology*. Epistemology is concerned with theories of knowledge, the ways in which man views the world, classifies events in it and relates them to each other in some kind of system. This can be done in terms of mathematics or one of the sciences. In fact, it was Piaget's discontent with current theories of knowledge that led him to try to trace the different ways in which the child views his world, as he develops from infancy to maturity. It was a new and important approach, culminating in the setting up of a centre for experimental genetic epistemology in Geneva, which tries to answer the questions of epistemology by reference to child development. In his introduction to Piaget's *Six Psychological Studies* (1969a) Elkind suggests that Piaget is best understood as a genetic epistemologist. In his studies of concept formation (chapter 3 onwards) Piaget is mainly concerned with the basic mathematical and scientific concepts which characterize the child's view of the world. This chapter is concerned with the development of the psychological structures which underlie the formation of those concepts (see also Pinard and Laurendean, 1969).

Before describing the stages which Piaget has traced in the intellectual (cognitive) development of the child, a few more of Piaget's basic concepts will be explained.

GROUPING

This is a mathematical concept which Piaget applies to the psychological relationships achieved by the child in the course of integrating his schemas (see above). For example, in classificatory studies, Piaget refers to the 'grouping' of classes. In the bead experiment (chapter 13) there is a group of wooden beads, containing a group of blue beads which is also part of the larger group. Numbers are not involved but the situation could be expressed as $A + B = B$, if A is included in B. Piaget calls this *Le groupement additif des classes*. When the classification is in terms of quality, e.g. colour, Piaget calls it a logical grouping. The same concept is used with reference to number. When the child can order his number concepts so that he understands its conservation whatever transformations may take place in its elements, e.g. $8 = 7 + 1$, $6 + 2$, $5 + 3$, $4 + 4$, 2×4, $2 \times 2 \times 2$, numerical 'grouping' has been achieved. More complex groupings are also described by Piaget.

INVARIANCE

This is a physical term which Piaget has adopted and given a psychological connotation. In the course of development (as illustrated by the tests in the following chapters), a child learns that certain properties of the things he handles do not change unless something is added to them or taken away. The best example will be found in chapter 6, where children are reported as justifying that the substance, weight or volume of a ball of plasticine does not change when it is deformed, i.e. it is invariant.

Piaget also believes that some of the characteristics of the child's mental structures are invariant. Although new structures are developed as the child grows from infancy into adulthood, the original structures remain. This may account for the fact that most adults at some time express themselves in anthropomorphic terms, which are characteristic of childish thinking. For example, one says that, if a picnic is arranged it will be sure to rain, whereas the sun shines when one's business is indoors, interpreting coincidence as the act of a malevolent power.

EQUILIBRIUM

This concept has been derived from the natural sciences. When we talk about the 'balance' of nature, we mean that, in the African jungle, for example, the different species of animals are balanced in numbers so that each has enough food and the right conditions for reproduction. When this balance is upset by indiscriminate hunting, a species may become extinct. Piaget believes that in mental life there are also regulatory mechanisms which balance what the organism gains from its environment and what it derives from maturational factors.

Equilibration plays an important part in Piaget's overall theory. Although it is the genetic factors of development which interest him most, his theory is not maturational in a narrow sense. Nor, of course, is it environmental in a narrow sense. Piaget believes in a fundamental interaction between internal and external which is taking place throughout life but which is especially significant in childhood. In growth there are three main influences: maturation, the physical environment and the social environment. To these Piaget adds a fourth, equilibrium, the mental mechanism which controls the other three. One of its important functions is the regulation of the growth of cognitive structures from the simple schemas of the baby to the complex coordinated structures of adulthood.

There is an important distinction between learning theories of development and Piaget's theory of equilibration. In learning theory, changes take place in the child's thinking and acting as a result of external reinforcement (reward and punishment, in the widest sense). According to Piaget's theory, such learning is not excluded, but it is insufficient to cover all the changes in behaviour resulting from the interaction of the three influences mentioned above. Equilibrium is an *internal* regulatory (balancing) mechanism, an active mental process which operates outside the individual's awareness, but which is brought about by the child reflecting in an auto-regulatory sense on his own activities.

STAGES OF DEVELOPMENT

Piaget has always quoted chronological ages with reference to stages of growth, which has resulted in a disproportionate amount of time being spent by investigators in disproving his norms. As his stages are related to intellectual development, mental ages would be more appropriate, but these also would not be comparable unless the same measuring technique were used. Chronological ages can be interesting in cross-cultural studies, where one may wish to explore cultural effects on progress, and mental ages where a high correlation with the results of Piaget-type tests might indicate that the latter would be an equally good test of intelligence. According to Piaget, age belongs to the group of factors in the development of concept formation which will vary between different social groups. He has never claimed that his norms of development are universal, although his earlier books did not make this clear.

Piaget's developmental pattern consists of three main stages:

Stage 1 (0–about 2 years)

This is the period of sensori-motor development. During these years the child extends his interest in his own body and bodily functions to include an ever-increasing variety of objects in his environment. Among his accomplishments he learns a great deal about the objects in his environment in relation to himself. He finds, for example, that they have a permanent identity, that they can be picked up and grasped as well as released by means of a sequence of motor acts and that they can be located after disappearing from sight. The discovery that he is something separate from these objects is the origin of his concept of self. His movements, at first random, become differentiated; he learns to repeat them and imitate others. He solves problems in space by trying out solutions after an accidental success with a random movement. In his second year he shows, by imitative gestures, the first signs of symbolic play. By the end of this period he has grasped a means–end relationship, so his behaviour becomes purposive. Piaget (1953) gives detailed examples of the infant's behaviour in his book, *The Origins of Intelligence in Children*.

Stage 2 (from about 2–11 years)

This period marks important changes in the child's capability and type of reasoning. During the first part (up to about 7 years) his actions become increasingly interiorized and he becomes capable of symbolic or 'representative' thought. This development becomes most apparent in his play which, instead of consisting solely of motor activities, becomes imaginative. The development of language enables the child to attach names to objects and events. He is also able to extend imitation of the actions of people around him to changes of role in his play: he *is* the train, the engine driver, the policeman, etc., and objects like chairs and tables, in fact, anything in his environment, undergo rapid changes to fit in with his activities. Although he is capable of distinguishing between reality and the symbol, the distinction becomes blurred at times. For much of the time he lives in a world of his own. Piaget describes his language as *egocentric* because its main purpose is not communication with other persons. Although he is learning to discriminate between objects and persons in his immediate surroundings, his classifications are still very primitive. His reasoning is dominated by what he perceives. Piaget refers to this period as the stage of 'intuitive' thought. By this he means that the child does not demand proof for his assertions. This is part of his egocentrism. Many illustrations of the child's mode of thinking during this period will be found in comments on the Aden tests.

In the second part of this period, actions have become interiorized thought operations. These are sufficiently coordinated to make logical thinking possible. However, the child's reasoning is still imperfect at this stage. Piaget describes it as 'concrete' because it only operates in a specific situation whereas later on he will be able to generalize from one situation to another. Perception still plays a part in his reasoning, but he depends less on it. He is most successful in a situation where he is able to manipulate actual objects and materials in the course of reasoning about them. For instance, in the conservation tests, he can, by his own actions, return the deformed ball of plasticine to its original shape. He has achieved the characteristic of 'reversibility', which, expressed mathematically, means that he is aware that if $a + b = c$, $c - a = b$ and $c - b = a$.

Stage 3 (about 11 years onwards)

Gradually the concrete aids needed by the child in his thinking become redundant and he becomes capable of 'formal', that is, what Piaget regards as 'logical' thinking. This development is greatly assisted by his increasing mastery of language. Other developments take place, for example, his moral values, which previously had depended very heavily on the attitudes and precepts of his parents, become organized into autonomous systems comparable to logical groupings. His equilibrium, that is, internal balance is superior to that which existed previously, in spite of a temporary disequilibrium during adolescence, due to the maturation of the sexual instincts. Piaget reminds us that at every transitional stage in development, temporary oscillations are likely to occur. The following is a summary of what Piaget has to say about the intellectual and emotional characteristics of adolescence. Further details can be found in his *Six Psychological Studies* (1969).

According to Piaget, one of the most striking characteristics of the adolescent is his interest in theoretical problems not related to everyday realities, and his facility for elaborating abstract theories. They talk, write and ruminate: 'all of them have systems and theories that transform the world in one way or another.' The transfer from 'concrete' thinking, with its support of perception, experience 'or even faith', has been gradual, but, having reached the stage of formal thought, the adolescent is able 'to draw conclusions from pure hypotheses and not merely from actual observation. This explains why formal thinking represents so much more difficulty and so much more mental work than concrete thought.'

Piaget (1969a) compares the intellectual egocentricity of the adolescent with the egocentricity of the infant who 'assimilates the universe into his corporal activity' (in other words, devours everything within reach), and the egocentricity of the young child 'who assimilates things into his own nascent thought', that is, indulges in symbolic play, etc.

Then, just as the sensori-motor egocentricity of early childhood as early childhood is progressively reduced by the organization of schemata of action and as the young child's egocentric thinking is replaced with the equilibrium of concrete operations, so the metaphysical egocentricity of the adolescent is gradually lessened as a reconciliation between formal thought and reality is effected. Equilibrium is attained when the adolescent understands that the proper function of reflection is not to contradict but to predict and interpret experience.

According to Piaget (1969a), personality, which has also been developing achieves its final form in adolescence. Personality results from submitting oneself to some kind of discipline. Its strength lies in a combination of personal autonomy and social cooperation. It cannot mature until the intellectual conditions of adolescence (described above) exist. The temporary disequilibrium of adolescence is sometimes revealed in 'the constant mixture of devotion to humanity and acute egocentricity. The phenomenon is the same whether it has to do with the misunderstood and anxious youngster convinced of failure who questions the value of life itself or with the active youngster convinced of his own genius.' During this period, disillusioned by the adult's imperfections, he transfers his filial feelings to his particular god, and attempts to integrate religion with his life systems. His intense feelings inspire a desire to play a decisive role in his chosen cause. Because of the discovery of love, his life plan is more concerned with specific interpersonal feelings than with general emotions.

The adolescent is constantly meditating about society, that is, the society he wants to reform, 'for he has nothing but disdain or disinterest for the real society he condemns.' As he comes into contact with the reality of the world in which he lives, he gradually adapts to it and disequilibrium gives way to equilibrium. 'Reason, which expresses the highest forms of equilibrium, reunites intelligence and effectivity.'

Piaget explains that his stages are both continuous and overlapping, but that the sequence is irreversible. Many investigations will need to take place before sequence is finally established, but few would deny the insights into child development contained in Piaget's descriptions of his stages of growth. He is often accused of producing an inadequate theory of child development because, it is said, he does not pay sufficient attention to important aspects, for example, experience, environmental and motivational factors. In fact such a 'theory' would need to embrace all up-to-date knowledge of human psychology. Each of the aspects mentioned is an area of study needing teams of experts to continue the investigation as knowledge increases. At the same time, because interaction takes place throughout life, for the developmentalist to ignore any aspect completely, would provide a distorted picture.

Like Freud, Piaget has tried to produce a framework which, ultimately, will be capable of explaining all human behaviour. Its superiority is that it would be much easier to fit Freud's important concepts into Piaget's scheme than vice versa, partly because Piaget's concepts are testable and capable of replication with all the refinements necessary to establish the significance of individual differences.

Maier (1966) has painstakingly compared Erikson's psychoanalytic theory (derived from Freudian principles), and Sears' social learning theory of development with Piaget's scheme, and found that they are not incompatible, that, when terminological difficulties are ironed out, much of their work appears to be complementary. Baldwin (1967), whose investigations of theories of child development cover an even wider field, has found large areas of agreement. Baldwin has suggested the possibility of 'an eclectic integration of the theories, provided that they can be reconciled in language.' His specifications include attention to changes in behaviour, 'hypothetical events, such as thoughts, feeling and inhibitory acts', as well as overt behaviour, levels of development and emotion, and their developmental aspects, the role of maturation, aspects of behaviour learned through reinforcement and conditioning and the incidence of new forms of behaviour. Baldwin concludes that

> the theories do not turn out badly. In many ways they support each other, and, in total, suggest a kind of prototheory of child development, which, although obviously incomplete, badly defined, and surely wrong in some respects, is a feasible and workable basis for further research and for more refined theory building.

If ever a group of psychologists decide to unite to produce such an integrated theory of child development, it seems possible that, with its firm biological basis of adaptation to the environment, the importance it attaches to both overt behaviour and its internalization, making possible the development of symbolic processes, and its unique contribution to knowledge about cognitive development, as well as the Genevan empirical studies which provide an endless source of material for testing Piaget's hypotheses against those of psychologists working in other fields, Piaget's framework is the best starting point at present.

Jerome S. Bruner

Inhelder et al. (1966) refer to Bruner's genetic approach to cognitive growth, so a brief account of his theories is included in this section, in spite of Wohlwill's criticism (in Sigel and Hooper, 1968) that he has failed to consider the developmental aspects of perception and thinking.

The original work on thinking by Bruner and his colleagues (1956) has been followed by a considerable number of studies of perception and con-

cept formation, very much of it inspired by the work of Piaget. The fusion
of his own theories of the strategies of thinking with the insights gained
from years of experiment to test his own and Piaget's hypotheses has
resulted in a theory of 'stages' not incompatible with Piaget's.

Stage 1
Enactive: characterized by adaptation at the motor level, moving, reaching,
grasping and a practical understanding of space.

Stage 2
Iconic: in which the child views the world in terms of percepts and concrete
images. Characteristically, one aspect of a situation dominates, e.g. colour
or shape.

Stage 3
Symbolic: a stage at which the child is able to express general and abstract
ideas in words and number. He has achieved the concept of conservation
and can translate action and image into action.

Bruner believes not only that the individual child internalizes the tech-
nologies of his culture as he develops, but that capacities slowly selected in
the course of evolution are represented genetically in the species: 'culture
then becomes the chief instrument for guaranteeing survival, with its
techniques of transmission being of the highest order of importance.'

In Piaget's theories of development, action becomes internalized as the
child passes from the stage of 'concrete' reasoning to formal reasoning. In
Bruner's theories, because it is the techniques which become internalized,
it seems possible to aid the maturational processes by giving instruction.
This apparent conflict of ideas is further discussed in chapters 7 and 16.

References

Adler, A. (1930). Individual psychology. In C. Murchison (Ed.), *Psy-
chologies of 1930*. Mass.: Clark University Press.
Baldwin, A. L. (1967). *Theories of Child Development*. New York: Wiley.
Bowlby, J. (1953). *J. ment. Sci.*, **99**, 265.
Bruner, J. S., J. J. Goodnow and G. A. Austin. (1956). *A Study of Thinking*.
New York: Wiley. (London: Chapman and Hall, 1957.)
Bühler, C. (1930). *The First Years of Life*. New York: Day.
Carmichael, L. (1926). *Psychol. Rev.*, **33**, 51–58; **34**, 34–47 (1927); **35**,
253–260 (1928).
Dennis, W. (1935). *J. genet. Psychol.*, **47**, 17–32; **53**, 149–158 (1938);
J. soc. Psychol., **12**, 305–317.
Erikson, E. H. (1965). *Childhood and Society*. Harmondsworth, Mddx.:
Penguin.

Freud, Sigmund. (1900 ed.), *The Interpretation of Dreams*. London: Allen and Unwin.

Freud, Sigmund. (1922 ed.). *Introductory Lectures on Psycho-Analysis*. London: Allen and Unwin.

Gates, A. L., and G. A. Taylor. (1925). *J. educ. Psychol.*, **16**, 583–592.

Gesell, A., and F. Ilg. (1946). *The Child from Five to Ten*. London: Hamish Hamilton.

Goodenough, F. L., and K. M. Maurer. (1942). *The Mental Growth of Children from Age 2 to 14 Years*. Minn: University of Minnesota Press.

Hilgard, E. R. (1956). *Theories of Learning*, 2nd ed. New York: Appleton-Century-Crofts.

Hilgard, J. R. (1932). *J. genet. Psychol.*, **41**, 36–56; *Genet. Psychol. Monogr.*, **14**, 493–567.

Inhelder, B., M. Bovet, H. Sinclair and C. Smock. (1966). Comments on Bruner's course of cognitive development. *Am. Psychol.*, **21**, 160–164.

Inhelder, B., and J. Piaget. (1964). *The Early Growth of Logic in the Child: Classification and Seriation*. London: Routledge and Kegan Paul.

Isaacs, Susan. (1930). *Intellectual Growth in Young Children*. London: Routledge and Kegan Paul.

Jung, C. (1939). *The Integration of Personality*. New York: Farrar and Rinehart.

Lewin, K. (1935). *A Dynamic Theory of Personality*. New York: McGraw-Hill.

Lewin, K., R. Lippitt and R. K. White. (1939). Patterns of aggressive behaviour in experimentally created 'social climates'. *J. soc. Psychol.*, **10**, 271–299.

Lovell, K. (1969). *An Introduction to Human Development*, 2nd ed. London: Macmillan.

Luria, A. R., and F. I. Yodovitch. (1960). *Speech and the Development of Mental Processes in the Child*. (Trans. J. Simon, 1960). London: Staples Press.

McGraw, M. B. (1951). Maturation of behaviour. In. L. Carmichael (Ed.), *Manual of Child Psychology*. New York: Wiley.

Maier, H. W. (1966). *Three Theories of Child Development*. New York: Harper and Row.

Pavlov, I. P. (1964 ed.) *Lectures on Conditioned Reflexes*. London: Lawrence and Wishart. (Also in N. L. Munn (1956). *Psychology*, 5th ed. Boston: Houghton Mifflin.)

Piaget, J. (1953). *The Origin of Intelligence in the Child*. London: Routledge and Kegan Paul.

Piaget, J. (1969a). *Six Psychological Studies*. (Ed. David Elkind). London: University of London Press.

Piaget, J. (1969b). *The Mechanisms of Perception.* London: Routledge and Kegan Paul.

Piaget, J., and B. Inhelder. (1969). *The Psychology of the Child.* London: Routledge and Kegan Paul.

Pinard, A., and M. Laurendean. (1969). 'Stage' in Piaget's cognitive-developmental theory: exegesis of a concept. In D. Elkind and J. H. Flavell (Eds.), *Studies in Cognitive Development.* New York: Oxford University Press.

Robertson, J., and J. Bowlby. (1952). Quoted in Yarrow (1961).

Shirley, M. M. (1951). In L. Carmichael (Ed.), *Manual of Child Psychology.* New York: Wiley.

Sigel, I. E., and F. H. Hooper, Eds. (1968). *Logical Thinking in Children.* New York: Holt, Rinehart and Winston.

Skard, A. G. (1968). Personal Communication.

Spalding, D. A. (1890). In W. James (Ed.), *Principles of Psychology*, vol. 2. New York: Holt. p. 396.

Spitz, R. A., and K. Wolf. (1946). Quoted in Yarrow (1961).

Stafford-Clark, D. (1965). *What Freud Really Said.* Harmondsworth, Mddx.: Penguin.

Terman, L. M., and M. A. Merrill. (1937). *Measuring Intelligence.* Boston: Houghton Mifflin.

Thomson, R. (1958). *The Psychology of Thinking.* Harmondsworth, Mddx.: Penguin.

Valentine, C. W. (1946). *The Psychology of Early Childhood*, 3rd ed. London: Methuen.

Valentine, C. W. (1956). *The Normal Child.* Harmondsworth, Mddx.: Penguin.

Vernon, P. E. (1965). *The Measurement of Abilities*, 2nd ed. London: University of London Press.

Vernon, P., and T. Husen. (1951). *Theoria*, **17**, 61–68.

Vygotsky, L. S. (1962). *Thought and Language.* (Trans. E. Haufmann and G. Vaker, 1962) Mass.: M.I.T. Press.

Watson, J. B. (1930). *Behaviourism.* New York: Norton. (Also in N. L. Munn (Ed.), *Psychology*, 5th ed. Boston: Houghton Mifflin, 1956.)

Yarrow, L. J. (1961). Maternal deprivation: toward an empirical and conceptual revaluation. *Psychol. Bull.*, **58**, 459–490.

Yerks, R. M., and L. Bloomfield. *Psychol. Bull.*, **7**, 253–263.

CHAPTER THREE

Piaget's work considered in relation to other studies of concept formation

Introduction

What is a concept? In everyday language we use the word 'idea', very often qualified by adjectives like 'loose' and 'exact' which indicate the degree of precision our thinking has reached. We say, for instance, 'I have a very vague idea about the procedure' and later on, 'now I have a very clear idea about what is involved'. However, like most common terms, 'idea' has collected many other meanings: the psychologist must aim at precision. The most fundamental and agreed properties of a concept are its complexity and its function in organizing thought. Concept formation is the mental process which enables the child to make sense out of the 'blooming buzzing confusion' which surrounds him at birth. Thomson (1958), in his useful chapter on concepts, defines them as 'complex systems of higher-order responses in terms of which our more basic response-patterns are organized'.

Organization takes place at various levels of mental functioning, and, as will be seen below, many psychologists prior to Piaget have equated 'concept formation' with the processes inherent in its operation. Piaget's main interest is in investigating the steps by which a child reaches his conception of the world around him. The level at which he can conceptualize will depend on the level of his intelligence and will influence his judgment and reasoning. Piaget uses his investigations of the formation of basic concepts in children to illustrate his overall theory of cognitive development discussed in chapter 2.

In this chapter there will be a short account of early work relevant to Piaget's work, followed by some discussion on the roles of perception and language in concept formation with special reference to the work of Piaget, Vygotsky, Luria and Bruner. This will be followed by a section on personality and concept formation.

Early work on concept formation

Basic to Piaget's theories of the growth of reasoning is his concept of 'grouping'. The child gradually builds up systems of thought structure, each of which serves as a sort of frame of reference throughout life and, at the same time, combines with others to form more complicated 'groupings'. In the first few years of his life, the child is largely concerned with classification, a mental operation fundamental to more advanced thinking. In its simplest form, classification is a perceptual exercise depending on discrimination. Many experimenters have demonstrated the capacity of animals as well as small children to respond to an abstract quality common to a group of objects. For example, by using a Yerkes apparatus, in which animals are required to turn into an alley on the side of the brighter of two lights in order to obtain food or avoid punishment, it is possible to train fish, mice, white rats, guinea pigs, rabbits, chickens, cattle, dogs, monkeys, etc., to form a brightness discrimination habit. Similarly, using many types of apparatus, the discrimination of form, colour, distance and relative versus absolute difference in stimuli have been tested. Munn (1950), for example, trained rats, monkeys and small children to respond to the quality of 'triangularity'. Notable in the field of visual discrimination is the work of Lashley (1938), whose experiments with racoons, cats, chimps and rats lead him to conclude that the ability to abstract and generalize is limited by the material and processes used.

This conclusion is relevant to the more complicated studies of abstraction and generalization carried out using child and adult subjects. Pioneer experiments were made by Hull (1920) and Kuo (1923) in which success in a task depended on the ability to abstract the radical from a Chinese character. Some of Kuo's students failed to reach generalization because their attention had not been drawn to the radicals. This aspect has been investigated by Reed (1946) who studied the influence of set, i.e. expectations, on concept formation. It seems possible that the same phenomenon may be at least partly responsible for the child's typical response to Piaget's 'Bead Test' described in chapter 13. The Subject classifies the beads according to their most prominent characteristic, colour, and fails, in spite of promptings, to attend to the less obvious quality of woodenness.

Smoke (1932), who criticizes earlier experiments for identifying abstraction with concept formation, devised situations in which the relationships and not the common elements in a stimulus pattern are the basis of the grouping process. These studies can be compared on the one hand with Fields' simple experiments (1932) with animals on relative brightness discrimination, and on the other with Piaget's tests used in this investigation, involving double seriation and the formation of asymmetrical relationships. In these the child builds parallel series and then demonstrates the relationship between their members.

According to Piaget, the development of the child's 'groupings' or systems of thought structure is marked by clearly defined irreversible stages. A detailed description of these will be found in chapter 2, their detailed application to the growth of the concept of number being described in the chapters on the Aden investigation. Most of the direct evidence of other investigators supports the existence of the types of thinking characteristic of these stages, but evidence of the sequence is less satisfactory. It is therefore interesting to see what indirect evidence can be found in investigations of children's and adults' thinking under abnormal conditions.

Inhelder (1943) herself has diagnosed the reasoning capacity of mentally defective children, using her tests on the conservation of matter, described in chapter 6. She claims that it is possible to distinguish between children whose 'groupings' are not yet fully developed, and those whose reasoning cannot develop beyond a certain stage. While not claiming to give a complete diagnosis of mental deficiency, she does suggest that, in the majority of cases, deficiency of reason shows itself as a fixation at one of the intermediate levels of operational thought. However, she confuses the issue by classifying in terms of difficulty the concepts themselves, so that, on the one hand, a defective can be said to be arrested, for example, at 'stage 2' of the growth cycle, and on the other, to have been arrested at the concept of substance which he has 'grasped in its entirety'. Inhelder herself, far from regarding this issue as subordinate to the main theory, quotes it as an example of *décalage horizontale* discussed in chapter 6. The present investigation does not support the order of acquisition of the concepts of substance, weight and volume even in normal children, but there is support elsewhere for Inhelder's theory of arrestment. Goldstein and Scheerer (1941), testing the impairment of mental functions in brain-injured patients, found that they were not only incapable of abstract thought, but could not manage a simple classification of objects containing a common characteristic, or shift from one type of classification to another. Weigh (in Humphrey, 1951), a pupil of Goldstein, had similar results with patients suffering cortical lesions, to whom he gave the task of grouping collections of articles, such as wools, coloured disks and common objects. In experiments with soldiers suffering traumatic lesions in the frontal areas, Goldstein and Gelb (1918) found loss of abstracting ability, performance being at the concrete level.

Some work on concept formation has also been done with children suffering from brain injuries. Strauss and Lehtinen (1947) used two types of test. In the first, the children were told to group fifty-six objects. The non-brain-injured Subjects based their classification on function or similar features, whereas the brain-injured, who chose more objects and formed more groups, used a wide range of criteria including colour, form, unessential details, vague and far-fetched functions, and relationships in hypothetical or imaginative situations. In the second test, children were asked to match pictures with objects, giving their reasons. Similar results were obtained. Unlike the deficient and normal children, they gave far-fetched choices which they justified by fantastic explanations.

At the discriminatory level of concept formation, many investigators have shown the detrimental effects of social and emotional factors on judgment. The size of a coin, for example, has been related to the economic position of the child who is exercising judgment, while even the judgment of the adult is affected by hunger and other forms of stress. More serious are the breakdowns and retrogressions due to mental illness, and in this field most work on concept formation has been done with schizophrenic patients. Typical experiments are those of Hanfmann and Kasanin (1937) using Vygotsky blocks of varying colours, shapes and sizes in two heights. The patients were asked to classify the blocks in terms of four nonsense syllables and to formulate the principle of classification. The experimenters found three types of response:

1. Trial and error behaviour: names of blocks not related to their properties.
2. Grouping according to rules, but without understanding the nature of the groups: only one possibility of grouping seen.
3. Task seen as a classification problem.

Haufmann found that the normal Subjects gave the best results followed by the schizophrenic patients, while the worst results were obtained from patients suffering from irreversible brain diseases. Within these groups better results were produced by patients with superior education. When the material was changed to pictures, schizophrenic patients described each separately, appearing to be incapable of classification. Cameron (1963), who made similar tests with schizophrenic patients, concluded that the ability to generalize was not itself impaired, but that there was a tendency to pay attention to irrelevancies, and that there was incongruity between the grouping of the blocks by the patient and his verbal expression of it. The first of these characteristics is also found in children who have reached Piaget's Stage 1, and the second in those who have reached Stage 2. The latter can solve the problem concretely, but cannot formulate their reasoning. Other investigators using schizophrenic subjects have described their results in terms of retrogression to childish thinking, while Hull (1920), whose Subjects included three each suffering from constitutional inferiority, dementia praecox and paresis, found a typical slowing down in the process of forming concepts. Finally, Petrie (1952) includes losses in capacity to generalize in his summary of the effects of different types of leucotomy on neurotic patients.

It will be seen that early experiments in abnormal psychology were exclusively concerned with the classificatory level of concept formation. Their results give positive, though inconclusive support to Piaget's 'stages' by suggesting that retrogression due to mental illness results in loss (or lack of) abstracting and generalizing ability, attention to 'global' factors and thinking at the concrete level. It seems that the crucial test of Piaget's theories is not to ascertain whether the types of thinking characteristic of his 'stages' exist, but whether they develop during childhood in an irreversible sequence. The problem is complicated by Piaget's contention that, although the later thought structures develop from the earlier ones, the latter persist, and continue to exert influence. Many critics of Piaget, who have set out to prove that adults also use the type of reasoning characteristic of his earlier 'stages' have, perhaps, unwittingly supported this contention. They have also shown, however, how difficult it is to prove whether the sequence exists, or whether the different methods of thinking can be found in varying degrees at all stages. Hazlitt (1930), for instance, carried out an investigation to see whether children who were unable to express verbally the relationship of 'except', would be able to show in a practical way that they understood it. She found that children under five years could, in fact, make an exception practically, although unable to formulate it. Smoke (1932) found, similarly, that some of his adult Subjects gave evidence of having acquired a concept which they could not formulate. From her intensive studies of young children, Susan Isaacs (1930) concluded that the difference between children and adults is not that the former do not reason, or that they only reason in the form of perceptual judgment or practical manipulation, but that children's reasoning, which is essentially based on their personal concrete problems, has less need of clear, verbal formulation. She cites, as an example, Dan (three years five months), who, when the stick with which Harold was threatening him was removed, protested, 'but he will hit me with his hand', that is, 'it was the quarrelsome Harold who should be removed, not the temporary tool he was using.'

Investigations which show that, even before they can verbalize, children can use the same type of reasoning as adults, and that adults frequently use childish thinking (as, for example, animistic thinking), illustrate the importance of content and method if a growth sequence is to be established. At the classificatory level, attempts have been made to grade concepts according to complexity. Welch and Long conceived of a hierarchical development of concepts from a simple discrimination of an object to its species and genus. The wider the classification, the more abstract the concept becomes. In relation to Piaget's theories, their most interesting

conclusion is that the genetic development of structures of abstract thinking seems to pass through rather definite stages. They found a pre-
abstract stage (up to about 21 months), followed by stages based on the
child's ability to learn concepts of the first, second and third hierarchies.
At the formal-reasoning level, Duncker (1926), investigating problem
solving with adult Subjects, concludes that insight is gradual and graduated. The degree, however, depends on the complexity of the problem
itself, which he breaks down into graded steps. Piaget's main interest is in
the period prior to formal reasoning, since he is concerned with its development. The very richness and variety of his material makes grading and
standardization a formidable task. One of the strongest impressions
resulting from the Aden investigation covering a large number of Piaget's
tests was that, unless the contents of the tests themselves are equated or
graded for difficulty, their usefulness as a basis for theory is greatly reduced.
Inhelder was exemplifying this, in effect, when she reported an unequal
grasp of the concepts of substance, weight and volume. She acknowledged
it openly at the World Health Organization discussions on Child Development (in Tanner and Inhelder, 1956) when she said, in reply to a question
on variation in the behaviour of children in generalization tests:

> We return to the form of reasoning and the content to be structured;
> the faculty of abstraction does not correspond to an operation which
> would appear at seven years whatever the object or situation. . . . The
> moment when the classification operations appear depends not only
> on the operational classification as such, but also, though in a lesser
> degree, on the content on which it operates.

This is precisely the conclusion reached by Lashley (1938) in connection
with his animals. It leaves the question of sequence within stages wide
open.

Perception and concept formation

The earlier work on concept formation already discussed illustrates that a
relationship exists between perception and conception. Perception is not
merely the sensation of seeing, feeling, hearing, touching, but the interpretation of the sense data in the light of previous experience. To say, for
example, that, through training in discrimination, a rat can acquire 'a
concept of triangularity' is implying that, basically, the same process is
responsible for perceptual and conceptual learning. This view is held by
the Gestalt school of psychology, referred to in chapter 2, whose theories
of perceptual organization are extended to the reasoning, that is, organization of thought, even in animals. Köhler (1925), for example, recounts how
his apes solved problems by seeing objects, not as recognizable 'things'
but in terms of their possible function in arriving at a solution. Discussing

space, G. A. Miller (1962) suggests that conceptual space is an extension of perceptual space, but 'It is almost impossible to keep them separate. As soon as one begins to consider even the simplest problems, one discovers that space perception is riddled with inferences, hypotheses, assumptions, meanings, expectations, that derive from conceptual space.' When judging distances, for example, we make considerable use of prior knowledge of the objects in sight. Miller gives as an example a ball seen from a distance: 'How far away you think the ball is depends on whether you think of the ball as a marble, a ping-pong ball, a billiard ball, or a large beach ball. Your *perception* changes directly as a function of your *conception* of the scene you are viewing.' Miller, however, is referring to adults, whose perceptual judgments are, as he states, influenced by considerable previous experience. This is not the case with children. Inhelder has studied the methods by which a child achieves the transition from a spatial configuration to a logical class. She found a series of intermediate and complicated steps between the two operations but came up against the difficulty that perception can be both an aid and a hindrance to classification. This is seen particularly in the Bead Test described in chapter 13. Many experiments in perception show that, like conception, it is subject to emotional, social and cultural influences.

The close relationship between the two functions is, perhaps, best seen in the constancy phenomena. In spite of changes in our retinal images, we still see objects like chairs and tables as having the same shape from whatever angle they may be viewed. Is the same mechanism at work when we realize that the amount of liquid is the same when poured from a narrow, tall glass into a wide, short glass? In other words, are perceptual constancy and the concept of conservation two sides of the same coin? When Lorenz (in Tanner and Inhelder, 1956) raised this matter with Piaget (albeit in more scientific terms), Piaget agreed that in perception it is the constancy phenomena which are closest to the phenomena of conservation. He does not, however, equate them, since logic, which is a necessary element in conceptual thinking, is often at variance with perception.

In attempting to discuss, even briefly, the contrasting attitudes of Piaget towards perception and concept formation, one is reminded of the large number of his articles and books which have not yet become available to the English-speaking public.* He has written so much on cognitive development that his concurrent experiments on perception have been largely neglected. In this book, discussion will be limited to the part played by perception in the development of concepts and some observations gleaned from Piaget's other writings.

For Piaget, perception, like concept formation, is a developmental

---

* However, since the time of writing this book, an important work has been made available in English translation (see Piaget, 1969b).

process, but not the same process. Some of his most interesting work, conducted with a rigour that is in contrast to his work on concept formation, has been in the field of perceptual illusions. As a developmentalist he is very much interested in the age at which the illusions operate. His investigations have shown that certain illusions, such as the overestimation of the vertical as compared with the horizontal, increase with age; the illusion of weight first increases and then decreases; while the Müller–Lyer illusion remains constant or decreases with age. He attributes the increase in errors to the wider experience of the adult, which involves him with distant relationships. Because the child's frame of reference is very limited, his margin for error is also limited, whereas the adult is subject not only to primary errors but also to secondary errors arising from his much greater experience of perceptual relations. The extent and direction of the error will vary with the physical properties and organization of the figures which provoke the illusion as well as with the nature of the person's perceptual experience. However, the illusion disappears more quickly with the adult, since his level of cognitive development makes him less liable to perseveration.

Piaget is also interested in the cognitive aspects of perceptual tasks. In three experiments with Morf, described in detail by Flavell (1963), he gives his Subjects the opportunity to add imaginary lines to figures to help in perceptual judgments. He finds stages in the extent to which the Subject, according to age, is able to make full use of data provided to solve his perceptual problems.

Two interesting conclusions from the above experiments are reached by Piaget: that 'at all levels perception is active and cannot be reduced to passive perception' and that environment plays a major role in perceptual development. He also stresses the active nature of concept formation but is constantly criticized for his limited interest in environmental influences.

Piaget regards perceptual development as highly complex and little understood. The fact that he uses different approaches and methods of evaluation from those he deems appropriate for the study of concept formation shows that he does not think of it as a continuous process. Both derive from sensori-motor development, but the pattern of growth is different.

In his studies of concept formation, and, in particular, those relating to the concepts of number and quantity, Piaget's theme is the gradual liberation of the child's thinking from perceptual evidence. The young child is constantly deceived by appearances, basing his judgments of 'more', 'less' and 'same' on such properties of objects as colour, shape, size and arrangement in space. Such judgments are immediate and wholly satisfying to the child. Only at a later stage does he question the evidence of his senses. At first his judgment is sound only in a practical situation where he can manipulate the evidence, but finally he can reason internally and generalize from one situation to another. To take a classic example from Piaget's conservation tests (described in more detail in the Aden project). The child, having estimated that two balls of clay contain the same amount, rolls one of them into a long, thin piece of string. When questioned about the amounts of clay in the ball and the string, he answers typically:

Either   'There is more clay in the string than the ball because the string is longer.

or   'They have the same because they've both got a lot of clay.'
'This one is round and fat and that one is long and thin.'

or   'It was the same when it was a ball, I could make it into a ball again.'
'Nothing has been added or taken away, so they must contain the same amount.'

Wohlwill criticizes Piaget's views of the relationship between perceptual and conceptual development for failing to link his theories rigorously with empirical evidence, for overestimating the rationality of adult thought while underestimating perceptual achievement and for exaggerating their functional independence. The last appears to be answerable: in descriptions of his first and intermediate 'stages', Piaget is very much concerned with the interaction of perception and conception. Other investigators are supplying the rigorous, empirical evidence to test this area of his theory, and attention is drawn to procedures used by Bruner (1966). An account of his screening experiment with the Genevan reaction will be found in chapter 7. Piaget, too, can be 'rigorous' when he deems the situation appropriate, and mention has already been made of his investigations (with Morf) of perceptual and conceptual judgments in the same stimulus situation. On the basis of these and other investigations, Wohlwill (1968) suggests that Piaget's analysis could be fruitfully supplemented by regarding perception and conception as the two poles of a continuum. For a full explanation of this point of view reference should be made to Wohlwill's own paper. This area of study is comparatively unexplored. One is reminded of the extraordinarily stimulating effect of Piaget's theories and experiments on other investigators.

Language and conceptual thought
Introduction

Mention has already been made of the use of the term 'concept formation' for discriminatory tasks which can be performed by animals and birds, who are motivated by rewards of food and sex. Monkeys can be trained to learn such tasks in return for plastic tokens which can be accumulated and later put in a slot machine which delivers grapes or peanuts. It could be argued that the recognition of the tokens as 'food-obtaining' is a continuation of the discriminatory process or that it is the outcome of rudimentary thought. Vygotsky (1962), whose theories are discussed later in this chapter, thinks that thought is firmly rooted in perceptual experience of the kind which enabled Köhler's apes to solve problems. In spite of his training as a zoologist, Piaget does not trace the process of concept formation from the lower animals, but from the sensori-motor experience of the new-born child. In his scheme the final stage is not reached until the child is capable of a level of thinking that involves 'interiorized' speech. The whole subject of the relationship between thought and speech is complicated by the interaction or feedback that takes place with development.

Psychologists concerned with cognitive development agree on the importance of language development for concept formation although they differ in the amount of attention they give to the relationship and theories to explain it. The following discussion will be confined to a brief outline of theories of the relationship between language and conceptual thinking held by Piaget, Vygotsky, Luria and Bruner.

Piaget

Prior to Piaget, a vast amount of work had been done by McCarthy (1951), Gesell and Ilg (1946), Bühler (1930) and others on the development of speech in infancy from the first babbling to the stage of constructing a finite sentence. It must be emphasized that the science of speech involves many disciplines: it has many sub-branches all of which are important in their own right. These include 'psycholinguistics' which focuses on language behaviour rather than child development or concept formation.* Although, of course, much work in this field must be relevant; a full discussion is outside the scope of this book.

Piaget's main interest is in the function of language, which he believes to have three consequences essential to mental development. To quote from his *Six Psychological Studies* (1969a), these are:

1. The possibility of verbal exchange with other persons, which heralds the onset of the socialization of action;
2. The internalization of words, i.e. the appearance of thought itself, supported by internal language and a system of signs;
3. Last and most important, the internalization of action as such which from now on, rather than being purely perceptual and motor as it has been heretofore, can represent itself intuitively by means of pictures and 'mental experiments'.

---

* The interested reader will find further details in Sinclair-de-Zwart (1969).

One of Piaget's earliest investigations, published in *The Language and Thought of the Child* (1952), was mainly concerned with the first of these functions. In a series of what could be regarded as pilot studies, he listened to the conversations of small children, alone and in groups, in the free atmosphere of Maison de Petits, the Institut J. J. Rousseau school attended mainly by children of professors and teachers. In his first study, he recorded all the utterances of two six-year-old children for a month. He found two main classes of speech, 'egocentric' speech in which there was no function of communication and 'socialized' speech in which the child was aiming to give information, to further his intentions or to influence the listener. In subsequent studies (see Inhelder and Piaget, 1964) he tried to trace the developmental sequence of speech. He concluded that the two classes 'egocentric' and 'socialized' were stages on a continuum, beginning with 'collective monologues', in which the child, stimulated by the speech of others, talks but does not pay any attention to the similar talk of his companions, to communication which is limited to collaboration on a common task and primitive argument of the 'I did', 'you didn't', type. He also found that children, up to roughly seven years, communicate imperfectly because of failure to listen to and comprehend information received.

Observation confirms the above descriptions of childish speech but Piaget has been criticized both for his analysis of the development of language and for the importance or lack of importance he attaches to speech in his studies of concept formation. Reference has already been made in this chapter to early criticism of his analysis of the results of his investigation. One gets the impression that resistance to Piaget's 'stages' is partly prompted by the knowledge that adults often display the kind of behaviour that he describes as typical of the small child. It is not uncommon to find adults engaging in 'collective monologues' in which each pursues his own line of thought, needing an audience, but failing to pay the slightest attention to what the other person is saying. Behaviour at the same level includes cursing the rain which always coincides with arrangements for an outing and the use of anthropomorphic terms to account for everyday happenings. Piaget's theories of the growth of mental structures take account of such behaviour since he says that, with the development of new structures, the earlier are superceded but still persist. This implies the possibility of retrogression to childish levels of language and thought in times of stress and emotional excitement, or fixation at a level of development because of congenital defects.

With regard to the second point quoted from Piaget (above), that is the internalization of words, reference can be made to his book *Play, Dreams and Imitation in Childhood* (1951), in which he describes how language enlarges the scope of the child's activity and, through communication, his knowledge of objects and events. However, Piaget emphasizes that it is only part of the symbolic function. The symbols which the child invents in his play are personal to himself but are partly the result of imitations which have become interiorized. Language plays an increasingly important role but it is only one part of the entire cognitive development during early infancy.

To Piaget, the third and most important function of language is the internalization of action as such, which enables the child not only to visualize real actions and speech, but to make 'mental experiments'. Here Piaget appears to be referring to the importance of language in conjunction with other symbolic processes, with reference to activities broadly termed 'creative'.

Early criticism of Piaget's use of language in his studies of concept formation was mainly that he equated language with thought (see Isaacs, 1930 and Hazlitt, 1930). A distinction needs to be made here between internalized and overt language. The child who is gradually learning his own language is in much the same position as the person who learns a foreign language: comprehension takes place in advance of facility and clarity of expression. Some experimenters feel so strongly that speech is a poor criterion for assessing the attainment of concepts that they devise tests which dispense with language altogether, apart from the instructions. At the other extreme, Whorf's theory is that it is the structure of language which determines a person's concepts. Piaget's later experiments still involve speech, but, beginning with his investigations of number and quantity, the emphasis is on activity: speech is limited to answers to questions arising from the manipulation of concrete materials. However it is the quality of the child's responses which determines for Piaget the quality of his thought processes: he cannot reach the final state of equilibrium unless he can explain his actions verbally. Kohnstamm (1967) sees this as a contradiction of Piaget's theory and experimental methods. He asks how Piaget's insistence on verbal justifications of the child's responses can be reconciled with his 'disdain for verbal learning'. This appears to be an attempt to compare two entirely different uses of language. Piaget is constantly being criticized for lack of rigour in his procedures, including the use of controls. It seems obvious that if the child is asked the kind of question used in the conservation tests, such as whether the ball or the string contains more clay, only two answers are possible. The justification demanded is a necessary control. It is also consistent with Piaget's theory of mental development which links the development of language with the development of thought. Once the child has mastered words he becomes immersed in a vast system of concepts and ideas that belong to everyone. Mastery of words, in the final stage, means the capability of 'formal' reasoning, sometimes described as 'hypothetico-deductive' thinking. It is difficult to believe that Piaget 'disdains' verbal learning although he has pointed out that, for example, being able to count does not mean that a child understands number. He looks at his experiments from the point of view of a genetic scientist, not as a schoolmaster exploring the efficiency of 'discovery' as opposed to 'formal' methods of teaching. Learning often takes place in a test situation regardless of whether the task is verbal or practical. Repetition is an important factor. For example, Arab children who had never had experience with mazes, failed on the easy Porteus Maze Tests, but, if allowed to continue, without instruction, managed some of the more difficult tests. In Piaget's tests, where the object is to examine the 'natural' thinking of the child in the course of development, the use of control groups as in a learning experiment would be inappropriate. One agrees, however, that Piaget has devised tests singularly suitable for use in testing environmental effects, social and cultural, on cognitive development as well as the importance of instruction. Further discussion on this subject will be found in the section on concept training in the final chapter. Inhelder's recent language experiments (Inhelder *et al.*, 1966) are discussed in connection with Bruner's theories at the end of this chapter.

Vygotsky

Vygotsky (1962), like Piaget, pays tribute to both the role of perception and the importance of language in the growth of concepts. 'The sensory material and the word', he says, 'are both indispensable parts of concept formation.' For this reason he is among those who do not regard abstraction studies which can be carried out using animal subjects as tests of concept formation. He has his own theory to explain the relationship between thought and speech. From his studies of ape language, he concludes that thought and speech have different genetic roots, speech being a development of the visual and vocal signs of animals, while thought is rooted in perceptual experience, of the kind responsible for the success in problem solving of Köhler's apes. It can be seen that this is a different view from that held by Piaget, who regards thought as a related, but not parallell, development of perception, with its roots in sensori-motor experience, which extends beyond perception. (Piaget uses the description 'part-isomorphic' for this complicated relationship.) Although, says Vygotsky, the growth of speech and thought are not parallel, 'at a certain point ... thought becomes verbal and speech rational'. Vygotsky thinks that the 'egocentric' stage in language development, described by Piaget, may be the link between external speech and inner speech, because the child is 'talking to himself' which is a kind of 'thinking aloud'. 'Egocentric' speech is of vital importance since it has a similar function to inner speech while at the same time it is overt and observable.

Vygotsky (1962) made some interesting experiments starting from Piaget's own observations that: (1) Egocentric speech occurs only in the presence of other children engaged in the same activity, and not when the child is alone, i.e. it is a collective monologue. (2) The child is under the illusion that his egocentric talk, directed to nobody, is understood by those who surround him. (3) Egocentric speech has the character of external speech: it is not inaudible or whispered. Vygotsky observes,

> These are certainly not chance peculiarities. From the child's own point of view, egocentric speech is not yet separated from social speech. It occurs under the subjective and objective conditions of social speech and may be considered a correlate of the insufficient isolation of the child's individual consciousness from the social whole.

In his first series of experiments, Vygotsky's hypothesis was that

> if egocentric talk results from egocentric thinking and its insufficient socialization, then any weakening in the social elements in the experimental setup, any factor contributing to the child's isolation from the group, must lead to a sudden increase in egocentric speech. But if the latter results from an insufficient differentiation of speech for oneself from speech for others, then the same changes must cause it to decrease.

In the first series of experiments, having measured the child's coefficient of egocentric speech, he put him with deaf-mute children or with children speaking a foreign language, in order to try to destroy the illusion of being understood. His interesting finding was that, in the absence of the feeling of being understood, the egocentric speech practically or entirely ceased. In the second series of experiments, by isolating the child or putting him in a group of strangers, the collective monologue was the variable excluded. Again, egocentric speech was reduced though not to the same extent as in the first experiments. In the final series, the experimental variable was the quality of egocentric speech: voices were drowned by loud noises and, in a variant of the experiment, the child was allowed to talk only in whispers. The results showed the basic trend.

From his experiments, Vygotsky concluded that egocentric speech 'is a form developing out of social speech and not yet separated from it in its manifestation, though already distinct in function and structure.' This is in distinct contrast to Piaget's view that egocentric speech has only the appearance of social speech and that it is only for the child himself. Yet Vygotsky believes that the child's egocentric speech is, to an extent, independent from social speech: it has already the function of inner speech, but remains similar to social speech in its expression.

In many ways Vygotsky's work complements that of Piaget: although expressed differently, his 'stages' overlap, he confirms the importance of perception and language in conceptual development and notes the progression from concrete to conceptual types of thought. He uses the development of the science of language rather as Piaget uses the development of the science of mathematics, to illustrate his overall theory of cognitive development.

Luria and Yodovitch

Like Vygotsky and Piaget, Luria and his colleague Yodovitch (1960) stress the role of language in the formation of mental processes. They are not, however, concerned with maturational factors and innate ability, but with the effects of experience in development. Experience includes environmental and social influences, but, above all, the acquisition of common experiences transmitted by speech, from which the maturational processes cannot be separated.

> This whole process of the transmission of knowledge and the formation of concepts, which is the basic way the adult influences the child, constitutes the central process of the child's intellectual development. If this formation of the child's mental activity in the process of education is left out of consideration, it is impossible either to understand or to explain causally any of the facts of child psychology.

The role of the adult in transmitting his culture to the younger generation is stressed throughout Luria's work. His analysis of the means by which this is done is based on the materialistic view of psychology rooted in Pavlov's conditioning theories (1964 ed.). At first learning leans heavily on reinforcement, but, as the higher mental processes develop, the child takes a more active part in his own development; stability brings with it what Pavlov calls 'self-regulation'.

Luria describes three methods of studying the role of speech in the formation of mental processes: concentrating on activity displayed during the development of speech, on language impairment due to brain injury and experiments including and excluding speech in the fulfilment of tasks. Reference has already been made to the indirect evidence of the nature of the higher processes, supplied by studies of their dysfunction resulting from illness, brain injury, emotional disturbance, etc. Luria believes that all three methods listed involve unresolvable problems which can be avoided by investigating cases of retardation of speech processes: 'in such cases the processes of higher nervous activity are so imperfect and the very speech of the child so defective—so poor are his connections, so immobile his dynamics—that the participation of speech in the formation of new connections becomes impossible and these are elaborated without the requisite participation of the abstract and generalizing function of the word.' Luria's experiments are founded on the work of the neurologists, such as Goldstein and Gelb (1918), already mentioned and on research by psychologists who have studied the impairment of perceptual functions in deaf-mutes.

By chance Luria and Yodovitch found ideal subjects for their experiments: uniovular twins who, although very retarded in their speech development, showed no signs of mental retardation. Details can be found in Simon's translation of their work (1960). This includes a detailed analysis of the slow development of their speech. For a period the twins were separated in the kindergarten to create a necessity for communicating with other children, and Yura, the weaker, was subjected to special speech training for ten months.

Luria's chief finding was the importance of social motivation in the development of speech shown by the children's improvement after separation, but even more significant was the improvement in the whole structure of their mental life. This took the form of meaningful play and purposeful constructive activity. Yura's speech not only improved grammatically as a result of his systematic training, but his quality of thinking exceeded that of his brother. The experimenters claim that their results testify to the importance of speech in the formation of many more complex mental processes.

Bruner

In Bruner's scheme of stages (discussed in chapter 2), language is the most important technique that the child internalizes during the 'symbol' stage of development. It enables him to translate his actions and images into a code with the aid of which he can express both general and abstract ideas. Language, like other behavioural techniques, is acquired from the child's culture, through the processes of imitation and education.

Bruner attributes much more importance than Piaget to the role of language in conceptual development. In his screening experiment described in chapter 7, he showed that, if not distracted by the perceptual characteristics of glasses into which water is poured, even a very young child is capable of using language as a medium of reasoning. Bruner does not equate language with thought, but he argues very convincingly that the quality of language and the full use of its various functions have a most powerful effect on the quality of thought. The implications of his views are discussed in the section on concept training in chapter 16.

Inhelder and her colleagues (1966) devised language experiments to determine (a) if there were changes in the child's descriptive language which accompanied acquisition of conservation; and (b) if performance on conservation tasks could be improved through systematic teaching of the language of description appropriate to that particular conservation concept. They found that the children's spontaneous descriptions at the different stages of conservation showed, as in Bruner's experiments, a parallel development in the structure of language patterns and their behavioural structure in the tasks. However a direct comparison with Bruner's analysis was difficult because he classified the children's responses in different terms. Conclusions with reference to the effects of linguistic training were more clear cut, showing some of the basic differences between the approaches to cognitive development of Harvard and Geneva. Briefly, linguistic training had two clear effects: in the post-tests children were able to express their arguments more clearly and consistently and those who in the pre-test on the conservation of liquids (described in detail in chapter 7) indicated that water level determined 'equality of amounts' in the post-tests mentioned the relationship between height and width. However, in spite of this, they had not achieved conservation: they did not see the *significance* of their observations: they had the tools but had not reached the stage for using them correctly. Inhelder concludes that language training helps to focus a child's attention on important aspects in a task and helps in the storage of information, but does not, of itself, integrate the information in a way to make achievement of the concept inevitable. This does not, according to Inhelder, exclude the possibility of feedback of language on the development of cognitive structures, which may be especially important at the formal-reasoning stage. Where Bruner puts the emphasis on interiorization of language in cognitive development, Piaget puts the emphasis on interiorization of action and regards language as a facilitating process.

Personality and concept formation

There is still much scope for the study of concept formation, notably in the field of personality. Sigel (in Sigel and Hooper, 1968) refers to the growing body of evidence indicating the relationship of types of personality traits to information processing, problem solving, etc. He uses the term 'cognitive style' to describe the variable that integrates personality and cognition. Dienes (1959), a pioneer in this field, has devised experiments to determine in what ways the ability to form abstract concepts is connected with other aspects of the personality. He approaches the problem as a Gestalt psychologist with his own interpretation of Piaget's stages. In his own words,

> The *first stage* is an arbitrary kind of stimulus-bombardment responded to by playful activity without any conscious aim. This play furnishes the fundamental reality experiences from which the concept will eventually be acquired.

The *second stage* is an intermediate one, in which it is beginning to be realized that some structurization of the play experiences is needed, and some of the component parts of the concept are beginning to be put together. This is a more purposeful stage, aiming at some final organization as yet unperceived.

The *third stage* is the formation of the final concept. The correct Gestalt of all the component parts is seen; in other words a measure of unity is achieved in the way the parts are seen to build up the whole.

Besides giving his experimental subjects material graded so that they could use the first level concepts for acquiring the second set and the second for the third, he also used Raven's Projection technique (1947) for investigating personality variables. His hypothesis was that the strategies used by the children would vary according to personality variables as well as intelligence test scores.

From his results, Dienes concluded that there are sex differences in the functioning of children's concept formation: 'Girls approach tasks more from the point of view of the construction of the whole, boys more from the point of view of analysis of the parts.' The girls also appeared in this investigation to be slightly more introverted than the boys. His main results from correlating intelligence and personality factors are as follows:

1. There is a positive relationship between intelligence and the personality factors of cohesion (integration) and introversion.
2. There is a negative relationship between constructive (creative) thinking and the extent of stereotypy (i.e. a rigid or authoritarian personality).
3. There is a positive relationship between the extent of the awareness of identification, general intelligence and capacity for constructive (creative) thinking.

Dienes' more complicated detailed analysis cannot be included here. His work indicates an aspect of conceptual development so far neglected by the Genevan school.

Goldschmid (1958), however, has noted Piaget's stress on the parallel development of reflective and intellectual life, which are interdependent 'since feelings express the interest and value given to actions of which intelligence provides the structure.' According to Goldschmid, children achieving higher conservation scores tend to possess personality characteristics which enhance cognitive functioning. His studies suggest to him 'the possibility that unstable or disturbed children develop conservation later than normal children of the same age, suggesting that disruptive personality characteristics may delay cognitive development'. This is in line with the earlier studies of concept formation using abnormal subjects discussed previously. Goldschmid tentatively links environment with personality as a factor in the development of personality.

References

Bruner, J. S. (1966). *Toward a Theory of Instruction.* Cambridge, Mass.: Harvard University Press.

Bruner, J. S., R. R. Olver and P. M. Greenfield, Eds. (1966). *Studies in Cognitive Growth.* New York: Wiley.

Bühler, C. (1930). *The First Years of Life.* New York: Day.

Cameron, N. (1963). *Personality Development and Psychopathology.* Boston: Houghton Mifflin.

7 Dienes, Z. P. (1959). *Concept Formation and Personality.* Leicester: Leicester University Press.

Duncker, K. (1926). *J. genet. Psychol.,* **33**, 642–708.

Fields, P. E. (1932). Studies in concept formation. *Comp. Psychol. Monogr.,* **9.** (Also in *J. Comp. Psychol.,* **21**, 341–355 (1936).)

Flavell, J. H. (1963). *The Developmental Psychology of Jean Piaget.* New York: Van Nostrand.

Gesell, A., and F. Ilg. (1946). *The Child from Five to Ten.* London: Hamish Hamilton.

Goldschmid, M. L. (1958). *Child Dev.,* 579–589.

Goldstein, K., and A. Gelb. (1918). *Z. ges. Neurol. Psychiat.,* **41**, 1–142.

Goldstein, K., and M. Scheerer. (1941). Abstract and concrete behaviour. *Psychol. Monogr.,* **53**, No. 2.

Hanfmann, E., and J. Kasanin. (1937). *J. Psychol.,* **3**, 521–540.

Hazlitt, V. (1930). Children's thinking. *Br. J. Psychol.,* **20**, 354–361.

Hull, C. L. (1920). Quantitative aspects of the evolution of concepts. *Psychol. Monogr.,* **28**, Whole No. 123.

Humphrey, G. (1951). *Thinking.* London: Methuen.

Inhelder, B. (1943). *Le Diagnostic du Raisonnement chez les Débiles mentaux.* Neuchâtel: Delachaux et Niestlé.

Inhelder, B., M. Bovet, H. Sinclair and C. Smock. (1966). Comments on Bruner's course of cognitive development. *Am. Psychol.,* **21**, 160–164.

Inhelder, B., and J. Piaget. (1964). *The Early Growth of Logic in the Child: Classification and Seriation.* London: Routledge and Kegan Paul.

Isaacs, Susan. (1930). *Intellectual Growth in Young Children.* London: Routledge and Kegan Paul.

Köhler, W. (1925). *The Mentality of Apes.* Harmondsworth, Mddx.: Penguin.

Kohnstamm, G. A. (1967). *Piaget's Analysis of Class Inclusion: Right or Wrong?* The Hague: Monton. (See also Sigel and Hooper, 1968.)

Kuo, Z. Y. (1923). *J. exp. Psychol.,* **6**, 247–293.

Lashley, K. S. (1938). The mechanism of vision. *XV J. gen. Psychol.,* **18**, 123–193.

Lorenz, K. Z. (1956). In J. M. Tanner and B. Inhelder (Eds.), *Discussions on Child Development.* London: Tavistock.

Luria, A. R., and F. I. Yodovitch. (1960). *Speech and the Development of Mental Processes in the Child.* (Trans. J. Simon, 1960). London: Staples Press.

McCarthy, D. (1951). Language development in children. In L. Carmichael (Ed.), *Manual of Child Psychology.* New York: Wiley.

Miller, G. A. (1962). *Psychology.* Harmondsworth, Mddx.: Penguin.

Munn, N. L. (1950). *Handbook of Psychological Research on the Rat.* Boston: Houghton Mifflin.

Pavlov, I. P. (1964 ed.). *Lectures on Conditioned Reflexes.* London: Lawrence and Wishart. (Also in N. L. Munn (1956). *Psychology,* 5th ed. Boston: Houghton Mifflin.)

Petrie, A. (1952). *Personality and the Frontal Lobes.* London.

Piaget, J. (1951). *Play, Dreams and Imitation in Childhood.* London: Routledge and Kegan Paul.

Piaget, J. (1952). *The Language and Thought of the Child.* London: Routledge and Kegan Paul.

Piaget, J. (1969a). *Six Psychological Studies.* (Ed. David Elkind) London: University of London Press.

Piaget, J. (1969b). *The Mechanisms of Perception.* London: Routledge and Kegan Paul.

Raven, J. C. (1947). *Progressive Matrices.* London: Harrap.

Reed, H. B. (1946). *J. exp. Psychol.,* **36,** 71–87, 252–261.

Sigel, I. E., and F. H. Hooper, Eds. (1968). *Logical Thinking in Children.* New York: Holt, Rinehart and Winston.

Sinclair-de-Zwart. (1969). In D. Elkind and J. H. Flavell (Eds.), *Studies in Cognitive Development.* New York: Oxford University Press.

Smoke, K. L. (1932). An objective study of concept formation. *Psychol. Monogr.*

Strauss, A. A., and L. E. Lehtinen. (1947). *Psychopathology and Education of the Brain-injured Child.* New York: Grune and Stratton.

Tanner, J. M., and B. Inhelder, Eds. (1956). *Discussions on Child Development.* London: Tavistock.

Thomson, R. (1958). *The Psychology of Thinking.* Harmondsworth, Mddx.: Penguin.

Vygotsky, L. S. (1962). *Thought and Language.* (Trans. E. Haufmann and G. Vaker, 1962) Mass.: M.I.T. Press.

Weigh, E. Z. Quoted in Humphrey (1951).

Welch, L., and L. Long. *J. Psychol.,* **9,** 59–95.

Wohlwill, J. F. (1968). In. I. E. Sigel and F. H. Hooper (Eds.), *Logical Thinking in Children.* New York: Holt, Rinehart and Winston.

CHAPTER FOUR

The child's conception of number

Introduction

The most comprehensive series of studies of the cognitive aspect of child development in existence has been produced by Jean Piaget and his co-workers in Geneva. So wide is their scope that it would be difficult to find any topic in this field which is not illuminated by a reference to them. By systematic questioning, valuable data have been collected on the child's concept of moral judgment, the world, causality, time, space and many other aspects of his environment.

These studies are valuable not only for the light they throw on the particular topics they discuss, but for their contribution to Piaget's general theories of the development of intelligence. Briefly, he sees the child's biological and cognitive developments as parallel processes. The infant by the processes of assimilation and accommodation becomes adapted to his psychological as well as his physical environment. His development involves the building up of systems of mental operations which follow a systematic order. The transition from one stage to the next is a gradual one during which, what Piaget refers to as 'group structures', are incomplete. The whole process is continuous, but at each stage his 'structures' or mental operations exhibit certain characteristics. His three main stages are outlined in chapter 2. Into his scheme, Piaget weaves the various studies referred to below.

The selection of his work on the child's conception of number for the following investigation had been dictated by several considerations. In spite of its interest and importance, it appeared to have received much less attention by investigators than other studies, such as language, for instance, which had provoked experimentation in all parts of the world. There is also the curious neglect of the subject of number in the usual textbooks. Garrett (1951) and others had drawn attention to the use of mathematics, mainly algebra, geometry and trigonometry, in early experiments on transfer of training by Thorndike and Woodworth, as a challenge to the doctrine of formal discipline, which held that training in mathematical skill would increase 'reasoning ability'. (This is more fully discussed in chapter 16 under 'concept training'.) However, in Carmichael's *Manual of Child Psychology* (1951) for instance, large sections are devoted to maturation, learning, mental growth, language development, etc., but not one word or reference relates to the psychology of number. It must be pointed out, however, that mathematicians, educationists and psychologists with a mathematical bent were carrying out many studies of number as a skill. It was left to Piaget to link that skill with the general characteristics of cognitive development. Other approaches to the subject are described below.

Some approaches to the child's conception of number

It is not proposed to give an exhaustive account of the literature dealing with the genesis of the concept of number, but to select a few examples of approaches to the subject which are interesting as a comparison to Piaget's approach.

For convenience of exposition, discussion of the main approaches to the child's conception of number will be arranged under sub-headings, such as *anthropological approach*, etc. It must be clearly understood, however, that there is much overlapping in the approaches to this subject. Stern (1949), for example, whose system of teaching is inspired by Gestalt doctrine, is also interested in the evolution of number concepts among primitive peoples. Similarly, Thorndike, who referred to arithmetical problems as training in thinking for problems of life, was responsible with Woodworth (1901, see also Woodworth, 1950), for a series of experiments attacking the whole doctrine of 'formal discipline'. Indeed, he could be described as an important forerunner of the 'Activity' movement in teaching, which advocates the development of number sense in children in a setting of vital experience. Again, Ballard (1928), with his practical outlook and real concern with the individual child's difficulties, approaches the subject with much the same attitude as Schonell (1958). It is with these reservations in mind that the following suggestions of approaches to the subject are offered.

Anthropological approach

Thorndike wrote in 1922 that very few of even the most enthusiastic supporters of the recapitulation theory or culture-epoch theory, which regards the development of the human race and development of an individual child as parallel at all stages, had attempted to apply either to the learning of arithmetic. He does, however, quote a mathematician named Branford, who applied the theory with great elaborations. A few sentences will suffice to illustrate the trend of his reflections:

> Thus the capacity of the infant and early childhood is comparable with the capacity of animal consciousness and primitive man. The mathematics suitable to later childhood and boyhood . . . is comparable with archaean mathematics passing on through Greek and Hindu to mediaeval European mathematics: while the Student is become sufficiently mature to begin the assimilation of modern and highly abstract European thought. (p. 198).

The use of ethnological data as a basis of biogenetic theories which compare the development of the child with the development of the race is summarized and condemned by Margaret Mead in her discussion on 'Research on Primitive Children' in Carmichael (1951).

A modern example of the anthropological approach is provided by a pupil of Max Wertheimer, Catherine Stern (1949), who traces the evolution of number concepts among primitive peoples and then illustrates how small children can be trained to solve their number problems by more efficient methods. The application of Piaget's tests to primitive tribes by Price-Williams, (1961, 1969) de Lemos (personal communication) and others suggests that limitations in the number concepts of primitive children may be linked more fruitfully with environmental than with biogenetic factors. Stern's approach is really an introduction to theories of number development based on *Gestalt Psychology*. Having given the child opportunity to play in situations carefully arranged to emphasize particular aspects of a potential number concept, she observed his spontaneous expressions, which, according to Wertheimer, would be recognized by trained mathematical observers 'as a first form of behaviour, which, repeated, could lead to a powerful mathematical motion' (Foreword to Stern, 1949). Her attempts to 'structure the field' can be compared with the approach of Montessori with its emphasis on provision of apparatus and careful training in the use of it.

The associationist approach

This is exemplified by Thorndike (1901, 1922, 1924) in America and Ballard (1928) in England. Fundamentally it regards reasoning not as an application of general principles but as the use of an organized hierarchy of habits to solve novel problems. The child's development of number concept will, therefore, depend on careful training with appropriate drill, the elimination of bad methods and useless examples and the provision for 'correct and economical response to genuine problems'.

Neither Thorndike nor Ballard deny the importance of maturation. Ballard (1928) supports Drummond's conclusions that 'The knowledge of number and the ability to perform number operations that is acquired in the Infants' Department (ages five to seven) are mainly the result of mental growth: this growth takes place not because of the teaching, but often, rather, in spite of it.' Thorndike thinks that the maturation of the capacities of the pupils affects in a general way the difficulty of tasks, but, he states 'there are, so far as is known, no special times and seasons at which the human animal by inner growth is specially ripe for one or other section or aspect of arithmetic'. It has been left to Piaget to test this assumption. Thorndike and Ballard examine underlying mathematical principles from the point of view of how they can be got over to the children in the most economical and pleasant way, whereas Piaget examines the children to learn from them in what way and in what order the basic principles are acquired. When Ballard uses such terms as 'addition age', 'subtraction age', etc., he is classifying in terms of performance rather than maturational stages, although these may be implicit. It is a question of emphasis.

The observational approach

In studies of child development, much valuable data has been accumulated by means of controlled observation. Gesell and his colleagues (1946) recorded detailed profiles of the behaviour of the child at each stage from birth until ten years old, covering traits, attitudes, interests, abilities, etc. In the field of number he records norms for different age groups, lists of accomplishment and attitude towards formal teaching. In this type of study use is made of a variety of observational techniques, such as screens, films, parent's reports, recorded play and clinical visits. The result is a collection of observations whose reliability depends on the wide and varied sources from which they are drawn. In a general way the development of number is linked up with other aspects of development, but its importance is its contribution towards the general picture, not the genesis of the notion of number itself. These studies, covering twenty years' work at the Yale Clinic of Child Development, can be used as a valuable check on experimental studies.

The statistical approach

Piaget's theories of the development of number concepts is an integral part of his general theory of the growth of intelligence. The belief that there is a close relationship between arithmetical ability and general intelligence is expressed by all the compilers of Intelligence Tests of the battery type, notably Binet (1937) and his adaptors and Wechsler (1944), who include many arithmetical items. Both Norsworthy (1906) and Merrill (1924) found feeble-minded groups below normal but less deficient in arithmetical *computation* than verbal subjects, but, as Anastasi and Foley (1949) point out, this may be partially due to the importance of verbal aptitude as a criterion of feeble-mindedness. Experience in teaching backward children leads to the conclusion that, given time and patience, a fairly high degree of accuracy can be obtained in mechanical arithmetic from less gifted children.

It should be noted that, whereas Binet and his adaptors include items testing arithmetical reasoning, other types of psychological tests, such as Differential Aptitude Tests (1947) and tests of traits, are mainly concerned with 'numerical ability' or 'computation'. There are some such groups of tests however which measure these two types of arithmetical ability separately. Anastasi and Foley (1949) give accounts of arithmetical prodigies and 'lightning calculators' who demonstrate that a high level of numerical aptitude can occur in people of average or low intelligence, and assert that some of them would probably be classified as 'borderline' or lower on current intelligence tests. It appears from the literature that even if arithmetical reasoning and computation are regarded as distinct abilities, the relationship between the development of number and the development of intelligence may be more complicated than Piaget's theories lead one to expect.

The diagnostic–remedial approach

The works of Schonell, which have been an inspiration to many teachers of arithmetic, have a special significance for those coping with the problems of the less gifted. His book (jointly with F. E. Schonell, 1958) sums up an approach to the development of number in children that has psychological as well as educational significance. He finds that the pattern of factors influencing arithmetical attainment are: general intelligence and experience, which influence reasoning power, memory, verbal ability, spatial ability, imagery and computational accuracy.

Briefly: he decides which of these factors can be helped in the practical school situation so that the right type of environment for number development can be achieved. He aims to provide the sort of experience which will ease the child's transition from stage to stage. (It was the same belief that inspired Susan Isaacs' (1930) well-known experiments at the Malting House School where learning was essentially linked with concrete experience.) Schonell then analyses difficulties experienced by children in manipulating numbers, solving arithmetical problems, etc., grades the difficulties and suggests practical means of overcoming and minimizing them.

His work and that of Piaget are complementary. He says, in effect, 'The manner in which children form number concepts and acquire verbal and spatial knowledge, on which will depend their later success in problem solving, depends partly on intellectual power, but I can do nothing about that.' But it also depends 'to a considerable degree upon the nature and extent of their experience with a variety of concrete materials in all sorts of situations', and about this he is ready with valuable help for the teacher. Piaget provides such situations in order to analyse the maturational stages through which the arithmetical reasoning of the child passes before he can solve his problems by 'operational' reasoning. Although he is aware of environmental factors, his main interest is in intellectual growth in terms of sequence. Schonell, on the other hand, is aware of the importance of maturation, as evidenced by his concept of 'number age', 'reading age', etc., but the sequence which interests him is the degree of difficulty of the tasks themselves, which are an essential part of the classroom environment.

Finally, whereas Piaget, having made his diagnosis leaves others to apply his theories to the teaching of arithmetic, and is himself mainly concerned with their importance in a comprehensive scheme of child development, Schonell, having diagnosed the subject matter of arithmetic in terms of its difficulty for the child, is mainly interested in remedying or minimizing the defects in reasoning which are so admirably demonstrated by Piaget. As Peel points out (see Carpenter, 1955) Piaget is not interested in the success or failure of a child to pass a test at a given level, but in the process by which he solves his problems.

The modern approach

The past decade has seen important new approaches to the teaching of mathematics including much lively experimentation in schools encouraged by the Nuffield Foundation, the Schools Council and the National Foundation for Educational Research (1960). Far-reaching changes have taken place in syllabuses, affecting both content and method: in primary schools the number of mathematical schemes has begun to rival the number of reading schemes, so that books and apparatus need constant renewal in order to be up to date. The main changes that have taken place with psychological implications can be summarized as follows:

1. Accuracy in computation is seen as less important than the understanding of mathematical principles.

Computational ability and mathematical understanding are not mutually exclusive: the results of experiments often show that children who achieve high standards in school tests also do well in Piaget-type tests. However, the learning of arithmetic by rote method is now recognized as of little value, either to the child or the computor-orientated society in which he lives, unless the pupil has some insight into the processes involved.

2. Learning is seen as an active process, involving the child at every level. In the modern classroom one does not expect to find rows of children painstakingly copying sums from the blackboard, all of which must be worked correctly before any individual child will be allowed a break for play. Instead, typically, the children will be grouped or working individually, playing 'shops' or number games, measuring, weighing and demonstrating in every possible way that numerical calculations are a necessary and meaningful asset in dealing with the problems of everyday life. (Gardner (1950) has produced evidence that young children's arithmetical progress, evaluated by orthodox tests, does not suffer as a result of this practical approach.)

3. With the increase in child activity, there has been a corresponding increase in apparatus designed to hasten the process of understanding.

Notably, Cuisenaire and Cattegno (1955) have devised apparatus to help children form basic mathematical concepts. Rods varying in length from 1 cm to 10 cm are used, all rods of the same length having the same colour. The child places the small rods end to end to form larger units, thinking in terms at first of colours rather than numbers. At a later stage the rods can be used for understanding more complicated mathematical processes, such as fractions and proportions. It is a method which seeks to use perception combined with action.

Dienes' (1959) apparatus is even more ambitious, his Multibase Arithmetical Blocks being designed to help children to develop concepts involving indices and logarithms. These, and his other apparatus, give children experience in handling mathematical relationships, aided by perceptual impressions of the visual, tactile and kinaesthetic kind.

In some schools formal apparatus is less favoured than everyday objects which the children can bring from home or construct in the classroom.

Piaget's theories of the development of the concept of number

Introduction

Piaget is not directly concerned with the teaching of mathematics or of mathematical concepts. A request to a School Mathematics Study Group in America for details of Piaget-type research brought the following reply from the Director:

> After a fairly careful review of Piaget's work on the Development of Number Concepts in children and the work of others along the same line, I have come to the conclusion that all of this has very little

relevance to mathematics education, and consequently I have not conducted any research of this kind.

My conclusion is based on two things. In the first place Piaget has a very incomplete understanding of the mathematical concepts that appear in the primary mathematics program. More important, Piaget is interested solely in how children develop concepts in the absence of instruction.

A full answer to this point of view must be left to the mathematicians themselves. However, many individuals as well as mathematical groups in Germany and England have thought it worth while to take a new look at their discipline in the light of Piaget's work. A few only will be mentioned. Williams (1958) compared Piaget's approach with the drills and practices arising from the Associationist approach (discussed above), with its theory of 'frequency, recency and intensity'. He verified Piaget's main hypotheses by matching a group of Piaget's tests with arithmetical tests in which the same principles were involved. The results confirmed Williams' belief in the importance of understanding relationships and of the usefulness of including some of the operations described by Piaget in a 'number readiness' programme. Hood (1962) who was also interested in the relationship between success on Piaget's tests and success in arithmetic reported that:

1. Pupils who failed most heavily on the pre-number concept tests were all very weak in arithmetic.
2. Those who passed Piaget tests successfully, with a few exceptions, were all making reasonable progress in arithmetic.
3. No instance of success in arithmetic and failure in Piaget tests was found in the same child.

The most comprehensive study by a mathematical group in England was that of the A.T.C.D.E. Research Group of the Mathematics Section (1963), also reported by Beard (1957, 1963). A standardized battery of three sets of four items of Piaget-type tests was given to large numbers of children in four areas. For full details the report should be read. Among the significant results were the following:

1. Confirmation of the order of difficulty of number concepts found by Piaget;
2. A sequential trend corresponding to Piaget's stages;
3. Ability to count did not necessarily imply understanding;
4. Individual differences possibly due to innate or experiential factors.

From a psychological point of view, it does appear that Piaget's work has drawn attention to the fact that young children have an imperfect understanding of number concepts and that learning to count or compute is not of itself sufficient to create understanding. His emphasis on the internalization of activity as a process in concept formation and the attention he pays to the period of 'concrete operational' thinking, which precedes formal reasoning are in line with changes in the approach to mathematical teaching listed above. As stated, he is not primarily interested in instruction, but, as a method of gaining insight into the way a child thinks, his tests are unrivalled. The author agrees with Lovell (1965) that 'all teachers in training should have the opportunity of observing children undertaking some of the Piaget-type experiments.'

Below is a condensed account of Piaget's theories of the development of the concept of number. It is intended to be a summary rather than a detailed criticism. It is hoped that the interpretation of Piaget's rather difficult terminology is approximately in accordance with his intention. Comments will be found in the accounts of the various tests. The main criticism is Piaget's assumption that because, logically or mathematically, a simple process, such as seriation, contains all the difficulties of a more complicated process, such as correspondence between two sets, the latter will be no more difficult for the child than the former, or that when a 'two to one' relationship is grasped, '3,4,5, etc.,' present no further difficulty. Long experience with teaching children, as well as the results of this investigation (see chapter 10), suggests that although this may ideally be the case, any addition of 'steps' in a process, however simple or repetitive, add to its difficulty for the normal child.

The child's conception of number

In the account of his investigations of the development of the child's conception of number, Piaget sets out to illustrate that arithmetical thought not only passes through the same stages of growth as logical thought, with which it is intimately linked, but that it exemplifies these stages par excellence.

The necessary condition for all rational activity, including arithmetical thought, says Piaget, is the concept of conservation. To the adult it is self-evident that liquids do not change in quantity when poured into glasses of different shapes, or that the number of objects under observation will not increase or decrease, according to their spatial arrangement. This knowledge, however, has been acquired by degrees throughout childhood, there being characteristic stages of development. The history of this acquisition can be described as the freeing of the child's reasoning from the influence of perception, which dominates his judgment in infancy, but progressively loses its hold as he becomes increasingly capable of operational thought.

The course of the struggle is complicated by what can be broadly termed as educational factors, the most important of which, language, is inseparable from formal reasoning. Although, according to Piaget, the development of language itself passes through stages comparable to those experienced in the growth of arithmetical notions, he believes and demonstrates in his tests that the ability to count does not imply understanding of number.

'Judgment', says Piaget, 'comes into play when perception proves inadequate, and only then. The problem is not why perception is deceptive, but why children at a certain level accept it whereas others correct it by the use of intelligence.' In tracing the growth of the child's conception of number, Piaget analyses the processes by which the concept itself derives from basic mathematical and logical principles. These two aspects are interwoven to produce a chain of theorems supported at each link by the results of his investigations with Genevan children. The following is a brief summary.

Arithmetical notions acquire their structure because 'a number is only intelligible if it remains identical with itself whatever the distribution of the elements of which it is composed', that is, because of its conservation. The first notions of number are based on perception and concrete judgment of objects. In describing these, the child relates one object to another, expressing resemblances ('symmetrical relations'), and differences ('asymmetrical relations'). Number is ultimately a fusion of classification (based on resemblances) and quantification (based on differences). The development of a child's ability to classify parallels that of his ability to quantify, a correlation of the two processes leading to a concept of number.

As language develops, a child learns to classify familiar objects in his environment. Classification involves correspondence, and the correspondence between objects that are alike is the beginning of cardination. The simplest and most direct measurement of the equivalence of two sets of objects is demonstrated by setting up a one–one correspondence. This is made easier if the objects are heterogeneous but qualitatively similar, e.g. eggs and egg-cups, but similar results are obtained when correspondence is not demanded by the investigator, but by the situation itself, as, for example, when the child is told, 'There is a number of objects: pick out the same number.'

Cardination involves ordination and vice versa. 'It is only when each element is combined with the preceding one that its position can be determined, just as it is only their position that can differentiate the units, which in other respects are all equivalent.' The ordinal aspect of a series is marked if the elements are not 'vicariant' (interchangeable) but differ from one another by characteristics capable of seriation. 'The child gradually learns that the position of any element in the series can be determined by considering the number of preceding elements.'

Cardinal and ordinal correspondence are combined when the problem involves correspondence between two sets qualitatively similar, each of which is capable of seriation. According to Piaget, this process is no more difficult for a child than constructing a single series. He solves the problem by double seriation, simple seriation and correspondence or direct correspondence. Displacement of one series forces the child, when making the correspondence, to keep both cardinal and ordinal values in mind.

Number involves both the combining of elements into a whole (by the process of addition or multiplication), and the breaking up of wholes into parts (by subtraction and division). The development of the composition of number is therefore linked with another aspect of classification, that of the relation between a whole (class), and its parts (sub-classes). The child gradually learns that a total class is wider than one included in it. Addition of classes involves finding the lowest common multiple, e.g. 'beads' in the case of 'brown round beads' and 'square blue beads'. This implies logical multiplication since 'each element belonging to a system of added classes necessarily belongs to two classes simultaneously.' The same mechanism is used in the grouping of numbers. Whereas grouping of classes involves 'intensive quantification', that is, the use of such words as 'more', 'less', 'one', 'none', 'all', the grouping of numbers involves iteration ('extensive quantification'). Classes are transformed into numbers when their terms are not only regarded as equivalent from every point of view, but remain distinct, i.e. capable of seriation. This appears to be contradictory, but in fact, class, asymmetrical relation and number are, says Piaget, 'three complementary manifestations of the same operational construction applied either to equivalences, differences or both together.'

Addition of number, unlike that of classes, involves iteration, since it produces a new number. The child has to learn that a whole remains constant irrespective of its parts, e.g. 4 plus 4 equals 7 plus 1, likewise that, by a system of compensation, differences can be equated. Equalization of parts involves division when the child is given a set of objects and told to make two equal heaps. 'Additive and multiplicative compositions, whether numerical or qualitative, are therefore correlative, and the mastery of one implies that of the other.'

That arithmetical multiplication results from the correspondence of two or more equivalent sets is gradually understood by the child. He learns that two sets each of which is equivalent to a third set, are equivalent to each other, irrespective of the arrangements of their contents. According to Piaget, the number of sets involved is immaterial once the child has grasped the lasting equivalence between two sets, since the mechanism of his thought does not change. As soon as a 'two to one' relationship is grasped, it becomes possible to generalize it to 3, 4, 5, etc. This principle is tested in the experiments described in chapter 10.

The interdependence and unity of the mechanisms underlying additive and multiplicative compositions of asymmetrical relations and of number is best seen, says Piaget, when continuous quantities are used to analyse the growth of the child's notion of measure. 'In measuring', he says, 'we compose units that are conserved, and introduce a system of equivalence between these compositions.' In order to understand this, the child must not only accept the conservation of liquids regardless of the number and variety of containers into which they are poured, but must also be able to create equivalences by the use of a common unit of measurement.(Processes involved include the relating of width to height ('multiplication of asymmetrical relations') and, by use of a measure, the reorganizing of units to produce an infinite number of compositions. Piaget concludes that:

> While multiplication of classes and multiplication of relations are two distinct operations, the one bringing into correspondence terms that are qualitatively equivalent, and the other asymmetrical relations between non-equivalent terms, all that is necessary in order to make the terms of these relations equivalent and thus to fuse multiplication of relations and that of classes into a single operational whole, is that the differences shall be equalized. We then have multiplication of numbers. Therefore Number is seen to be a synthesis of class and asymmetrical relations.

It will be seen that at every point in his argument, Piaget stresses the importance of the principle of conservation to the understanding of arithmetical notions. The signs of development reached by the child, can, he believes, be determined by the extent to which perception dominates his reasoning, blinding him to the facts of conservation. Although the process is gradual, the transition from childish to adult reasoning is marked by three definite stages. In the first, the child is completely deceived by appearances. He believes that a quantity varies according to its container, or bases his judgment on some qualitative factor such as height or width. He is confused by changes in spatial arrangements, sometimes thinking that density can increase or decrease the number of elements. When he seriates, his 'global' outlook leads him to concentrate on the large or small elements, ignoring the finer graduations, or to pay attention to one aspect, such as the tops of the sticks, while ignoring another, such as the base. When one series is displaced with respect to another, he can no longer see the correspondence. Perception again intervenes to prevent him from thinking simultaneously of a whole, such as a set of wooden beads, and its parts (blue or red beads). When the whole is decomposed, he is incapable of including one of the parts in it. Asked to divide a numerical whole into equal parts, he is satisfied with an appearance of equivalence. At no time is equivalence lasting. To sum up, the child at this stage, limited by his perceptual outlook, is incapable of appreciating conservation, equivalence, part–whole relationships, measure and all the processes necessary for an understanding of number.

At the transitional stage, the child contradicts himself frequently, sometimes basing his reasoning on conservation and sometimes on appearances, often arriving at a correct solution by trial and error. His judgment is still largely controlled by perception, but he differs from children in the first stage by his practical skill in making relationships, seriating, constructing correspondences, etc. In Piaget's terms he is capable of 'concrete operations': he is able to solve an immediate problem, but fails to generalize the results. He can, for example, allow for the height and width of jars when comparing quantities, because he can visualize a system of compensation, but, if one of the quantities is subdivided, his system breaks down, because it is not based on conservation. He knows, intuitively, that a correspondence can be remade after it has been destroyed, but he cannot keep both cardinal and ordinal values in mind at the same time. This frequently leads to a mistake of one unit. For example, when asked how many elements precede a unit, he will include the unit itself, or he will exclude it when calculating its position. His reliance on visual evidence leads him to reconstruct a whole series in order to evaluate one of its elements. It also prevents him from foreseeing the result of addition and subtraction, his ability being limited to the making of rigid reproductions of a numerical model. However, as Piaget points out, the very contradictions in his compositions at this stage are a proof of the conflict between perception and reasoning, and thus a sign that perception is beginning to lose its hold.

The process is completed in the final stage, when the child achieves understanding of conservation because his reasoning, freed from the bonds of perception, is capable of logical and mathematical operations. He grasps both reversibility and equivalence, but, in contrast to the intermediate stage, the equivalence is lasting. The correspondences made by him are of an intellectual nature, so he uses concrete groupings only as a check. Freed from perceptual and spatial limitations, the correspondences persist and thus are truly quantifying. The child at this level can correlate cardination and ordination, recognizing that the element n represents both the nth position and the cardinal value of n. Having achieved mobility of thought, he can construct and reconstruct systems of classes simultaneously, for example, thinking of a quantity of beads in terms of substance, colour or shape, without forgetting one attribute while considering another. He is capable of measuring by using a common unit, and of composing complex systems of relationships, involving both logical and numerical reasoning.

Techniques

Piaget's work on the child's conception of number marks a stage in the development of his techniques. In his earlier work, the investigator questioned a child closely on a number of subjects without the aid of concrete material. From now on, the child will be placed in a carefully devised situation in which he can observe and manipulate concrete material. His answers will be made to questions on observed facts. In his investigations on number concepts, Piaget and his colleagues have, at each point in his argument, devised simple experiments in which the child is asked to handle familiar material such as plasticine, glasses of water, wooden blocks, beads, etc., to describe what he is doing, and give reasons for his actions and their results. The two main features of his method are:

1. The simplicity both of the material used and of the operations demanded from the child. It is this that makes his tests particularly suitable for repetition with children of varying backgrounds and environment. Even the most primitive peoples are likely to be familiar with clay, water and simple vessels.

2. The 'clinical' approach. Each child is interviewed separately, manipulates the material himself, works at his own rate in an atmosphere of play, and is encouraged to express his ideas to the best of his ability. This seems to the investigator not only the most suitable, but the only possible approach for research with very young children. The questionnaire method is economical of time and effort, but its resemblance to the school examination situation subjects it to the same disadvantages. In the interview, the investigator has a better opportunity to assess and increase the cooperation between himself and his child subject, as well as collecting valuable incidental information.

The disadvantage of this method is its lack of precision, controls and exact repeatability, now considered to be almost indispensable in a scientific investigation. A compromise is needed: one that will satisfy these requirements but retain the informal atmosphere characteristic of Piaget's investigations.

References

Anastasi, A., and J. P. Foley. (1949). *Differential Psychology*. New York: Collier-Macmillan.

A.T.C.D.E. (1963). Report on Primary Mathematics.

Ballard, P. B. (1928). *Teaching the Essentials of Arithmetic*. London: University of London Press.

Beard, R. (1957). An investigation of concept formation among infant school children. Unpublished Ph.D. Thesis: University of London.

Beard, R. (1963). The order of concept studies in two fields (i) Number concept in the infant school (ii) Conception of conservation of quantity among primary school children. *Educ. Rev.*, **XV**, Nos. 2, 3.

Binet, A. (1937). In L. M. Terman and M. A. Merrill (Eds.), *Measuring Intelligence*. Boston: Houghton Mifflin.

Carmichael, L., Ed. (1951). *Manual of Child Psychology*. New York: Wiley.

Carpenter, T. E. (1955). A pilot study for a quantitative investigation of Jean Piaget's original work on concept formation. *Educ. Rev.*, **7**, 142–149.

Cuisenaire, G., and C. Cattegno. (1955). *Numbers in Colour*. London: Heinemann.

Dienes, Z. P. (1959). *Concept Formation and Personality*. Leicester: Leicester University Press.

Gardner, D. E. M. (1950). *Long Term Results of Infant School Methods*. London: Methuen.

Garrett, H. E. (1951). *Great Experiments in Psychology*. New York: Appleton-Century-Crofts.

Gesell, A., and F. Ilg. (1946). *The Child from Five to Ten*. London: Hamish Hamilton.

Hood, H. B. (1962). An experimental study of Piaget's theory of the development of number in children. *Br. J. Psychol.*, **53**, 273–286.

Isaacs, Susan. (1930). *Intellectual Growth in Young Children*. London: Routledge and Kegan Paul.

de Lemos, M. Personal Communication.

Lovell, K. (1965). *The Growth of Basic Mathematical Concepts in Children*. London: University of London Press.

N.F.E.R. (1960). National Survey of Attainments: Number Concepts Test (7 plus).

Norsworthy, M. (1906). *Psychology of Mentally Deficient Children*. New York.

Piaget, J. (1952). *The Child's Conception of Number*. London: Routledge and Kegan Paul.

Piaget, J. (1953). *The Origin of Intelligence in the Child*. London: Routledge and Kegan Paul.

Price-Williams, D. R. A. (1961). A study concerning concepts of quantities among primitive children. *Acta Psychol.*, **18**, 293–305. (Reprinted in Price-Williams, 1969.)

Price-Williams, D. R. A., Ed. (1969). *Cross-Cultural Studies*. Harmondsworth, Mddx.: Penguin.

Schonell, F. J., and F. E. Schonell. (1958). *Diagnostic and Remedial Teaching in Arithmetic*. Edinburgh: Oliver and Boyd.

Stern, C. (1949). *Children Discover Arithmetic*. New York. (London: Harrap, 1953.)

Thorndike, E. L. (1922). *The Psychology of Arithmetic*. New York.

Thorndike, E. L. (1924). Mental discipline in high school studies. *J. educ. Psychol.*, **15**, 1–22, 83–98.

Thorndike, E. L., and R. S. Woodworth. (1901). The influence of improvement in one mental function upon efficiency of other functions. *Psychol. Rev.*, **8**, 247–261, 384–395, 553–564.

Wechsler, D. (1944). *The Measurement of Adult Intelligence.* Baltimore: Williams and Wilkins.

Williams, A. A. (1958). Number readiness. *Educ. Rev.*, **11**, 31–45.

Woodworth, R. S. (1950). *Experimental Psychology.* London: Methuen.

Part II
A cross-cultural investigation in Aden, South Arabia*

* Now the Republic of South Yemen.

CHAPTER FIVE

Background to the investigation

Synopsis

This chapter deals with the background to the investigation in Aden, a place which offers great scope to the research worker but also some disadvantages. This is followed by nine chapters each of which describes a test or tests adapted from Piaget or Inhelder for the purpose of the investigation. Reasons for the order of the tests and modifications of Piaget's techniques will be found, while details of the modifications have been included in a description of the relevant test. Although a brief account of Piaget's theories and techniques is included in chapter 4, it has been assumed that the reader is familiar with Piaget's book *The Child's Conception of Number* (1952) or that, if his interest is aroused, he will refer to it.

Chapter 15 discusses four non-verbal tests which were given to the Subjects in conjunction with the Piaget-type tests in order to provide some other yardstick in addition to the latter for ranking Subjects. A brief description of the tests is included.

The final chapter contains a general discussion of the results of this research and their implication for Piaget's theories of the development of number. In addition there are some general comments by the investigator.

Method of presentation

The work is arranged so that each chapter is complete in itself: it introduces a test used, discusses the procedure and analyses the results obtained. In each chapter there is a frequency table, to which reference is made in the discussion of the results, and a bibliography.

The order of tests, however, is not haphazard, since it follows Piaget's own order. This makes it possible to follow the investigations side by side with Piaget's own chapters on the subject, bearing in mind that some of the conservation tests are more fully described by Inhelder (1943). The links between tests or aspects of tests are discussed in the text and illustrated by cross-references. Throughout this section, unless specifically stated otherwise, any reference to Piaget's book is a reference to *The Child's Conception of Number* (1952).

At the end of this work can be found a comprehensive table of the data and a Bibliography and general reference sources.

Aims

The aims of this investigation can be summed up as the quest for answers to the following questions:

1. Do the Arabs, Indians, Somalis and European children living in Aden, faced with the same type of problem as Genevan children, exhibit characteristic responses analysable in terms of Piaget's 'stages'?
2. Are the 'stages' applicable to each test independently or do the tests represent a definite progression in the child's conception of number?
3. Is there any significant difference in the results obtained from children of different communities in Aden with respect to:
   (a) Characteristic responses;
   (b) Average age at which these appear?
   How do they compare with Piaget's norms?

Scope of investigation

This investigation is based on tests described by Piaget in *The Child's Conception of Number* (English edition, 1952), and Bärbel Inhelder's tests reported in *Le Diagnostic du Raisonnement chez les Debiles mentaux* (1943). From a practical point of view it was impossible to give all the tests, so the selection was made from two points of view:

1. At least one test should be selected to illustrate each main stage in the child's development of number as maintained by Piaget.
2. Within the range, tests most enjoyed by children should be selected.

Before the main investigation was begun, while the investigator was improving her Arabic, a pilot study was carried out on 14 English and Arab children. As a result of this study the procedure was streamlined to minimize fatigue in the subjects, and the following tests were rejected:

(a) The bead test (chapter 2, Piaget, 1952, illustrating conservation of discontinuous quantities). This test was unsatisfactory since the beads made different heights in the glasses according to the way they were placed. Several children pointed this out. The subject of conservation was well covered by other, better tests.

(b) The glass and bottle test (chapter 3, Piaget, 1952), which, in the pilot study, was given alternately with the bath and doll test, was dropped in favour of the latter which was much more popular.

(c) The first experiment (chapter 8, Piaget, 1952) on the arithmetical relation of part to whole was found to be unsatisfactory. In the brief time that could be allotted to it there was hardly any pause between the investigator's assertion that the number of sweets for the following day would be the same, and her question 'Will you have the same number of sweets both days?' The shell test was also preferred because the children manipulated the material themselves.

(d) In the pilot study, the test on reproduction of figures (chapter 4, Piaget, 1952) was tried out, using coins instead of counters. In order to make it practicable in the time available, the number of operations had to be reduced. This was unsatisfactory so the test was later omitted.

Subjects

144 children living in Aden: 72 male, 72 female, consisting of 48 Europeans (mainly British), 48 Arabs, 24 Indians and 24 Somalis.

For a number of reasons the Subjects were, in a sense, self-selected. They were, unless under school age, attending local schools with the same type of syllabus, though taught in different languages but, as the investigation had to take place entirely out of school hours, nothing could be done without the cooperation of parents, friends and the children themselves. The investigator made a blank list of races, numbers and sex required in the different groups and filled it in as volunteers were found. The finding of the Subjects was partly done by the children themselves who told their friends and brought them along in large numbers sometimes at very inconvenient times. In a sense, the European group was not a cross-section of a normal population. They were the children of Government Officials, business men and R.A.F. personnel domiciled in Aden, whose economic position was mostly higher than that of the majority of the local Subjects. In a country where there is no compulsory education and girls have only recently competed for school places it could be said that the local Subjects were also the children of the more enlightened section of the population. They were, however, random samples of a much larger group.

For practical reasons the investigation could not take place in one particular room. The investigator used her flat in Khormaksar and schools in different parts of Aden, by kind permission of the Head Teachers, the main consideration being transport. Local friends helped to collect the children but the investigator had to see them home. In order to be able to grade the answers, no child was accepted without a birth certificate unless the school had a record. Many local children turned up with their framed birth certificate removed from its place of honour on the sitting room wall.

Some explanation had to be given to parents and friends. They were told that the investigator had a number of toys and puzzles, and that she wanted to see how children of different races would play with them. No child was allowed to take part without permission of the parents. The whole situation was so novel, that in some child circles you were not 'in the swim' unless you had played with Miss H's toys. The refusal of children who were over or under age sometimes needed delicate handling. One kind friend seeking Indian Subjects among his neighbours was asked, 'Why does she want Indians? There are plenty of Arabs about!'

Special problems

It is difficult to foresee all the problems and difficulties involved in research in a backward country, and, as an alternative to abandoning the project, the best has to be done in the circumstances. Most of Piaget's Subjects were between the ages of four and nine years old so it was desirable to choose children as young as possible. There are no nursery schools in Aden and it was quite unrealistic to think of enticing little Arabs, Somalis and Indians from their mothers to play for long periods with a foreigner, even if the mothers had been willing and the children as fluent as Aes, Geo, etc., who expressed their reactions so clearly to Piaget. It was, therefore, decided to start with the official school age (six years) and take children under nine years. Unfortunately, whereas there was no European child of six who was not attending school, many local children begin school between seven and eight years, owing to shortage of places. In the end a few children who had not started school, some of them not quite six, had to be accepted in the six-year-old group. Somalis of the right age were a problem too, as many of them stay with relations in Somaliland to learn their mother tongue before beginning their lessons in Arabic in Aden. In the end, one or two just turned nine had to be accepted in the eight-year-old group.

The investigation was conducted in two languages: English and Aden Arabic. With one exception, no child was accepted who could not speak and understand one of these languages. The Somalis and Indians formed a bilingual group: they spoke their own tongue in the home but used Arabic in the street and often at school. The exception was brought by an enthusiastic father when the investigator had despaired of finishing the youngest Indian group. Having sent the father away she had to call him back as an interpreter since Maboub could not understand a word of Arabic. The investigator was much indebted to an Arab Education Officer, who not only acted the child's part in order to test her Arabic version of the tests, but observed the first 20 Arabic-speaking Subjects in case a language difficulty arose. He was quite confident that the investigator and the children understood each other but stayed on out of interest. He was the only helper who knew what took place at the sessions.

On some Sundays the whole morning was wasted waiting for children who had promised to come but had not arrived. A sense of time is not highly developed in the Middle East countries. The only way to make sure of getting a reasonable number of Subjects for the morning was to arrange for them to be collected and brought to the centre, and then to keep them there until the last one had been tested. They played games while waiting their turn. Testing had to stop at the beginning of the Ramadhan Fast which lasts from dawn until sunset for a month, as, although the children themselves were not fasting, one could not reasonably expect their parents to cooperate. Also testing in the worst of the hot weather was avoided.

There are many advantages for the research worker in Aden to offset the difficulties. There are a number of communities living in the same environment, but maintaining their own social and religious customs and speaking their own languages. One criticism of Piaget is that he has generalized from results of investigations with a small and highly selected group of Genevan children. If similar results are obtained when children are tested in such different circumstances, this criticism loses its validity.

Finally must be mentioned the satisfaction gained from being the first in the field. The children were not bored because it was an entirely new experience for them. In fact their enthusiasm was embarrassing at times. Whereas on some days none turned up, on others certain 'regulars' appeared for the fourth, fifth or sixth time and could not be discouraged. No doubt the sweets and ride home in a car were responsible. Many of the parents became very interested and were promised a demonstration at some future date. There was the feeling that in any future research in Aden it would be possible to improve the conditions, since contact has been established with a reliable group of helpers as a result of this investigation.

The tests: introduction

The Piaget tests

Following the order of Piaget's chapters in *The Child's Conception of Number*, the tests can be grouped as follows:

Part I. Conservation of Quantities and Invariance of Wholes.

Deformed Ball: Substance⎫
Deformed Ball: Weight   ⎬Inhelder.
Deformed Ball: Volume   ⎭

Ch. 1   Water Tests⎫
        Block Test ⎬Inhelder.
        Sugar Test ⎭

Part II. Cardinal and Ordinal one–one Correspondence.

Ch. 3   Bath and Doll Test
Ch. 5   House and Door Test
Ch. 6   Staircase Tests

Part III. Additive and Multiplicative Compositions.

Ch. 7   The Bead Test
Ch. 8   The Shell Tests
Ch. 9   Bath, Towel and Doll Test
Ch. 10 The Parallel Glass Test

ORDER OF TESTS

The tests were divided into two groups:

Group I

The three Plasticine Conservation Tests
The Bath and Doll Test
The House and Door Test
The Staircase Tests
The Bead Test
The Shell Tests

Group II

The Water Tests
The Block Test
The Sugar Test
The Bath, Towel and Doll Test
The Parallel Glass Test

Within these groups the order of tests was randomized. The aim was to allow for randomization and, at the same time, minimize the risks of collusion between Subjects, help from home and learning from test to test. At the same time, the more popular tests needed to be divided between the sessions in order to maintain interest. All these considerations had to be balanced. It would have been preferred not to have given the three

Plasticine Tests on the same day but in view of the hypothesis on the order in which conservation of substance, weight and volume are acquired, it was essential that outside learning should not take place between the tests. They were, of course, randomized and separated as far as possible from each other during the session.

A warning was given by Arab friends that no Arab child would be able to keep the tests secret, as this is against their social custom, but it was found that children from all communities responded when told that it would spoil the fun for their friends if they knew what was going to happen beforehand. A special pact was made that if parents were very insistent the children could say 'we played with plasticine, water, blocks, etc.,' but would not mention details of questions or answers. A group of children brought together played games while waiting for their turn but the variety of responses from any one group convinced the investigator that the promise of secrecy was being kept. Where possible, children were separated from the group, after being tested, so that they only played with someone who had done the same tests, but to have kept strictly to this arrangement would not only have invited tears and non-cooperation, but would have defeated randomization. In family groups and, as a general rule, the youngest children were tested first. As a final precaution each child took the following note (in English or Arabic) home with him at the end of the first session:

> There are no right or wrong answers in this investigation. Each answer is equally valuable. I should be very grateful if you would not discuss with your child any questions or answers he may remember, to avoid influencing subsequent items, though he will naturally want to tell you what he has been doing. In an investigation of this type it is better to defer discussion until the conclusion. Thank you very much for your cooperation.

Many parents said that their children refused even to mention the tests, taking pride in being able to keep a secret.

The length of sessions and the number of tests given at a sitting had to be varied since, while in view of the wide scope of the investigation time was an important factor, it was even more important to keep the child's interest and cooperation. The investigator, therefore, judged when a child needed a break or had had enough for one day. As all the tests could not be given on one day, it was most important that the child would not refuse to return willingly another time. There were Subjects who had to be replaced because they did not complete the tests, but this was not the fault of the children who, however apprehensive on the first occasion, clamoured for another visit; it was because a few parents found the effort inconvenient. One British mother, having failed to cancel three afternoon appointments,

withdrew her support, but the majority of the parents were most coopera-
tive, bringing not only their own children but others in their neighbour-
hood.

Modifications of Piaget's techniques and procedure

An attempt was made to combine the procedural advantages of the
'clinical method' adopted by Piaget and his colleagues with the statistical
advantages of more refined scientific methods. Thus the child's 'irrelevant'
remarks during the course of the tests were tolerated: he was encouraged
to expand his explanations in order to clarify his ideas and, within the
limits of the design, the investigator adopted his phraseology. In the course
of each test however, certain crucial questions were put, the answers to
which were recorded verbatim and used in quantifying results.

Modifications in procedure and content were of two kinds:

1. Those depending on the time factor, length of test, variations in
   material, subsidiary tests, etc. It is quite patent that one investigator
   using 144 Subjects could not hope to cover in detail with each one of
   them the ground covered by Piaget, Inhelder and a team of workers in
   the course of years. There had to be a selection and streamlining of
   procedure. Each original test was studied from the point of view of its
   basic importance to Piaget's theories, and an endeavour was made to
   preserve its essence even when different material was selected. (There
   is no implication that the tests used were in any way superior to the
   original versions: quite the contrary. The modifications were justified
   by the circumstances of this investigation.)
2. A set of changes included in the above was also made on other grounds.
   In the original tests the child was frequently invited to verify his results.
   For example, scales were used by Inhelder in her conservation tests on
   weight and, in Piaget's Water Test, the child, having compared the
   amount of water in one of the pair of jars with that of its companion
   after pouring into a cylinder, pours it back again before making a second
   comparison using a wide jar. It seems to the investigator that, although
   the child's responses are in all circumstances 'grist to the mill', knowledge of results and learning during the tests had to be kept to a minimum
   in order not to confuse the issue in this particular investigation.

Grading system

Grades for individual tests are discussed separately. The task set was to
keep the divisions as clear cut and unambiguous as possible using Piaget's
classification.

Grade 'C'

Answers in this category showed a complete lack of understanding of the problem. The child failed to grasp relationships, was sidetracked by irrelevances or deceived by appearances. This is sometimes referred to as the 'global stage' by Piaget.

Grade 'B'

Answers in this category illustrate the intermediary reactions described by Piaget. The child recognizes a relationship but cannot explain it: he is deceived by appearance in one case but not in another: he can solve the problem when it is straightforward but not when it is reversed. Piaget sometimes refers to this as the 'intuitive' stage.

Grade 'A'

In these answers the problem was solved: the answer including or implying some ability for abstract reasoning. The problem is seen not in isolation but as an example of a general law. This law can be applied whatever form the problem takes. Piaget sometimes calls this the 'operational' stage.

These categories were sufficiently clear cut in the children's answers for a regrading in England to be substantially the same as an original grading in Aden some months before. In fact, changes made were due not to a change in judgment but to one or two slight changes made in sub-grouping answers. These sub-groupings were additions to the main analysis, e.g. noting that some children referred to the weight of the ball in the Conservation of Volume Test. They do not appear in the statistical tables, which deal with main categories, but references to them can be found in the author's comments on performance in some of the tests.

The non-verbal intelligence tests

In addition to the tests adapted from Piaget and Inhelder four non-verbal intelligence tests were given to each Subject. These are discussed in chapter 15.

References

Hickinbotham, Sir Tom. (1958). *Aden.* London: Constable.
Ingrams, Harold. (1966). *Arabia and the Isles,* 3rd ed. London: Murray.
Inhelder, B. (1943). *Le Diagnostic du Raisonnement chez les Débiles mentaux.* Neuchâtel: Delachaux et Niestlé.
Little, T. (1968). *South Arabia.* London: Pall Mall.

Lunt, J. (1966). *The Barren Rocks of Aden.* London: Jenkins.
Piaget, J. (1952). *The Child's Conception of Number.* London: Routledge and Kegan Paul.
Price-Williams, D. R. A., Ed. (1969). *Cross-Cultural Studies.* Harmondsworth, Mddx.: Penguin.
Van der Meulen, D., and H. Von Wissmann. (1964). *Hadramant: Some of its Mysteries Unveiled.* Leyden: Brill.
Waterfield, G. (1968). *Sultans of Aden.* London: Murray.

CHAPTER SIX

Concepts of the conservation of substance, weight and volume

General introduction to the conservation tests

Fundamental to all scientific thought is the principle of conservation, so the child's development in the understanding of the 'invariance' of number and quantity forms the basis of Piaget's theories. On this understanding depends the whole structure of the child's arithmetical reasoning. Indeed, all Piaget's carefully devised tests on seriation, part–whole relationships, correspondence under different conditions and equalization of differences are an elaboration or development of his basic tests on the concept of conservation.

In this investigation most of the conservation tests were adapted from those reported by Piaget's colleague, Bärbel Inhelder, in *Le Diagnostic du Raisonnement chez les Débiles mentaux* (1943), the remainder being included by Piaget in *The Child's Conception of Number* (1952).

One important adaptation of Inhelder's tests was adopted in this investigation. Although, as Inhelder herself observed, children will insist on the correctness of their answers in spite of evidence to the contrary, according to her table, some of her Subjects passed from Stage 2 to Stage 4 during the tests. This learning which may have resulted from verification of results after each test is interesting, but confuses the issue. In this investigation no verification (as, for instance, by the use of scales in the weighing tests) was allowed, and no comments were made on the child's observations, although his handiwork was admired. The lack of verification also minimized perseveration, which is a danger to be faced when so many of the answers use the word 'same'.

During the last ten years the conservation tests have been the most popular for replication, partly because of their importance for Piaget's theories, and partly for simplicity of materials and ease of administration. These factors also make them particularly suitable for cross-cultural studies. In even the most primitive countries, clay vessels are in common use, so that children are familiar with the material used by the potters. This means that investigators, mindful of the importance of using indigenous material in cross-cultural studies can, by using clay in these tests, make direct comparison with the results of tests carried out both in Geneva and other parts of the world.

Although reference will be made to some of the more important individual tests of substance, weight and volume, carried out by individual investigators, notably Lovell and Ogilvie (1960, 1961), interest in this chapter is centred on the order of acquisition, cited by Inhelder as an example of *décalage horizontale*.

Deformed Ball: conservation of substance

Introduction

The use of plasticine (referred to as 'clay' by the local children of Aden) in this and other tests to study the child's understanding of conservation was one of those brilliant ideas, so simple that one cannot imagine not thinking of it oneself! Not only is the material admirably suited to the investigator's purpose, but it can be relied on to give pleasure to all the child Subjects, of whatever race or background. This is especially true of the modern odourless forms, which, being clean to handle, cause no revulsion from even the most particular little girls. Many a child, whose parents have made him nervous by telling him (in spite of instructions) that he is about to be 'examined', has taken courage at the sight of the familiar material, especially if, before testing was begun, he was allowed to play freely with it.

In this test, the problem is straightforward. Will two balls, which originally contained the same amount of plasticine, still contain the same amount when the shape of one is altered?

Description of the test

MATERIALS

2 balls of Aloplast the same colour
A plasticine board

PROCEDURE

The child was given the two balls of Aloplast and asked if there was the same amount of plasticine in them. If he thought that there was not, he was asked to make them both the same. When he was quite satisfied that there was no difference in the balls, he was told to put one on one side and with the other to make a long sausage (snake, piece of string, and so forth, according to taste, string being substituted for sausage with local children who were mainly Moslems). He was then asked to compare the amount of plasticine in the ball and the sausage (Question 1). After this he was told to make the sausage into a ball again. This time he had the two balls to compare: one which had never lost its ball shape, and the other which had suffered changes in shape (Question 2).

QUESTIONS

1. Have the ball and the sausage the same amount of plasticine in them, or has one more than the other? Why?
2. Have these balls the same amount of plasticine in them or has one more than the other?

Comments on performance

As in the original experiment, the children who gave non-conservation answers were deceived by the appearance of the deformed ball. Their judgment was based on perception instead of reasoning. Typical conservation answers (graded 'A') were:

No. 2   'The same: the sausage looks bigger but it's not, because we equalled it out before: That's fat and round and this is long and thin.'

No. 49   'The same, because at first they were the same but I only rolled that one.'

No. 15   'The same because the balls were the same when I rolled the sausage.'

Some children were intuitively sure of the sameness of the two pieces of plasticine, but were less able to formulate the reason (Grade 'B' answers). Among these Subjects were:

No. 6   'The same because this is big and this is big.'
No. 9   'The same because this is a big rope and this is a big ball.'

The non-conservation answers (graded 'C') mostly referred to the length of the sausage, string, etc.

No. 74   'The string is more because it's long.'
No. 83   'The string is more because it's big.'
No. 26   'There's a little more in the sausage because the sausage is longer: at first they were the same.'

Many children, however, thought that the ball contained more plasticine:

No. 3   'The ball has more because it's rounder.'

No. 42   'The ball has more because the string is long.'

No. 43   'The ball has more because it's bigger and solid.'

No. 70   'The ball has more because the string is weak.'

The answers to the second question fell into two groups. Those who had given a perceptual response to the first question either thought that its change in substance had been temporary and that a return to its ball shape would right matters, or that a permanent transformation had taken place. The following are examples of the two groups:

Group I

No. 52   'The same: none is small: they are brothers.'

No. 53   'The same, because this one is like that one.'

No. 75   'The same, because both balls.'

No. 113   'The same, because the snake has got rolled up.'

Group II

No. 8   'There is more in this ball because the other has been made into a rope.'

No. 51   'This ball is more because at first it was string.'

No. 103   'This ball (string) is more because I rolled it.'

Grading system

'A' Conservation

'B' Right answer but inadequate reason

'C' Non-conservation

N.B. If a child thought that the deformation had permanently changed the amount of plasticine in the second ball, this was indicated by (p.c.).

Results (Table 1)

In terms of age the trend in this test is in the right direction. At first glance boys appear to be better than girls, but in the combined results of tests 1, 2 and 3 the difference is insignificant. When the communities are compared, the Arabs were a little better than the Indians and Somalis. Although the European children's results were better, they were still poor. Out of 48 such children 22 used global comparison, including five eight-year olds. Nearly one third of the Subjects who gave non-conservation answers thought that the deformation had permanently changed the amount of plasticine in the second ball. The rest thought that with the return of its ball shape, the sausage reverted to its original quantity.

Discussion

The quantitative results of this test are discussed in conjunction with those of test 2 and test 3.

Table 1

Conservation of Substance Test

Frequency distribution of results obtained with test no. 1

Group	Rating	Age 6+ M	F	Total	Age 7+ M	F	Total	Age 8+ M	F	Total	Total M	F	Total
European	A	3	2	5	5	4	9	6	3	9	14	9	23
	B	—	—	—	1	—	1	1	1	2	2	1	3
	C	5	6	11	2	4	6	1	4	5	8	14	22
	Total	8	8	16	8	8	16	8	8	16	24	24	48
Arab	A	—	1	1	1	—	1	3	1	4	4	2	6
	B	—	—	—	—	—	—	1	—	1	1	—	1
	C	8	7	15	7	8	15	4	7	11	19	22	41
	Total	8	8	16	8	8	16	8	8	16	24	24	48
Indian	A	—	—	—	—	—	—	1	2	3	1	2	3
	B	—	—	—	—	—	—	—	—	—	—	—	—
	C	4	4	8	4	4	8	3	2	5	11	10	21
	Total	4	4	8	4	4	8	4	4	8	12	12	24
Somali	A	—	—	—	—	—	—	1	1	2	1	1	2
	B	—	—	—	—	—	—	—	—	—	—	—	—
	C	4	4	8	4	4	8	3	3	6	11	11	22
	Total	4	4	8	4	4	8	4	4	8	12	12	24
Total	A	3	3	6	6	4	10	11	7	18	20	14	34
	B	—	—	—	1	—	1	2	1	3	3	1	4
	C	21	21	42	17	20	37	11	16	27	49	57	106
	Total	24	24	48	24	24	48	24	24	48	72	72	144

According to Piaget, the child's attainment of the concept of substance (or quantity) follows the stages characteristic of his general cognitive development. At first he is deceived by the appearance of the object made by the second ball of clay, thinking that change of shape may imply change of amount. This is because he is exclusively occupied with one aspect of the situation. During a transition period he sometimes arrives intuitively at the right answer, but his formulation of it is imperfect, depending no doubt partly on his language development but also on the particular concrete situation to which his judgment is related. Lovell and Ogilvie (1960) found that some children who were non-conservers in this experiment when plasticine was used, were conservers when tested with rubber bands. As reported later in this book, the author, like Beard (1957), found that conservation of quantity was achieved more quickly when liquid was poured from one vessel to another than in the test above using plasticine. This was also found in the Geneva tests. In Piaget's third stage, the child gives a 'conservation' answer. All these stages were found, as described above. It seems that once the concept of the conservation of substance has been obtained using one material, such as plasticine, it does not necessarily follow that it will hold in all situations involving conservation of substance. Lovell suggests: 'It seems rather that the concept is applicable only to highly specific situations at first and that it increases in depth and complexity with experience and maturation.' Perhaps Lunzer's (1968) suggestion that a fourth stage be added 'in which insightful application is added to complete appreciation' is the answer here. It would make the task of validating Piaget's stages less difficult.

Deformed Ball: conservation of weight

Introduction

According to Piaget, the development of the concept of the conservation of weight is a later stage than that of substance: the child can accept the latter and deny the former but not vice versa. In this investigation the test chosen from Inhelder's group follows closely the technique used in the Conservation of Substance Test, so that at a later point a fair comparison can be made between the results. The problem for the child is: will two balls of plasticine which originally weighed the same still weigh the same after the shape of one of them has been altered?

Description of the test

MATERIALS

2 balls of Aloplast of the same colour
A plasticine board

In the original test scales were used to weigh the plasticine balls. This must have given great joy to the young Subjects who, if they were like the children in this investigation, would have prolonged the process as long as possible! So, for practical reasons, the scales were dispensed with and the child was simply asked to weigh the two balls by balancing them in his hands and to say whether they were the same weight. If they were not, he was told to adjust the plasticine until they were. He then had to put one ball to the side and with the other make a large plate. This, as in the original, was to show that length as such was not responsible for the results in the previous test. He was *not* then asked to weigh the ball and plate to make a comparison, because this would be a judgment of how they *felt*, and they might easily feel different. Instead of this, the investigator placed them in her hands and pretended to balance one against the other. She then said 'I wonder how the weight will be. What do you think?, etc.' The child was asked to justify his belief (Question 1). Then he was told to make the plate into a ball again and once more to compare the weight of the two balls (Question 2).

QUESTIONS

1. Will the plate weigh heavier than the ball, or are they the same, or does the ball weigh heavier than the plate? Why?
2. Is one ball heavier than the other or not? Why?

Comments on performance

It is interesting that among all the 144 Subjects, not one child, including a very precocious scientifically minded young American, questioned the validity of weighing the balls with hands! The investigator had fully expected some of the eight-year olds to demand a balance, instead of which, like the younger ones, they solemnly balanced one ball against the other, confident in their judgment.

As in the Substance Test, non-conservation answers were given by children deceived by the shape of the plate. Typical conservation answers (graded 'A') were:

No. 1 'The same, because they were the same weight when they were in balls.'
No. 15 'The same, because when I made the plate they were the same weight.'
No. 94 'The same, because I made them the same: I put a little bit from one ball to the other.'

In this test, and indeed in all the tests using plasticine one or two were confused by their original adjustment of the balls. Having made it, they forgot that the purpose was equivalence. An example is No. 30: 'The plate is heavier because it was lighter at first and then I took a little from the other ball.'

As before, some children gave inadequate reasons for their correct judgment (graded 'B').

No. 8   'The same, because at the beginning they were both balls.'

The non-conservation answers (graded 'C') mostly referred to the flatness or thinness of the plate as compared with the solid ball:

No. 27 'The ball is heavier because it's fat and the plate is thin.'

No. 26 'The ball is heavier because when the plate is flattened out it feels lighter.'

No. 25 'The ball weighs heavier because it is round.'

No. 11 'The plate is light: at first it was heavy, but now it is weak.'

There were exceptions:

No. 24 'The plate is heavier because it's got weight on the sides.'

As in the Substance Test, the deformed ball either returned to its former state or its weight was permanently affected by the deformation.

Group I

No. 11 'The same: this was weak but now it is the same.'

No. 21 'The same, because I have put them in a ball again.'

No. 95 'They weigh the same because the plate has been made into a ball.'

Group II

No. 3   'That one (not plate) is heavier because it is round.'

No. 37   'The ball that wasn't a plate is heavier because the other one is soft.'

No. 19 groped for a reason to explain more frequent changes in weight. He started off with the balls weighing the same, then found the ball heavier 'because the ball is not flattened out like a plate.' Finally he decided that 'The one the plate is made from is a little bit heavier because I must have added a little more when weighing them.'

Grading system

'A' Conservation

'B' Right answer: inadequate reason

'C' Non-conservation

N.B. If a child thought that the deformation had permanently changed the weight of the second ball, this was indicated by (p.c.).

Results (Table 2)

The results of the seven plus group of European children are slightly better than the eight plus group. Apart from this the trend, in terms of age,

Table 2

Conservation of Weight Test

Frequency distribution of results obtained with test no. 2

Group	Rating	Age 6+ M	F	Total	Age 7+ M	F	Total	Age 8+ M	F	Total	Total M	F	Total
European	A	1	1	2	3	3	6	4	1	5	8	5	13
	B	—	—	—	1	1	2	—	—	—	1	1	2
	C	7	7	14	4	4	8	4	7	11	15	18	33
	Total	8	8	16	8	8	16	8	8	16	24	24	48
Arab	A	—	1	1	—	—	—	3	—	3	3	1	4
	B	—	—	—	—	—	—	1	1	2	1	1	2
	C	8	7	15	8	8	16	4	7	11	20	22	42
	Total	8	8	16	8	8	16	8	8	16	24	24	48
Indian	A	—	—	—	—	1	1	—	1	1	—	2	2
	B	—	—	—	—	—	—	—	—	—	—	—	—
	C	4	4	8	4	3	7	4	3	7	12	10	22
	Total	4	4	8	4	4	8	4	4	8	12	12	24
Somali	A	—	—	—	—	1	1	1	1	2	1	2	3
	B	—	—	—	—	—	—	—	—	—	—	—	—
	C	4	4	8	4	3	7	3	3	6	11	10	21
	Total	4	4	8	4	4	8	4	4	8	12	12	24
Total	A	1	2	3	3	5	8	8	3	11	12	10	22
	B	—	—	—	1	1	2	1	1	2	2	2	4
	C	23	22	45	20	18	38	15	20	35	58	60	118
	Total	24	24	48	24	24	48	24	24	48	72	72	144

is in the right direction. The European and Arab boys have slightly better results than the girls, but in the Indian and Somali groups the opposite obtains, so that there is very little difference in the totals. The results for the Aden communities are uniformly low: only four Arabs, two Indians and three Somalis gave 'conservation' answers. The European children's results are a little better but very weak. Out of 48 children in this group, 33 used global comparison, including eleven aged eight years.

Discussion

The quantitative results of this test are discussed at the end of this chapter in conjunction with the results of tests 1 and 3. It is worth noting, however, that the relative difficulty of the concept of weight compared with substance, as found in the group as a whole, is in line with Piaget's hypothesis concerning individual children, which is discussed later in this chapter.

From experience using this test in Aden and elsewhere, it seems certain that for many young children there is no dividing line between the concepts of substance and weight. When asked in the previous test whether there was more plasticine in the ball or the string or in the two balls, they frequently justified their answers by saying 'they weigh the same'. Many of them responded to the question by spontaneously picking up the two objects and weighing them in their hands. Piaget noted this confusion in another experiment in which five objects were used of the same weight but with one having a different amount. It is therefore not surprising if the gap between acquiring the concepts of the conservation of substance and weight is not as wide as that between weight and volume, if the same material is used.

Once again the children could be grouped according to Piaget's stages. Typical answers showing conservation, an intermediate stage and non-conservation can be seen above. Further confirmation resulted from the studies of Lovell and Ogilvie (1961). However, when they varied the procedure using a third heavier ball with which to compare the other two, it was found that non-conservers and children at the intermediate stage could see the relationship between the weights of the three balls. (In Piaget's terminology, they were capable of transitivity although not of conservation.) Ironically, Inhelder pointed out that Lovell's experiment differed in essential details from the Genevan experiment, which makes comparison difficult. Smedslund (1959, 1961), studying transitivity of weight concluded, unlike Lovell, that conservation occurs before transitivity, but his procedure differed materially from Lovell's. Varying the procedure is not only a legitimate but necessary experimental device, but it is a two-edged weapon in validation studies.

Deformed Ball: conservation of volume

Introduction

This test, adapted from Inhelder's group, completes the plasticine tests on substance, weight and volume. It will be considered separately in this section after which a comparison will be made between the results of the three tests. An extra interesting feature of this test is the child's explanation of the increased volume of the contents of the glass after the plasticine ball has been put into the water.

Description of the tests

MATERIALS

2 balls of Aloplast of the same colour
A plasticine board
A glass half filled with water

PROCEDURE

As before, the child started with two balls of plasticine which he was told to compare for size and adjust for size if necessary. His attention was then drawn to the glass of water and he was asked what would happen if either of the balls was put into the water. If his answers were not concerned with volume, he was asked to look at the height of the water in the glass and say whether it would stay where it was or go up or down (Question 1). A reason was required for his answer (Question 2).

He was then told to put one of the balls to one side and with the other to make whatever he liked: a doll, cat, aeroplane, etc. Only one model was required and every bit of plasticine must be used. When this was finished he was asked to compare the amount of room that the ball or his model would take up in the water (Question 3). If he appeared not to understand the question, he was asked to put his finger on the glass to show where the water would come if the ball were put in, and then to show where it would come for his model. (In the original experiment rubber bands were used. They would have been introduced in this investigation if found to be necessary, but in each case the answer was quite clear without.) The child was asked to account for his reply. He was then told to make his model into a ball again and then compare the room taken up by the two balls respectively in the water (Question 4).

QUESTIONS

1. What will happen if you put the ball of plasticine into the jar of water?
2. Why will the water go up? (down?)

3. Do you think that the aeroplane, (cat, doll, etc.) will take up more room in the water than the ball, or less, or the same? Why?
4. Will one ball take up more or the same or less room than the other? Why?

Comments on performance

Most of the children thought that the water would rise after the ball of plasticine had been put in it. If they had no idea what would happen or needed encouragement, the investigator allowed them to see for themselves as the real interest in this question was the child's reasoning. Some children thought that the water would go down. As Piaget observed, many children think that the weight of the ball or the force behind it is responsible for the change in the height of the water. Such answers included the following:

No. 1   'The weight makes the water go a bit higher.'
No. 3   'The ball of plasticine is heavy so it makes the water go up.'
No. 5   'The ball is so heavy that it sinks down and pushes the water up.'
No. 21   'The plasticine goes in and pushes the water away and gets it higher.'

Among the good answers were the following:

No. 2   'It takes up some room and the water still in comes higher because it can't get into the place where the ball is.'
No. 8   'The ball is in the water and the water must go up because the ball has no room.'
No. 12   'Now the water's a little: then you need more room and it goes up.'

No. 11 insisted that the water stayed where it was in spite of many demonstrations, while No. 30 thought that the water would go down because 'the ball is heavy and the water is light.'

The reasoning in Question 3 and 4 followed the same pattern as in the substance and weight tests. The following are examples of single 'conservation' answers in Question 3 (graded 'A').

No. 46   'They will take up the same room because when they were balls they were the same.'
No. 50   'Both the same, because when the aeroplane was a ball the balls were both the same.'
No. 94   'The same room because they were both the same to begin with.'

Two children thought that the ball and model would take up the same room because of equal weight. Their answers were graded 'B'.

e.g.   'The water will be the same height because the plate is as heavy as the ball.'

In the non-conservation answers (graded 'C') explanation was found in the shape of the model, its size and its weight.

No. 135 'The water would not go up as high for the boat as for the ball because the boat is lighter.'

No. 131 'The water will go down more for the snake because it is longer.'

No. 19 'The water would come a bit higher because the plate is a bit wider than the ball.'

In the last question there were again those who thought the volume was equalized by the return of the model to its former condition, and others who considered the change in volume permanent. Among the latter were:

No. 70 'The water is higher for the ball that was a plate.'

No. 73 'The water is higher for the ball that was a rope.'

No. 14 'The water is down for the ball that was a rope.'

No. 69 gave a very clear answer with suitable gestures:

'It is higher for this because I haven't rolled it up properly.' (He finished the job) 'Now they are the same.'

Grading system

'A' Conservation

'B' Right answer: inadequate or wrong reason

e.g.   'The water will be the same height because the plate is as heavy as the ball.'

'C' Non-conservation

N.B. (i) Weight causing water to rise (Question 2) was indicated by 'w'.
     (ii) Permanent change as the result of deformation (Question 4) was indicated by (p.c.).

Results (Table 3)

The results of the Indians and Somalis show a normal trend in each age group, but as only three of them gave 'A' grade answers, and none gave 'B' grade, this trend cannot be taken very seriously. The European children, as in the previous test, were better at the seven-year than the eight-year level whose results were even slightly worse than those of the six-year olds. In the Arab group, too, the six-year group was slightly better than the others, but as only three children in the whole group achieved an 'A' grade, this anomaly could be attributed to sampling. In the European community the boys were better than the girls, but in the totals there is very little difference between the sexes. There is little difference in the results of the Aden communities which are well below those of the European children. Among the latter, 27 out of 48 used global comparison, including, as in test 2, eleven children aged eight years.

Table 3

Conservation of Volume Test

Frequency distribution of results obtained with test no. 3

Group	Rating	Age 6+ M	F	Total	Age 7+ M	F	Total	Age 8+ M	F	Total	Total M	F	Total
European	A	4	1	5	5	4	9	2	2	4	11	7	18
	B	—	1	1	1	—	1	—	1	1	1	2	3
	C	4	6	10	2	4	6	6	5	11	12	15	27
	Total	8	8	16	8	8	16	8	8	16	24	24	48
Arab	A	—	2	2	—	—	—	1	—	1	1	2	3
	B	—	—	—	—	—	—	1	—	1	1	—	1
	C	8	6	14	8	8	16	6	8	14	22	22	44
	Total	8	8	16	8	8	16	8	8	16	24	24	48
Indian	A	—	—	—	1	—	1	—	1	1	1	1	2
	B	—	—	—	—	—	—	—	—	—	—	—	—
	C	4	4	8	3	4	7	4	3	7	11	11	22
	Total	4	4	8	4	4	8	4	4	8	12	12	24
Somali	A	—	—	—	—	—	—	—	1	1	—	1	1
	B	—	—	—	—	—	—	—	—	—	—	—	—
	C	4	4	8	4	4	8	4	3	7	12	11	23
	Total	4	4	8	4	4	8	4	4	8	12	12	24
Total	A	4	3	7	6	4	10	3	4	7	13	11	24
	B	—	1	1	1	—	1	1	1	2	2	2	4
	C	20	20	40	17	20	37	20	19	39	57	59	116
	Total	24	24	48	24	24	48	24	24	48	72	72	144

Discussion

The quantitative results of this test are discussed in conjunction with the results of tests 1 and 2 in the next section of this chapter. In the total results there is very little difference indeed between the Weight and Volume Tests. When the results of the Weight and Substance Tests were compared, the extra two successes at the 'A' level in the Weight Test lessened support for Piaget's theory of comparative difficulty which was upheld in the previous test.

An additional interest in this test is the reason given for the rise in the level of the water after a ball of plasticine has been put into it. Piaget noted that many children attribute it to the weight of the plasticine which forces the displacement of the water. In this investigation, 57 out of 144 Subjects gave 'weight' answers. As roughly the same proportion of children at each 'stage' gave this answer it does not appear to have any fundamental connection with the transition from stage to stage. In this test 46 children thought that after the deformed ball had been restored to its original shape its volume would still be affected by the changes it had suffered. Out of these only nine were consistent in all three tests, so it appears to be just part of the confusion caused in the child's mind by the changes perceived to have taken place in the plasticine.

Elkind (1961) who also repeated Piaget's study confirmed the Geneva pattern of responses. Beard (1963) using a test of displacement volume but different apparatus, found a wide range of success in 70 children from seven to sixteen. Other studies of volume, e.g. by Lovell and Ogilvie (1961), have used different procedures, so comparison is not possible. A survey of the literature however, gives the impression that, while it is legitimate to compare the results of this test with test 1 and test 2 using the same material, and, as far as possible, a similar procedure, the concept of volume is far too complicated to be exemplified by such a simple test. For an account of tests not used in this investigation, students are recommended to consult Lovell's text (1961).

Order of acquiring concepts of substance, weight, volume

Bärbel Inhelder has made use of the concept of 'grouping' in testing reasoning power. She was able to show that the order of acquiring the concepts of conservation of substance, weight and volume recurs in its entirety in mental deficients; the last of these three constants (present only in slightly backward individuals and unknown in really deficient cases) is never found without the other two, nor the second without the first, while conservation of substance occurs without conservation of weight and volume, and that of substance and weight without volume.

Piaget (1950): *The Psychology of Intelligence*

Introduction

HYPOTHESIS

The concepts of conservation of substance, weight and volume are acquired in that order: that the last is never found without the other two, nor the second without the first: that conservation of substance occurs without conservation of weight and volume, and that of substance and weight without that of volume.

A separate section has been devoted to the above hypothesis for two reasons. First, it is a clear-cut unequivocal statement which invites confirmation, and secondly, if true, it could have not only important applications in the grading of mental defectives, but could be used as a possible intelligence test for grading say, illiterate peoples.

Inhelder (1943) claims that it is possible to differentiate between different types of mental deficiency according to the way in which an individual reasons about these concepts, the main division being between the 'deficients' who are fixated at different levels, and the 'retarded' who are progressing through the stages at a less than normal rate.

Piaget states further (1953) that in the case of normal children: 'From 7 to 8 children become aware of the transitive character of equalities in the case of lengths, etc., but only towards 9 and 10 in the case of weight and towards 11 and 12 for volume.' He also claims that a child uses the same arguments at each of the levels, so that, for example, when he reaches the stage of conservation of weight, he uses the same arguments as he had previously used in the case of substance, while continuing to deny conservation of volume for the same reasons he had previously used in the case of substance and weight.

Out of all the possibilities suggested by the above assumptions, only the order of acquiring the concepts could be studied in this investigation, though some reference to other points will be made in the discussion.

INVESTIGATIONS

In her study, Inhelder used Subjects from the ages of 7·6 to 5·2, having an IQ range from 45 to 105. She admits that her IQs are very unreliable, as the subjects were tested by all sorts of people using a variety of tests.

In a previous investigation by the writer (unpublished: a dissertation submitted as part of the practical examination offered for a first degree), Inhelder's tests were given to a group of thirteen children having about the same range of intelligence as Inhelder's, the raw scores of the Wechsler Intelligence Scale for Children (1944) being used for comparative purposes. In view of Inhelder's claim that even the tests on volume could be done by the slightly backward, Subjects (not including any cases of known organic injury) were selected from a mental hospital. However, as even the most promising Subject, a girl nearly fifteen years old, with a Wechsler IQ Full Scale 83 and Performance Scale 101, only managed to get two of the tests right, the group had to be widened to include children of normal intelligence. This is not surprising if the ages suggested by Piaget for the acquisition of these concepts is approximately correct.

Peel of Birmingham University (1955) reports a study by Carpenter (1955) assisted by Lunzer in which tests on substance, weight and volume were included in an investigation of Piaget's work on number. Her Subjects, who were also tested on the Terman–Merrill version (1937) of the Stanford–Binet Scale, were twenty girls with a chronological age of five to nine years. Their mental ages ranged from 14 to 5·8 years.

In the present study there were 144 children, half male and half female, with an age range of five to nine years (although, as stated elsewhere, only one or two children under six or over eight years had to be included to complete the groups), so this makes possible some comparison with the Birmingham results. In both studies, too, the hypothesis was limited to the conservation of substance, weight and volume of a solid, plasticine being used in each test, so that differences in results could not be attributed to variety in material. Carpenter's procedure was apparently less rigid and her choice of test different in some respects, but substantially there is enough in common between the two investigations for a comparison to be made. The details of the present tests have already been described in chapters 3, 4 and 5, so they will not be repeated here.

Results

In order to make a rough comparison, the main results of the previous investigation mentioned above and the Birmingham tests will precede the results of the Aden investigation, details of which may be found in Table 4.

PREVIOUS INVESTIGATION

1. Many of the answers bore a close resemblance to the answers reported by Piaget and Inhelder.
2. The concepts of the conservation of substance, weight and volume are only sometimes acquired in that order.
3. The gap between the acquisition of these three concepts if it exists, is much narrower than Piaget suggests. Out of twenty Subjects, sixteen had either all tests right or no tests right, or some tests right for more than one concept.

Table 4

Order of acquisition of conservation concepts

Ratings on tests 1, 2 and 3 in that order

Group	Age 6+ M	Age 6+ F	Age 7+ M	Age 7+ F	Age 8+ M	Age 8+ F
	16 CCC	27 CCC	2 AAA	1 AAA	5 AAC	3 CCC
	45 CAC	66 ACA	21 ACA	19 ACC	23 ACC	15 AAA
	57 CCC	69 CCC	34 BBB[a]	24 CCA[a]	28 AAA	22 ACC
European	67 CCA[a]	75 CCC	50 ACA	25 CCC	35 BCC[a]	26 CCB
	68 ACA	77 CCC	64 CCC	38 AAC	49 ACC	37 CCC
	132 CCA	82 CCC[a]	112 AAA	56 ABA	90 ACC	65 BCA
	133 ACA	93 ACC	114 ACA	94 CAA[a]	133 CAA[a]	97 CCC
	135 ACC	134 CAB[a]	131 CAC	130 CCC[a]	119 AAC	98 ACC
	47 CCC	10 AAC	39 CCC	14 CCC	6 BBA[a]	4 CCC
	58 CCC	46 CCA	48 ACC	29 CCC	8 CAC[a]	7 CCC
	59 CCC	51 CCA	52 CCC	43 CCC	11 CCC	32 CCC
	60 CCC	62 CCC	53 CCC	85 CCC	12 AAB	33 CBC
Arab	117 CCC	81 CCC	54 CCC	87 CCC	13 ACC	40 ACC
	118 CCC	86 CCC	55 CCC	89 CCC	20 CCC	41 CCC[a]
	126 CCC	88 CCC	61 CCC	100 CCC[a]	31 ACA	42 CCC[a]
	129 CCC	136 CCC	69 CCC	105 CCC	70 CCC	44 CCC
	18 CCC	73 CCC	30 CCC	36 CCC[a]	9 ACC	74 CCC
Indian	78 CCC	79 CCC	76 CCC	72 AAC	17 CCC	80 ACC
	140 CCC	83 CCC	95 CCA	101 CCC	71 CCC	122 CCC[a]
	142 CCC	99 CCC	96 CCC	102 CCC	84 CCC	138 AAA
	91 CCC	103 CCC	92 CCC	106 CCC	108 CCC[a]	104 CCC[a]
	127 CCC	124 CCC	115 CCC	107 CAC	109 CCC[a]	120 CCC[a]
Somali	139 CCC	141 CCC	116 CCC	123 CCC	110 CCC[a]	121 CCC
	144 CCC	143 CCC	128 CCC	125 CCC	111 AAC	137 AAA

[a] Children who got A on test 4 but not on test 1 (*n* = 20);
Children who got A on test 1 but not on test 4 (*n* = 6).

4. There was a very high correlation between the Piaget-type test scores and the raw scores on the Wechsler Intelligence Scale for Children (1944).

1. From the original dissertation, kindly lent by Miss Carpenter, it appears that many of the answers bore a close resemblance to the answers reported by Piaget and Inhelder.
2. One Subject reversed Piaget's findings by acknowledging the conservation of weight, but denying the conservation of substance. Results on the conservation of volume supported Piaget.
3. The period of transition was not very well demonstrated. On the whole, the children either seemed to have no real understanding of the problem, or else full realization seemed to be present.
4. There appeared to be a close correlation between Piaget's reasoning tests and the Terman–Merrill Intelligence Tests. (Note: In both of these investigations the Piaget scores used for comparison with Intelligence Test Scores included tests other than the three plasticine tests.)

1. Many of the answers bore a close resemblance to those reported by Piaget and Inhelder.
2. 21 Subjects supported Piaget's hypothesis, and 25 did not.
3. The period of transition was not very well demonstrated; out of 144 Subjects, 98 were at the same stage in each test and 16 had some tests right for more than one concept.
4. No satisfactory comparison could be made between these tests and the non-verbal intelligence tests which appeared to be unsuitable for local children. (For a discussion of this point see chapter 15.)

Discussion

Although no exact comparison can be made, it appears that the results of these three investigations are very similar. In none was the word 'never' in Piaget's statement justified. With regard to the transition from one stage to the next, it is particularly difficult to compare the data with Inhelder's, as she only indicates one stage in her table for all three concepts, in spite of Piaget's assertion that even in a normal child there may be a difference of as much as five years between acquiring the concepts of substance and volume. It is, however, clearly shown that the majority of Subjects in these investigations showed no gap between acquisition of the three concepts. This is in line with Piaget's general theme of the development of intelligence as a whole and of number and quantity in particular, for if his 'stages' represent a maturational progression, it is difficult to understand how this particular hypothesis fits in.

In the Aden results the trend for age was in the right direction but the tests were found difficult for the majority of Subjects in all communities. There was very little sex difference. The European children had better results but Aden children reached the top grade. The fact that 29 children who failed the substance tests (1) with plasticine, but passed the continuous substance test (4) with water, and six vice versa, suggests that a different set of results might be obtained using different material.

For this reason a recent study by de Lemos (personal communication) is difficult to fit into this comparative study: she used sugar for continuous quantity (similar to Price-Williams' (1969) use of fine earth), tea-leaf for weight and Inhelder's Displacement Test for volume. The Aden investigation confirms the Genevan finding that children reach the 'conservation' stage in relation to Continuous Substance Test before substance in the form of a ball of plasticine. In de Lemos' tests the results for weight were consistently best for both her groups of Australian Aboriginal children while one group produced almost the same results for quantity and volume.

Elkind's Piaget Replication Study 2 (1961) provides a more satisfactory basis for comparison as he introduced standardization of Piaget's procedures and the use of a statistical design. However, he expresses his results in age groups, not in terms of the individual child. But the present author feels strongly that sequence is not only the most crucial factor in Piaget's overall theory, but the main interest of this experiment. To quote Elkind:

> The results of the present study agreed with Piaget's findings regarding the ages at which children discover the conservation of mass, weight and volume. In both studies: the conservation of mass *did not usually appear* before the ages 7–8; the conservation of weight *did not usually appear* before the ages 9–10; and the conservation of volume *did not in most cases appear* before the age of 11. [italics added]

Elkind's discussion of his experiment is limited to Piaget's description of the main three stages of the growth of the concept of conservation as demonstrated in all three parts of his experiment: he does not attempt to explain except in very general terms why there should be a wide age gap between the three concepts nor why, using his standardized procedures, he found exceptions. (Inhelder, who apparently used procedures lacking standardization and no statistical design, found no exceptions to the rule.) She has, however, fitted her results into Piaget's general theory of development in terms of her concept of *décalage* (horizontal). This refers to sub-stages of growth within a single level of functioning. Piaget has always emphasized that his stages, although well marked, are continuous. Thus, at the intermediate level, certain cognitive structures are available, but not perfected. This makes possible a different level of conceptualization depending on the difficulty of the concept for the child. So, to quote Flavell (1963),

> *it so happens* that invariance of mass is typically achieved by children a year or two earlier than invariance of weight. [italics added]

From the evidence above, we now encounter within the classic stages of Piaget's theory:
1. Variations depending on the material and procedure used in an experiment, e.g. children acquiring the concept of the conservation of quantity earlier when the quantity is continuous (water) than when it is not (plasticine), described by Inhelder as *décalage verticale*.
2. Variations (which can follow an invariable order) depending on the difficulty of the concept, described by Inhelder as *décalage horizontale*.

All the evidence appears to invalidate 2 (above) with reference to the concepts of substance, weight and volume, but not, if order is ignored, the fact that some basic concepts are acquired with greater difficulty than others. The main problem is how it will ever be possible to *prove* invariable sequence of Piaget's stages of cognitive growth when so many variables are involved in the test situation.

References

Beard, R. (1957). An investigation of concept formation among infant school children. Unpublished Ph.D. Thesis: University of London.

Beard, R. (1963). The order of concept studies in two fields (i) Number concept in the infant school (ii) Conception of conservation of quantity among primary school children. *Educ. Rev.*, **XV**, Nos. 2, 3.

Carpenter, T. E. (1955). A pilot study for a quantitative investigation of Jean Piaget's original work on concept formation, *Educ. Rev.*, **7**, 142–149.

Elkind, D. (1961). Children's discovery of the conservation of mass, weight and volume. *J. genet. Psychol.*, **98**, 219–227. (Reprinted in I. E. Sigel and F. H. Hooper (Eds.), *Logical Thinking in Children*. New York: Holt, Rinehart and Winston, 1968.)

Flavell, J. H. (1963). *The Developmental Psychology of Jean Piaget*. New York: Van Nostrand.

Inhelder, B. (1943). *Le Diagnostic du Raisonnement chez les Débiles mentaux*. Neuchâtel: Delachaux et Niestlé.

de Lemos, M. Personal Communication.

Lovell, K., and E. Ogilvie. (1960). A Study of the conservation of substance in the junior school child. *Br. J. educ. Psychol.*, **30**, 109–118.

Lovell, K., and E. Ogilvie. (1961). A study of the conservation of weight in the junior school child. *Br. J. educ. Psychol.*, **31**, 138–144.

Lovell, K., and E. Ogilvie. (1961). The growth of the concept of volume in junior school children. *J. Child Psychol. Psychiat.*, **2**, 118–126.

Lunzer, E. A. (1968). Children's thinking. In H. J. Butcher (Ed.), *Educational Research in Britain*. London: University of London Press.

Piaget, J. (1950). *The Psychology of Intelligence*. London: Routledge and Kegan Paul.

Piaget, J. (1952). *The Child's Conception of Number*. London: Routledge and Kegan Paul.

Piaget, J. (1953). *The Origin of Intelligence in the Child*. London: Routledge and Kegan Paul.

Piaget, J. (1953). *Logic and Psychology*. Manchester: Manchester University Press.

Price-Williams, D. R. A., Ed. (1969). *Cross-Cultural Studies*. Harmondsworth, Mddx.: Penguin.

Smedslund, J. (1959). Apprentissage des notions de la conservation et de la transivité du poids. In J. Piaget (Ed.), *Etudes d'Epistémologie génétique*, vol. 9. Paris: Presses Universitaires. pp. 85–124.

Smedslund, J. (1961). The acquisition of conservation of substance and weight in children. *Scand. J. Psychol.*, **2**, 203–210.

Terman, L. M., and M. A. Merrill. (1937). *Measuring Intelligence*. Boston: Houghton Mifflin.

University of Birmingham Educational Review (1955). Vol. 8, No. 3.

Wallace, J. G. (1965). *Concept Growth and the Education of the Child*. Slough, Bucks. National Foundation for Educational Research.

Wechsler, D. (1944). *The Measurement of Adult Intelligence*. Baltimore: Williams and Wilkins.

CHAPTER SEVEN

Water Tests and
Parallel Glass Test

Water Tests: conservation of continuous quantities

Introduction

There are two parts to this test, the first being adapted from Inhelder's conservation tests (1943) already mentioned, and the second from chapter 1 of Piaget's *The Child's Conception of Number* (1952). The former deals with the perceptual illusion based on shape and the latter with that based on number. The technique was basically the same as in the original tests but the procedure was simplified and shortened.

Description of the tests

MATERIALS

2 glass beakers of the same size and shape (A_1, A_2)
1 narrow glass cylinder closed at one end (C)
1 wide, shallow wine glass (B)
3 sherry glasses of equal dimensions (D_1, D_2, D_3)
Water coloured with ink

PROCEDURE

Part (i)

The two glass beakers (A_1, A_2) of the same size and shape were placed in front of the child, and the investigator poured the coloured water into them until they were three-quarters full. As she poured the water into the second glass she asked the child to say 'Stop!' when the two amounts of liquid were the same. The child was allowed to adjust the water until he was quite satisfied on this point. The water was then poured from one of the beakers (A_1) into the wide, shallow wine glass (B) and the child was asked to compare the amount of water in this glass and the remaining beaker (A_2)

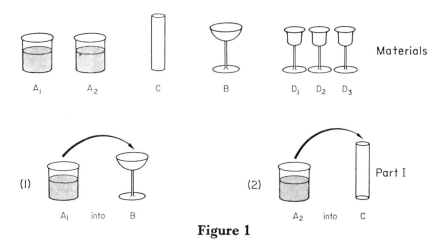

Figure 1

Water Test—materials

(Question 1). The water from the second beaker (A_2) was then poured into the tall, narrow cylinder (C), and the child was asked to compare the amount of water in this and in the wide glass (B) (Question 2). After the water had been returned to the beakers $(A_1$ and $A_2)$, the child was asked once more to compare the amounts (Question 3). It should be noted that in Piaget's test the water is returned to the original container after the first comparison so that A_1 is compared with A_2, B and C but B and C are not compared. The task in this test is more complicated since A_1 and A_2 have been poured into B and C respectively. The reasoning thus becomes: if $A_1 = A_2$ and $A_2 = B$ and $A_1 = C$ then $B = C$.

Apart from lessening the possibility of learning during the test, this variation illustrates the extent of perceptual illusion, for the child who has just declared that B contains more than A_1 will, after A_1 has been poured into C, declare with equal confidence that B is less than C.

Part (ii)

If the child thought that the amount of water in the two beakers was different, it was once more readjusted for the second part of the test. The three sherry glasses (D_1, D_2, D_3) were placed close together. The investigator pointed first to one beaker and then the other, saying, 'This is your drink and this is mine, but I prefer my drink in these glasses.' She poured her drink into the three sherry glasses making the amount about equal in each. Then, placing her hand over the three glasses, she repeated 'This is my drink and that is yours.' The child was again asked to compare the two amounts (Question 4).

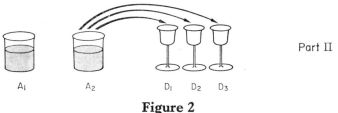

Part II

A₁   A₂   D₁   D₂   D₃

Figure 2

Water Test—procedure

QUESTIONS

1. Do you think that there is the same amount of water in this glass (beaker) and this glass (cylinder) or has one more than the other?
2. Compare the amount of water in this glass (wine glass) and this glass (cylinder). How are they?
3. What about the glasses (beakers) now: how is the water in them?
4. Who has more to drink, you or me?

Comments on performance

The tests using water were the next in popularity to those using dolls and baths, both with the European and local children. The answers given were very clear cut, words being accompanied by unambiguous and expressive gestures.

Grading system

In cases where a different type of answer was given for Part (i) (Questions 1–3) and Part (ii) (Question 4) two separate grades were given, indicating that the child who is deceived by shape may not be deceived by subdivision.

'A' CONSERVATION

No. 138 'The same, because one glass is fat and the other thin but the water was the same in the other glasses' [Part (i)].
No. 119 'The same, because yours was first in that jar and it was like mine then' [Part (ii)].

'B' RIGHT ANSWER: INADEQUATE OR WRONG REASON

No. 48   'The same, because that is blue and that is blue' [Part (i)].
No. 63   'The same, because it is all from the tap' [Part (i)].
No. 3   'The same' (No reason). [This was the only answer in this category in Part (ii).]

'C' NON-CONSERVATION

No. 16   'The *other* one has more now, because this one is much thinner than this one, so it takes much more water' [Part (i)].

No. 96   'You have more because you have three glasses' [Part (ii)].

'C/A' NON-CONSERVATION FOR PART (i)/CONSERVATION FOR PART (ii)

No. 4   'This one has more, because it is a big glass' [Part (i)].

No.   'They are the same, because when yours was in the other glass they were the same' [Part (ii)].

N.B. As in the previous conservation tests, a permanent change in the water resulting from its manipulation was indicated by (p.c.).

Results (Tables 5 and 6)

PART (i): SHAPE

In this test there are no anomalies in the age groups and very little difference between the results of one sex compared with the other, though the Arab males are slightly better and the Indian females much better. Nearly half the Subjects were graded 'A' or 'B' on this test. In the European community a third failed, in the Arab and Indian communities two-thirds, and in the Somali community just over half.

PART (ii): NUMBER (3 GLASSES)

In this part also, the age trend is in the right direction for all groups and there is not much difference in the overall results arranged according to sex, although, as in Part (i), the Arab males are slightly better, and the Indian girls very much better.

Discussion

After an account of the original study an attempt will be made to co-ordinate the main results of a few studies of the conservation of continuous quantities available at the time of the Aden investigation. This will be followed by a short account of Price-Williams' researches in Nigeria and a fuller account of Bruner's screening procedure which has provoked a reply from Inhelder and her colleagues.

INVESTIGATIONS BY PIAGET AND INHELDER (the original tests)

Piaget, who quotes the answers of children aged four to eight years, uses the following procedure:

The child is first given two cylindrical containers of equal dimensions

(A_1 and A_2), containing the same quantity of liquid, as measured by the levels. The contents of A_2 are then poured into two smaller containers of equal dimensions (B_1 and B_2) so that the height of the water is equal. The child is asked to compare the liquid in A_1 with that in $B_1 + B_2$. If neces-

Table 5

Water Test [Part (i)]

Frequency distribution of results obtained with test no. 4(i)

Group	Rating	Age 6+ M	F	Total	Age 7+ M	F	Total	Age 8+ M	F	Total	Total M	F	Total
European	A	5	4	9	4	6	10	7	5	12	16	15	31
	B	—	—	—	—	—	—	—	1	1	—	1	1
	C	3	4	7	4	2	6	1	2	3	8	8	16
	Total	8	8	16	8	8	16	8	8	16	24	24	48
Arab	A	1	1	2	1	1	2	5	3	8	7	5	12
	B	—	1	1	2	—	2	—	—	—	2	1	3
	C	7	6	13	5	7	12	3	5	8	15	18	33
	Total	8	8	16	8	8	16	8	8	16	24	24	48
Indian	A	—	—	—	—	2	2	—	3	3	—	5	5
	B	—	2	2	2	—	2	—	—	—	2	2	4
	C	4	2	6	2	2	4	4	1	5	10	5	15
	Total	4	4	8	4	4	8	4	4	8	12	12	24
Somali	A	—	—	—	—	—	—	3	3	6	3	3	6
	B	—	1	1	2	2	4	—	—	—	2	3	5
	C	4	3	7	2	2	4	1	1	2	7	6	13
	Total	4	4	8	4	4	8	4	4	8	12	12	24
Total	A	6	5	11	5	9	14	15	14	29	26	28	54
	B	—	4	4	6	2	8	—	1	1	6	7	13
	C	18	15	33	13	13	26	9	9	18	40	37	77
	Total	24	24	48	24	24	48	24	24	48	72	72	144

sary, the liquid in B_1 can then be poured into two smaller, equal containers, C_1 and C_2, and if thought desirable, the liquid in B_2 can be poured into two further containers, C_3 and C_4, identical with C_1 and C_2. Questions can be asked with reference to the equality between $C_1 + C_2$ and B_2, or

Table 6
Water Test [Part (ii)]
Frequency distribution of results obtained with test no. 4(ii)

Group	Rating	Age 6+ M	F	Total	Age 7+ M	F	Total	Age 8+ M	F	Total	Total M	F	Total
European	A	3	3	6	4	5	9	7	5	12	14	13	27
	B	—	—	—	—	—	—	—	1	1	—	1	1
	C	5	5	10	4	3	7	1	2	3	10	10	20
	Total	8	8	16	8	8	16	8	8	16	24	24	48
Arab	A	—	1	1	2	1	3	5	4	9	7	6	13
	B	—	—	—	—	—	—	—	—	—	—	—	—
	C	8	7	15	6	7	13	3	4	7	17	18	35
	Total	8	8	16	8	8	16	8	8	16	24	24	48
Indian	A	—	—	—	—	1	1	—	2	2	—	3	3
	B	—	—	—	—	—	—	—	—	—	—	—	—
	C	4	4	8	4	3	7	4	2	6	12	9	21
	Total	4	4	8	4	4	8	4	4	8	12	12	24
Somali	A	—	—	—	2	—	2	4	2	6	6	2	8
	B	—	—	—	—	—	—	—	—	—	—	—	—
	C	4	4	8	2	4	6	—	2	2	6	10	16
	Total	4	4	8	4	4	8	4	4	8	12	12	24
Total	A	3	4	7	8	7	15	16	13	29	27	24	51
	B	—	—	—	—	—	—	—	1	1	—	1	1
	C	21	20	41	16	17	33	8	10	18	45	47	92
	Total	24	24	48	24	24	48	24	24	48	72	72	144

between $C_1 + C_2 + C_3 + C_4$ and A_1, etc. In this way, the liquids are sub-divided in a variety of ways, the child being asked to compare the quantity after sub-division with the quantity in one of the original containers. As a check to his answers, the child may be asked to pour into a glass of a different shape a quantity of liquid approximately the same as that in a given glass.

Using a similar procedure, Piaget used beads instead of water for experiments on the conservation of discontinuous quantities.

Inhelder used differently shaped containers in her investigations. Liquid was poured into containers of equal dimensions, A_1 and A_2. The liquid from A_2 was then poured into a wide container, and at a later stage from A_2 into a narrow container. With each pouring, the child was asked to compare the amount of liquid in the new container with the amount in A_1.

THE BIRMINGHAM INVESTIGATION

Other references to this investigation have already been made. The Subjects were twenty girls, aged five to nine years, with mental ages ranging from 14 to 5·8 years. The investigator, Carpenter, adapted the techniques of Piaget and Inhelder, using two procedures:

(a) Inhelder's procedure, except that, as in the present investigation, the liquids in the wide and narrow containers were compared directly, instead of a second comparison being made with A_2.

(b) The liquid, as in Piaget's procedure was poured first into A_1 and A_2, and then from A_1 into B_1 and B_2. At this stage the procedure was modified. The liquid from A_2 was divided between a narrow container (C) and a wide container (D), and the child was asked to compare the contents of $B_1 + B_2$ and $C + D$.

THE TORONTO INVESTIGATION

This investigation was carried out in the Institute of Child Study of Toronto University, by Dr. Lamaimas Serradatta of Thailand. The work is unpublished, but a report has kindly been forwarded by the Director, Dr. Blatz.

Using eighteen kindergarten children Dr. Serradatta adopted the exact procedure of Piaget.

A PREVIOUS INVESTIGATION BY THE AUTHOR

Reference has already been made to this investigation (p. 96). The Subjects consisted of twenty children, thirteen of whom were patients in a mental hospital, the remaining seven being residents in the same neighbour-hood. Chronological ages ranged from 7·1 to 14·11 years, and raw scores on the Wechsler Scale for children from 61 to 329. The only test given on the conservation of continuous substance followed exactly the same pro-cedure as in the first of the Birmingham tests, except that the liquid was returned from the narrow and wide containers to the original parallel containers for a final comparison.

In the present study there were 144 children aged five to nine years, living in Aden. Two procedures were adopted to test the notion of conservation of continuous quantities:

(a) The procedure adopted in the previous investigation and in the first of the Birmingham tests.
(b) In a shortened form of Piaget's experiment, the liquid was poured from one of the identical glasses A_1 and A_2 into three smaller identical glasses, B_1, B_2 and B_3, and the child was asked to compare the quantity in A_1 with the quantity in $B_1 + B_2 + B_3$.

Below is a summary which can be used for comparing the results of these investigations.

From his results Piaget concluded that a child does not at first realize that continuous quantities are constant, but arrives at this notion gradually by way of three main stages which correspond to the stages of his intellectual development.

Stage 1
Up to the age of five years the child thinks that the quantity of the liquid will vary according to the shape and dimensions of the containers into which it is poured. 'Quantification is restricted to the immediate perceptual relationships.'

Stage 2
From the age of five to seven or eight years, there is a period of transition. The chief reactions observable at this stage are his acceptance of conserva-tion when sub-divisions of the liquid are large, but not when they are small, and again when differences in the dimensions of the containers are slight, but not when they are gross.

Stage 3
Between the ages of seven to eight and ten to eleven years, children dis-cover 'invariance'. They state immediately or almost immediately that the

quantities of liquid are conserved, irrespective of the number and nature of the changes made.

All the investigators mentioned above received responses from their Subjects which could be fitted into the above scheme. In the Toronto group it was noted that conservation broke down with the increase of sub-divisions, in the Birmingham group that the progression of the three stages was borne out. In the present investigation, many children who upheld conservation when glasses of different shapes were used, denied it when the liquid had been sub-divided. Whereas 77 gave 'perceptual' answers for shape, 92 children gave the same type of answer for subdivision. This inconsistency existed in all age groups, there being no appreciable difference between the sexes or different communities.

THE TRANSITION STAGE

In the Toronto Study, the seven out of the eighteen children who had reached Piaget's second stage, gave answers corresponding to the Geneva pattern. Three had their notion of correspondence destroyed when three or four glasses were used, two when differences in the levels of the liquids in the glasses was increased, and two gave inconsistent answers. These children were 'kindergarten age', presumably about five to seven years old. Carpenter (1955) found that her Subjects reached the transition stage at a later age than Piaget's, their ages ranging from six years ten months to nine years seven months.

In the investigator's own previous study, in only one case, a child of eleven years, were answers corresponding to the transition stage given, while in the present investigation, there were thirteen such answers when shape was being considered (including four aged six, eight aged seven and one aged eight), while, when number of glasses was being considered, only one eight-year-old child came into this category. As in the 'conservation' tests using plasticine, evidence for the existence and characteristics of this stage is not as clear cut as Piaget's scheme leads one to expect.

Price-Williams (1961) investigated the concept of the conservation of continuous quantities using for his subjects illiterate children of the Tiv tribe of Central Nigeria. Piaget's techniques were followed as closely as possible, but he used fine earth instead of water. With slight variations, including the use of more containers, the procedure was similar to that used in the Aden investigation. The non-conservers clearly based their answers on the level of the earth and the number of containers, whereas the subjects who judged the various examples to be equal justified their answers 'in terms of the actual operations which the experimenter performed. The experimenter had taken the glass and poured the earth into two other glasses—it must be the same.' Price-Williams also noted that the

Tiv children spontaneously reversed the sequence of operations by pouring back the earth from the second containers to the first. Similar responses were obtained from the Arab, Somali and Indian children. The Tiv children gave less correct responses when more containers were involved. It will be seen from the tables that the trend was the same with the Aden subjects, although the differences were not great. From the point of view of Piaget's main theory, Price-Williams' most important observation was that, within the limits of his experiments, sequence of operations was found to be the same in Africa as in Europe.

Reference has already been made to the importance of reversibility and compensation as factors in conservation. Bruner and his colleagues (1966) have devised a series of experiments to show whether, as Piaget indicates, the operation of reversibility precedes, developmentally, the operation of compensation. In the experiments described in this chapter, reversibility is a recognition that the water is the same in spite of its changed appearance when poured into glasses of different shapes and numbers because it can be poured back again. Compensation is at work when attention is drawn to the shape of the vessels, the child reasoning that, when the water is poured into a wide beaker it will be lower than when poured into a narrow beaker: height compensates for width. This is an example of what Piaget calls 'the multiplying of relations' also discussed in chapter 15.

One only of several experiments will be described. Bruner (in Bruner *et al.*, 1966) noted that children of his subjects' ages (four to eight) depend for judgment on the perceptual properties of objects, but that they are also in the process of developing symbolic techniques of representation. His hypothesis was that, if they could be shielded from the full impact of perceptual factors in a Piaget-type experiment, they would be able to represent the situation in language *before* they could see it and 'perhaps the language would serve as a guide for organizing their perceptions in a new way.'

Forty children were subjected to the following procedure:

A pre-test using four pairs of beakers, each containing the standard

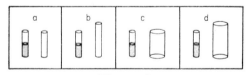

Figure 3
Pairs of beakers used in screening experiments
Reproduced by permission from Bruner *et al.* (1966)

beaker and one other (figure 3). Standard procedure involved pouring the liquid from the standard beaker into the empty beaker, and asking the child if there was still the same amount of liquid.

I. The standard beaker, half full of coloured water, and one empty comparison beaker at a time were shown to the subject and then placed behind a screen twelve inches wide and five inches high, so that only the tops of the beakers showed. The standard procedure was then followed, but the screen was never taken away, so the child never saw the level of the water in the second beaker.

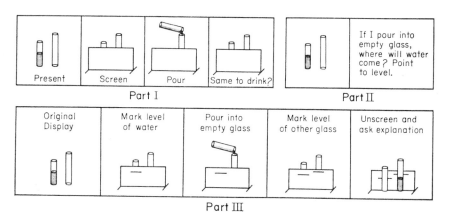

Part I   Part II

Part III

Figure 4

Three screening procedures. Part I unmarked screening procedure; Part II water-level guessing procedure; Part III screening–marking procedure

Reproduced by permission from Bruner et al. (1966)

II. The beakers were presented, as in (I) but the screen was not used and the subject was asked, giving reason, whether there would be the same amount of water if it were poured from the standard beaker to the comparison, and to indicate with his finger the level to which the water would come. The water was never poured, so the child did not see the level of the water in the second beaker.

III. The beakers were presented as in (I) but before a screen. The child was asked to draw a line on the screen that corresponded to the level of the water in the standard beaker. Then, as in (I), the pair of beakers was placed behind the screen, the water poured from the standard to the comparison beaker, and the child asked if there was still the same amount of water. He was also asked to draw a second line that predicted the level of water in the second beaker, using the line he had already drawn as a reference. Then the screen was taken away, so for the first time, the child saw the level of the water in the comparison beaker. He was asked to judge (giving reasons) whether there was still the same amount of water as there had been before pouring.

IV. Repeat of pre-test.

Briefly, Bruner's results were as follows. Training has a marked effect on all but the four-year olds, who, if they have given a conservation judgment when the screen was present, regress to non-conservation when they can see the beakers. The older children, however, consciously resist the visual presence of the beakers, mostly insisting on identity of substance in spite of change of appearance. Reversibility and compensation are represented not only in the reasons given for conservation, but also in some of the reasons given for non-conservation, so Bruner concludes that they cannot by themselves be *producing* conservation: compensation can exist without conservation. In a further experiment in which the subjects were asked what would happen if the water were poured back, and to justify their answers, Bruner satisfied himself that reversibility also can exist without conservation. Greenfield (in Bruner *et al.*, 1966) confirmed these results using Wolof child subjects in Senegal.

The answer by Inhelder *et al.* (1966) to Bruner's conclusions is to clarify some of the basic differences in theory and methodology between the Harvard and Genevan cognitive growth projects. Those concerned with language are discussed in chapter 3, here only those aspects relevant to Bruner's experiments above, will be mentioned. First, Inhelder points out that 'in Piaget's developmental theory, cognitive development consists of a progressive structuralization whereby actions and intellectual operations become organized into coherent systems,' whereas, 'according to Bruner, cognitive development consists in the acquisition of 'techniques' of information processing.' Whereas Bruner's techniques, through an 'interiorization' process form the basis for three information-processing systems, Piaget's 'structures' are characterized by laws such as reversibility and compensation, which apply throughout the system as a whole. His stages are stages in the structuralization process; Bruner's stages, on the other hand, represent *levels* in cognitive functioning. To summarize, the basic difference between the approaches of Piaget and Bruner is that whereas Piaget's overall theory is concerned with the development of mental structures, Bruner is concerned with function at the different developmental stages. The implication is that structure, that is the underlying mental processes, follows an invariant pattern, the analysis of which is Piaget's main interest; whereas, at each level of intelligence, function, according to Bruner, can be improved by the use of appropriate techniques.

Reversibility is present at all of the three main stages of development: the purpose of the Genevan studies is to study the transition between one stage and the next. For example, at the sensori-motor stage, the child is able to coordinate his movements with the concurrent changing perceptions and this gives rise to the permanence of objects. At the concrete–operational stage, in discovering the conservation of substance, weight, volume, length, etc., despite alterations of their perceptual aspects, they are depending on thought reversibility rather than action reversibility. The Geneva school is not just concerned with the transformation of information but with its coordination with underlying developmental processes. Inhelder agrees with Bruner that information-processing techniques are very important in the study of cognitive development but thinks that Bruner's studies of them are inadequate to account for the implied transformation of information and its coordination with structural development.

Further discussions of the Genevan attitude to learning procedures and reference to some of their studies will be found in chapter 3 on 'concept attainment', which again refers to the work of Bruner and his colleagues, and in the section on 'training procedures' in the final chapter.

Parallel Glass Test: coordination of inverse relations*

Introduction

Piaget used six distinct problems to demonstrate that measuring implies a logic. The tests progress from conservation of quantity when vessels of different shapes and numbers are used (described above) to more complicated tests in which equivalences must be established by the child himself, using a variety of vessels. In establishing these equivalences, the child utilizes the processes already demonstrated in previous tests, showing 'the interdependence and deep-seated unity of the mechanisms that explain the psychological construction of number.'

Out of Piaget's tests the fourth was selected and simplified, as the sixth had already been included in a conservation test, and these two tests appeared to be basic in the series.

Description of the test

MATERIALS

3 pairs of glasses:
2 sherry glasses (A_1, A_2)
2 glass beakers wider and taller than the sherry glasses (B_1, B_2)
2 glass beakers about the same size but wide at the bottom and narrow at the top (C_1, C_2)
A jug of water coloured by ink

---

* Test 13 has been removed from its position in the Aden investigation and has been included in this chapter to facilitate comparison with test 4.

The three sets of glasses, A_1, A_2, B_1, B_2, and C_1, C_2, were placed in front of the child as follows:

$$C_1 \qquad C_2$$
$$B_1 \qquad B_2$$
$$A_1 \qquad A_2$$
$$\text{child}$$

The investigator then poured the liquid into A_2 until it was about three-quarters full. The child was then asked if he could pour the same amount of liquid into B_2. If he estimated the amount and ignored all the other glasses, the investigator said 'This is your drink, and this is mine. Show me what you can do to make sure that we have got the same amount to drink.'
The procedure was then repeated, using B_1 and C_2.

Comments on performance

There was very little variety in the responses to this test. Most of the children judged the amount of the liquid by its height in the glass. Some of them made the heights exactly the same, while others allowed for the differently shaped glasses. The pouring was done very carefully. No. 4 said 'They are the same because I put a little in at a time to make them the same.' And when asked to prove that he was right just went on protesting that they were the same. No. 9 said that they were the same because they were both red. The proof for most of the children was to place the two glasses side by side and compare the height of the water or explain how they had allowed for differences in the width of the glasses.

The second attempt added nothing to the result. It was interesting to note that the children who started off by measuring and then used a spare glass for proof at the first attempt, repeated the whole process in the second attempt. No. 3 used the spare glass for checking, but when it was found to be the wrong amount he poured the whole lot back and started again. This trial and error continued until his guess was correct. Most of the children who used a spare glass for proof were quite satisfied when the liquid was the same in the parallel glasses, failing to pour it back into the selected glass. Various methods of using the parallel glasses were adopted. These included in the first test:

1. (after estimation) B_2 into A_1
2. A_2 into B_1
3. A_2 and B_2 into C_1 and C_2.

Grading system
'A' Using the spare glass spontaneously.
'B' Checking with a spare glass.
'C' Estimating.

Results (Table 7)

Apart from the European and Somali eight-year groups, whose results are a little superior, there is no difference in results tabled according to age.

Table 7
Parallel Glass Test
Frequency distribution of results obtained with test no. 13

Group	Rating	Age 6+			Age 7+			Age 8+			Total		
		M	F	Total	M	F	Total	M	F	Total	M	F	Total
European	A	—	—	—	—	—	—	2	—	2	2	—	2
	B	4	3	7	4	3	7	4	7	11	12	13	25
	C	4	5	9	4	5	9	2	1	3	10	11	21
	Total	8	8	16	8	8	16	8	8	16	24	24	48
Arab	A	—	—	—	—	—	—	—	—	—	—	—	—
	B	—	1	1	1	—	1	—	1	1	1	2	3
	C	8	7	15	7	8	15	8	7	15	23	22	45
	Total	8	8	16	8	8	16	8	8	16	24	24	48
Indian	A	—	—	—	—	—	—	—	—	—	—	—	—
	B	—	—	—	—	—	—	—	—	—	—	—	—
	C	4	4	8	4	4	8	4	4	8	4	4	8
	Total	4	4	8	4	4	8	4	4	8	12	12	24
Somali	A	—	—	—	—	—	—	—	—	—	—	—	—
	B	—	—	—	—	—	—	—	1	1	—	1	1
	C	4	4	8	4	4	8	4	3	7	12	12	23
	Total	4	4	8	4	4	8	4	4	8	12	12	24
Total	A	—	—	—	—	—	—	2	—	2	2	—	2
	B	4	4	8	5	3	8	4	9	13	13	16	29
	C	20	20	40	19	21	40	18	15	33	57	56	113
	Total	24	24	48	24	24	48	24	24	48	72	72	144

This was a very difficult problem for all communities and both sexes. Out of 144 Subjects, only two European children (males), used the spare glass spontaneously to solve the problem. Half the Europeans, three Arabs and one Somali used the spare glass for proof, but all the Indians were satisfied with their estimation.

Discussion

In view of the general lack of understanding of the principle of conservation revealed in this investigation it is not surprising that so many children failed to apply it in this test. Whereas in test 4 they had to make judgments on situations provided by the investigator, that is, to *recognize* equivalence under differing circumstances, in this test they had to *create* the equivalence for themselves. It is interesting to compare the results in this test with those in test 4, to see whether the children who at least used the spare glass after being prompted by the investigator, had also appeared to understand the principle of conservation in test 4. It will be seen that the two children who spontaneously used the glass had also expressed the notion of conservation of continuous substances. Also out of 29 children who could solve the problem, although they had not done so spontaneously, twenty had been successful in both parts of test 4, and two in one part. This means that seven children who were uncertain about the principle behind equivalence, were yet able to make use of it when confronted with a suitable problem.

Peel (see Carpenter, 1955, University of Birmingham, 1955) reports a study by Lunzer using Carpenter's older group supplemented by twelve girls between ten and twelve years, in which Piaget's test was further adapted. He used different glass receptacles, including a graduated feeding bottle, and asked for the same amount of liquid to be poured into a glass and a dish. He analysed his answers into four categories, corresponding to four stages:

Stage 1
No appreciation of the problem. (Little or no allowance for the greater width of the dish, height being used as a criterion.)

Stage 2
Partial and inadequate appreciation. (Allowance made for difference in shape, but the significance of the graduations on the feeding bottle not grasped.)

Stage 3
Complete appreciation, but the knowledge not yet available for insightful application. (Failure to use the feeding bottle (and funnel) until prompted.)

Stage 4

Complete appreciation and insightful application. (The problem solved correctly without assistance.)

Very few children failed to make allowance for the extra width of the dish. In this investigation more than half the children who failed to use the spare glass ignored the differences in the shapes of the glasses, but in the results the first two categories above were combined. Lunzer found that the true age for success was about eleven to twelve years, so it is not surprising that the problem in this test (which may have been harder, since no graduated container was available) was solved by two eight-year-old children only.

References

Bruner, J. S., R. R. Olver and P. M. Greenfield, Eds. (1966). *Studies in Cognitive Growth*. New York: Wiley. (Greenfield's study is also in D. R. A. Price-Williams (Ed.), *Cross-Cultural Studies*. Harmondsworth, Mddx.: Penguin, 1969.)

Carpenter, T. E. (1955). A pilot study for a quantitative investigation of Jean Piaget's original work on concept formation. *Educ. Rev.*, **7**, 142–149.

Inhelder, B. (1943). *Le Diagnostic du Raisonnement chez les Débiles mentaux*. Neuchâtel: Delachaux et Niestlé.

Inhelder, B., M. Bovet, H. Sinclair and C. Smock. (1966). Comments on Bruner's course of cognitive development. *Am. Psychol.*, **21**, 160–164.

Piaget, J. (1952). *The Child's Conception of Number*. London: Routledge and Kegan Paul.

Piaget, J. (1953). *The Origin of Intelligence in the Child*. London: Routledge and Kegan Paul.

Price-Williams, D. R. A. (1961). A study concerning concepts of quantities among primitive children. *Acta Psychol.*, **18**, 293–305. (Reprinted in Price-Williams, 1969.)

University of Birmingham Educational Review (1955). Vol. 7, No. 2.

University of Birmingham Educational Review (1955). Vol. 8, No. 3.

CHAPTER EIGHT

Block Test: transitivity of equal weight

Block Test

Introduction

This is a very much simplified version of one of Inhelder's tests (1943). It was included because it gives an opportunity to note colour responses and to see whether the Subjects can formulate the principle that if $A = B$, and $B = C$ and $C = D$, then $A = D$.

Description of the test

MATERIALS

4 blocks, size 1 cubic inch, coloured red, blue, yellow and green respectively on all sides

PROCEDURE

The four blocks were placed in a row in front of the child who was asked in turn to weigh with his hands A and B, B and C, C and D to see if they weighed the same. A box of square blocks of the same size and colours formed a reserve for the children who were not satisfied with the investigator's choice. After the child had agreed that $A = B$ and $B = C$ and $C = D$, the investigator picked up A and D, pretended to weigh them, and asked the child whether the weight would be the same (Question 1). She then, in the same way, balanced A and D against C and B and asked the child his opinion of the weights and the reason for his answer (Question 2).

QUESTIONS

1. What about the yellow and red? Will they be the same or different? Why?

2. Now suppose we put the yellow and red on one side and the blue and green on the other, will they weigh differently or the same? (N.B. Colours were randomized.) Why?

Comments on performance

This test was, above everything else, a demonstration of the faith which children put in their hand weighing judgments. No one asked for a balance, but the spare box of bricks was used in every possible combination before some of the Subjects were satisfied. An extreme case was an Indian girl of seven years who weighed every block carefully about a dozen times but would not agree that any one was the same weight as another. After using the spare box three times in various combinations, the investigator had to abandon the test! There were, however, many children who were prepared to say at a glance that the blocks weighed the same, and only tested them at the behest of the investigator.

Grading system

'A' REASONING

No. 28   '1 = 2, and 2 = 3, and 3 = 4, so 4 = 1' (Question 1).
The two and two are the same because they all weigh the same (see above) (Question 2).

'B' CORRECT: APPEARANCE OF FAULTY REASONING

No. 1   'The same, because they were made in the same factory.'
No. 3   'The same, because they look the same.'
No. 8   'The same, because they are both blocks of wood.'
No. 17   'The same, because that is heavy and that is heavy.'

'C' INCORRECT

No. 16   'The green will be lighter because the yellow one will weigh the green one down' (Question 1).
'These two are heavier because the blue is the second strongest (Why?) Because the blue one will come down a bit' (Question 2).

N.B. If colour appeared to be the main factor in the response it was indicated by (c).

Results (Table 8)

On the whole the age trend in this test was in the right direction, although in the Arab community the seven-year group was slightly better than the eight-year group. The only 'A' grade answer from an Arab was given by a six-year old. In the group as a whole there was very little difference between male and female subjects although the latter were slightly better in the European and Indian communities. The Arab 'A' grade answer was given by a girl.

Table 8

Block Test

Frequency distribution of results obtained with test no. 5

Group	Rating	Age 6+			Age 7+			Age 8+			Total		
		M	F	Total	M	F	Total	M	F	Total	M	F	Total
European	A	—	—	—	1	—	1	2	1	3	3	1	4
	B	6	5	11	5	8	13	5	6	11	16	19	35
	C	2	3	5	2	—	2	1	1	2	5	4	9
	Total	8	8	16	8	8	16	8	8	16	24	24	48
Arab	A	—	1	1	—	—	—	—	—	—	—	1	1
	B	4	4	8	7	7	14	7	3	10	18	14	32
	C	4	3	7	1	1	2	1	5	6	6	9	15
	Total	8	8	16	8	8	16	8	8	16	24	24	48
Indian	A	—	—	—	—	—	—	—	—	—	—	—	—
	B	3	2	5	3	2	5	3	4	7	9	8	17
	C	1	2	3	1	2	3	1	—	1	3	4	7
	Total	4	4	8	4	4	8	4	4	8	12	12	24
Somali	A	—	—	—	—	—	—	—	—	—	—	—	—
	B	2	4	6	2	3	5	4	2	6	8	9	17
	C	2	—	2	2	1	3	—	2	2	4	3	7
	Total	4	4	8	4	4	8	4	4	8	12	12	24
Total	A	—	1	1	1	—	1	2	1	3	3	2	5
	B	15	15	30	17	20	37	19	15	34	51	50	101
	C	9	8	17	6	4	10	3	8	11	18	20	38
	Total	24	24	48	24	24	48	24	24	48	72	72	144

In all communities the majority of answers were graded 'B'. Only four Europeans and one Arab gave reasoning answers. Both these communities had nine 'C' grade answers, while the other communities each had seven. It appears that, apart from the five children who gave 'A' grade answers, the communities were about equal in this test.

Discussion

This test differs from the preceding ones because, unlike the plasticine and the water, the blocks remained the same throughout the proceedings. Consequently an answer based on perceptual characteristics was, in fact, a correct answer. This accounts for the unusually large number of answers graded 'B'. So few reasoning answers were given that it is worth examining them. The four European children gave reasoning answers for both questions and the Arab for only the second question. The wording of their answers varied a little, but there was no essential difference. The clearest answer was given by No. 28, a boy of eight years whose answer is quoted on the preceding page. The others pointed to the blocks saying: 'That's the same as that, and that's the same as that, etc., so that (1) is the same as that (4)'. The little Arab girl just reiterated that they were all the same in answer to the first question, but in answer to the second she pointed to one in each hand saying, 'That one and that one are the same, and you added that one and that one the same' (pointing to the other two). She made it quite clear that she was not judging by appearance only.

Apart from the intelligence tests this was the only test in which colour was a prominent feature, so a special note was made of answers in which reasoning was linked with the colour of the block. Out of 144 children, sixteen gave 'colour' responses, but they either could not or would not explain why the colour influenced their answers, so no conclusions can be formed. No. 72 for example, who said that two blocks were the same weight 'because that is yellow and that is red', might have been trying to convey that colour was the only difference between them. To test the colour factor satisfactorily, it would be necessary not only to press for fuller answers, but to follow Inhelder's technique more closely by using both plain and coloured blocks.

Researchers who have investigated children's understanding of transitivity of weight have been concerned with factors not included in the Aden test, which, as stated, was a simplification of Inhelder's procedures. Smedslund (1959), for example, designed an experiment to show the effects of direct external reinforcement on the acquisition of concepts of conservation and transitivity of weight. He found evidence of learning in his results, but suggested that what the learners had acquired might be a 'pseudo-concept', lacking the quality of insight and necessity characterizing genuine

P.C.D.—5*

concepts. In later experiments (Smedslund, 1961), he sought association between conservation of weight and transitivity of weight with the factor of age, but found evidence only of a correlation between conservation and transitivity. This finding is in line with the view of Piaget and Inhelder who regard the mental structures of conservation and transitivity as corresponding when applied to any particular concept. Lovell and Ogilvie (1961), however, claimed that a large percentage of their subjects at the transition stage of the concept of weight as well as a large percentage of non-conservers had achieved transitivity. In a recent study by Guyler (1966), conservation of weight precedes transitivity of weight. If the results of test 2 and test 5 in the Aden study are compared, it will be seen that there was only one case where transitivity of weight preceded conservation of weight as against sixteen where conservation preceded transitivity. Guyler attributes the difference between her results and those of Lovell and Ogilvie to the methodology of the latter. In fact, if the Aden criteria of success had been used, some of their achievers of transitivity would have been considered in the transition stage. In trying to compare the results of replications of Piaget-type tests one is constantly reminded of the need for standardization.

In her study Guyler also explored the relative effects of both chronological and mental age on the acquisition of conservation and transitivity. As one would expect, correlation was higher with mental age than chronological age: Piaget's tests are designed to demonstrate stages in the development of reasoning. A wide discrepancy, such as that found by Goodnow (1962), may be due to using Raven's Progressive Matrices (1947) as a test of mental age in a cross-cultural study. The author, who tried this test out on her non-European subjects (chapter 15), found that the difference between the results of the British and local groups became more marked with age, which, in Aden, meant a wider gap also in educational experience. The problem involved here is discussed in chapter 16 in the section on cross-cultural studies.

References

Goodnow, J. J. (1962). A test for milieu effects with some of Piaget's tasks. *Psychol. Monogr.*, **76**, Whole No. 555.

Guyler, K. R. (1966). The effects of variations in task content and materials on conservation and transitivity. Unpublished M.Ed. Thesis: Manchester University.

Inhelder, B. (1943). *Le Diagnostic du Raisonnement chez les Débiles mentaux*. Neuchâtel: Delachaux et Niestlé.

Lovell, K., and E. Ogilvie. (1961). A study of the conservation of weight in the junior school child. *Br. J. educ. Psychol.*, **31**, 138–144.

Piaget, J. (1952). *The Child's Conception of Number.* London: Routledge and Kegan Paul.

Piaget, J., and B. Inhelder. (1941). *Le Développement des Quantités chez l'Enfant.* Neuchâtel: Delachaux et Niestlé.

Raven, J. C. (1947). *Progressive Matrices.* London: Harrap.

Smedslund, J. (1959). Apprentissage des notions de la conservation et de la transitivité du poids. In. J. Piaget (Ed.), *Etudes d'Epistémologie génétique,* vol. 9. Paris: Presses Universitaires. pp. 85–124.

Smedslund, J. (1961). The acquisition of conservation of substance and weight in children. *Scand. J. Psychol.,* **2,** 203–210.

CHAPTER NINE

Sugar Test: conservation

Sugar Test

Introduction

This is one of the most fascinating of Inhelder's tests, and the investigator very much regrets that the procedure had to be reduced to a minimum in this investigation. Inhelder (1943) used lump sugar so that, not only could the child watch it dissolve in the water, but she was able to include questions on the conservation of substance, weight and volume, thus providing a useful check on the results of the plasticine tests. The Aden children are not familiar with lump sugar as their tea is made in the kettle, the tea, milk and sugar being boiled together, but in any case, time only allowed for easily dissolved sugar to be used. The weighing of the jars with and without sugar had to be omitted.

Description of the test

MATERIALS

A glass of water
A supply of granulated sugar

PROCEDURE

A glass about three-quarters filled with water was placed in front of the child who was then shown a pot of granulated sugar and asked what it was. If he had any doubt he was given some to taste. (One or two children thought it was salt.) The child was then asked what would happen to the sugar if it were put into the water (Question 1), and whether the water level would stay where it was or go up, or down (Question 2). Some grains of sugar were then put into the water and the child watched them dissolve.

While this was happening, the child was asked whether, when the sugar had dissolved (melted, gone away, etc.), the water would stay where it was (Question 3). When the sugar could no longer be seen the child was then asked whether there was anything in its place (Question 4) and whether the water was then like tap water (Question 5).

QUESTIONS

1. What will happen if you put the sugar into the water?
2. What will happen to the water? Will it stay where it is, or go up, or down?
3. When the sugar is dissolved (melted, gone away, etc.) will the water stay where it is or not?
4. When the sugar is all gone, will there be anything in its place?
5. Is this water like tap water now?

Comments on performance

Descriptions of what happens to the sugar in the water included: 'It would go to the bottom of the water and melt away' (many Subjects). 'It would go to a sort of water: you wouldn't be able to see it' (No. 3). 'It goes to the bottom: after a time it goes away' (No. 6). 'It would dissolve' (No. 23). 'The sugar goes down, down, down. You can't see it because it's down.' Nearly all the children expressed in some form or other that the sugar would disappear, but opinion was divided as to whether it had vanished completely or was merely out of sight. Question 2 was asked in a more interesting context in the test on the conservation of volume, using plasticine. It is merely included here as a prelude to Question 3 which provides a new situation. Actually most of the children thought that the water would rise a little, but a few held the opposite opinion. Much thought was given to the behaviour of the water after the dissolution of the sugar. To avoid misunderstanding, the question was repeated substituting for 'stay where it is', 'stay up' or 'stay down', according to the child's previous answer. Quite a number of the children were puzzled about the final fate of the sugar, which, in some cases, they thought was not in the water at all once it had disappeared from sight. Many conservation answers broke down at Question 5. In case some of the local children might not understand 'tap' water, if the sink was not handy, 'water in the house', 'school water', 'water from the zeer' was added, and a sugarless glass of water was kept for comparison.

Grading system

Answers 1 and 2 were not graded since they were important only as a preliminary to the other questions.

'A' Conservation throughout:
(i) Volume unchanged when the sugar was dissolved (Questions 1 and 3).
(ii) The sugar remaining after dissolution (Questions 4 and 5). (Both correct.)
'B' (i) or (ii) correct, but not both
'C' Non-conservation, (i) or (ii) correct

Results (Table 9)

In the European group the trend for age was normal, with no 'A' grade answers at six years, one at seven years and five at eight years. The Arabs had very similar results for seven and eight years although the former achieved one extra 'A' grade. In the Somali community the trend was normal while the seven-year Indians were better than the eight-year olds, who were even slightly less successful than the six-year olds. In the overall results, the trend was normal, but there was very little difference at the 'C' grade level.

Throughout the groups, the girls are slightly better than the boys in this test. When the communities are compared, the Europeans are better, but the margin between the groups is not as wide as in many of the other tests. At the six-year level the Arab results were slightly better than the European. This was a difficult test for all the Subjects, since only eleven out of 144 gave 'A' grade answers.

Discussion

There is very little to add to the comments already made on this test. In an earlier investigation, referred to previously, five out of twenty Subjects gave 'Conservation' answers, the youngest being an eight-year-old girl patient at the mental hospital. The other successes were achieved by normal children aged eleven and thirteen years. On that occasion, much more time was given to the test, and the procedure approximated that of Inhelder. It seems likely that the actual disappearance of the sugar from sight increases the difficulties experienced when considering the changed shape of the plasticine or dimensions of the water. This for some children was obviously a kind of magic, which, perhaps, can be explained in the same kind of terms as those used by Greenfield who gave conservation tests to children of the Wolof tribe in Senegal, West Africa. (Reference to these experiments is also made in chapter 7.) Greenfield (1966) suggests that the Wolof child, 'while perfectly willing to attribute "magical" powers to an authority figure like the experimenter, would not attribute any special powers to himself.' The Aden children are very used to the addition of sugar in the making of tea, but as, like the milk and tea, it is added while the water is still in the kettle, they have little experience of seeing it 'disappear' or of observing differences in the volume of the liquid. Because of the time factor, the experimenter herself added a few grains of sugar to the water, instead of inviting the child to do so, and, for many children, it was fascinating to be able to see its gradual dissolution.

Table 9
Sugar Test
Frequency distribution of results obtained with test no. 6

Group	Rating	Age 6+ M	F	Total	Age 7+ M	F	Total	Age 8+ M	F	Total	Total M	F	Total
European	A	—	—	—	—	1	1	2	3	5	2	4	6
	B	6	3	9	7	4	11	3	5	8	16	12	28
	C	2	5	7	1	3	4	3	—	3	6	8	14
	Total	8	8	16	8	8	16	8	8	16	24	24	48
Arab	A	—	—	—	1	1	2	—	1	1	1	2	3
	B	5	5	10	2	2	4	3	3	6	10	10	20
	C	3	3	6	5	5	10	5	4	9	13	12	25
	Total	8	8	16	8	8	16	8	8	16	24	24	48
Indian	A	—	—	—	—	—	—	—	—	—	—	—	—
	B	—	4	4	4	2	6	2	1	3	6	7	13
	C	4	—	4	—	2	2	2	3	5	6	5	11
	Total	4	4	8	4	4	8	4	4	8	12	12	24
Somali	A	—	—	—	—	—	—	1	1	2	1	1	2
	B	1	2	3	2	3	5	2	1	3	5	6	11
	C	3	2	5	2	1	3	1	2	3	6	5	11
	Total	4	4	8	4	4	8	4	4	8	12	12	24
Total	A	—	—	—	1	2	3	3	5	8	4	7	11
	B	12	14	26	15	11	26	10	10	20	37	35	72
	C	12	10	22	8	11	19	11	9	20	31	30	61
	Total	24	24	48	24	24	48	24	24	48	72	72	144

A more likely explanation of the poor results in this test is that given by Flavell (1963), who points out that, for the younger child, 'the sugar becomes completely annihilated as an existent when it dissolves, much as the infant regards an object as no longer existing which has passed out of the visual field,' and that the tiny grains of sugar are not endowed with weight or volume. This is certainly not a simple test of conservation since it involves both substance, including a transformation far more radical than that involved in the plasticine and water tests, and volume, as affecting both the water and the sugar.

References

Flavell, J. H. (1963). *The Developmental Psychology of Jean Piaget*. New York: Van Nostrand.

Greenfield, P. M. (1966). On culture and conservation. In. J. S. Bruner, R. R. Olver and P. M. Greenfield (Eds.), *Studies in Cognitive Growth*. New York: Wiley, pp. 225–256.

Inhelder, B. (1943). *Le Diagnostic du Raisonnement chez les Débiles mentaux*. Neuchâtel: Delachaux et Niestlé.

Piaget, J. (1952). *The Child's Conception of Number*. London: Routledge and Kegan Paul.

CHAPTER TEN

Bath and Doll Tests: numerical equivalence

Bath and Doll Test: constancy of numerical equivalence

Introduction

This test is concerned with the problem of correspondence between objects that are heterogeneous but qualitatively supplementary. The aim, to quote Piaget, is to discover whether 'the one–one correspondence made by the child, or with his help, necessarily entails in his mind the idea of lasting equivalence between the corresponding sets.'

Piaget used three sets of material for this test: glasses and bottles, flowers and vases, eggs and egg-cups. In this investigation small baby dolls and baths were substituted, as they were easier to handle and more attractive to the Subjects than glasses and bottles. The other material was impracticable. The same technique was used as in Piaget's test, but the procedure was limited to two groupings of the material.

Description of the test

MATERIALS

A tin containing 12 rubber dolls 2 inches in length
6 tin toy baths slightly bigger than the dolls

PROCEDURE

The six baths were placed side by side as close together as possible, in front of the child, who was handed the tin of dolls and told to put one baby in each bath. After Question 1, the child helped to make a heap of the dolls. After Question 2, the dolls were spaced out evenly in front of the baths so that the end ones were about a foot from the end bath. After Question 3, the child returned the dolls to the baths (see figure 5).

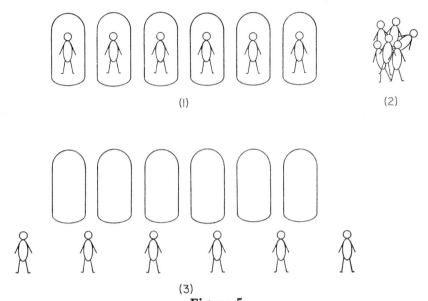

(1)

(2)

(3)

Figure 5

Bath and Doll Test—procedure

QUESTIONS

1. Is there the same number of baths and dollies?
2. Are they the same? Why?
3. Are they the same now? Why?
4. Is there the same number of baths and dollies?

Comments on performance

This was a very popular test with the boys as well as the girls. The most revealing answers resulted from Question 2 since spacing the dolls made them easy to count, whereas some other reason for equivalence or otherwise had to be supplied in the case of the heaped dolls. Thus No. 133 said: 'There are more baths because you have hidden the dollies.' whereas No. 113 said: 'They are the same because the babies are all bunged up together.'

Grading system

In cases where different types of answer were given for Question 2 and 3 separate grades were given.

'A' REASONING

No. 1   'Yes you didn't take any baths away.'

No. 4   'Yes, because each one was in a bath.'

'B' COUNTING OR INADEQUATE REASONING

No. 22   'There are 6 babies and 6 baths.'

No. 23   'Yes, because I reckoned it out in my head.'

N.B. If a child found the answer by counting, he was asked: 'Is there any other reason why they are the same?'

'C' NON-CORRESPONDENCE

No. 32   'No, because the dolls are far.'

No. 78   'The dolls are more because the baths are small and the dolls big.' (Pointed to spaces.)

Results (Tables 10 and 11)

HEAPED DOLLS (i)

In three groups, European, Indian and Somali, the seven-year groups were better than the eight-year groups, while in the Arab community, there was little difference between groups but the trend was in the right direction.

The results for girls and boys are similar at the lowest level, but at the top level, the girls are better than the boys in the European and Somali groups.

In the European community, nearly all the answers were graded 'A' or 'B', while the Arab answers were nearly evenly distributed between the three categories. The Indian and Somali groups had similar results, with more 'C' grades than 'A's' or 'B's'.

SPACED DOLLS (ii)

Again the seven-year group showed slightly better results than the eight-year groups. The results, arranged according to sex, favour the girls slightly at the 'A' level in the European and Somali groups.

In the European community, only five out of 48 children gave 'C' grade answers, but less than half 'A' grade replies. The Arab totals were approximately the same at all levels with sixteen rating as 'A', seventeen 'B' and fifteen 'C', while the Indian and Somalis were less successful with fourteen 'A's', thirteen 'B's' and twenty-one 'C's'.

Discussion

In Piaget's tests, the child was asked to put out enough glasses so that each bottle in a row of six would have one. The child was later asked to compare the number of glasses and bottles after the glasses had been put close together, and again after they had been spread out. This technique was adopted in the test under discussion.

PIAGET AND CONCEPTUAL DEVELOPMENT

The children found what appeared to be a very simple test surprisingly difficult, considering that their ages ranged from five to nine years, and only six objects were rearranged. Nearly a third did not even see the numerical equivalence of the two sets although even the youngest could

Table 10

Bath and Doll Test

Frequency distribution of results obtained with test no. 7(i)

Group	Rating	Age 6+			Age 7+			Age 8+			Total		
		M	F	Total	M	F	Total	M	F	Total	M	F	Total
	A	2	5	7	4	6	10	3	4	7	9	15	24
European	B	5	3	8	4	2	6	4	2	6	13	7	20
	C	1	—	1	—	—	—	1	2	3	2	2	4
	Total	8	8	16	8	8	16	8	8	16	24	24	48
	A	2	2	4	3	2	5	3	4	7	8	8	16
Arab	B	3	4	7	3	3	6	2	2	4	8	9	17
	C	2	3	5	2	3	5	3	2	5	8	7	15
	Total	8	8	16	8	8	16	8	8	16	24	24	48
	A	—	1	1	3	—	3	1	2	3	4	3	7
Indian	B	2	—	2	1	3	4	—	—	—	3	3	6
	C	2	3	5	—	1	1	3	2	5	5	6	11
	Total	4	4	8	4	4	8	4	4	8	12	12	24
	A	—	—	—	2	2	4	—	3	3	2	5	7
Somali	B	1	1	2	1	1	2	3	—	3	5	2	7
	C	3	3	6	1	1	2	1	1	2	5	5	10
	Total	4	4	8	4	4	8	4	4	8	12	12	24
	A	4	8	12	12	10	22	7	13	20	23	31	54
Total	B	11	8	19	9	9	18	9	4	13	29	21	50
	C	9	8	17	3	5	8	8	7	15	20	20	40
	Total	24	24	48	24	24	48	24	24	48	72	72	144

count up to six or beyond. During the investigation the impression was given that results would be better for the spaced arrangement, because counting was easier, but a comparison between tables 10 and 11 shows that results on the two halves of the test were almost identical. In her pilot

Table 11

Bath and Doll Test

Frequency distribution of results obtained with test no. 7(ii)

Group	Rating	Age 6+			Age 7+			Age 8+			Total		
		M	F	Total	M	F	Total	M	F	Total	M	F	Total
European	A	2	3	5	4	6	10	3	4	7	9	13	22
	B	5	2	7	4	2	6	5	3	8	14	7	21
	C	1	3	4	—	—	—	—	1	1	1	4	5
	Total	8	8	16	8	8	16	8	8	16	24	24	48
Arab	A	2	2	4	3	2	5	3	4	7	8	8	16
	B	3	4	7	3	3	6	2	2	4	8	9	17
	C	3	2	5	2	3	5	3	2	5	8	7	15
	Total	8	8	16	8	8	16	8	8	16	24	24	48
Indian	A	—	1	1	2	—	2	1	2	3	3	3	6
	B	2	—	2	1	3	4	—	—	—	3	3	6
	C	2	3	5	1	1	2	3	2	5	6	6	12
	Total	4	4	8	4	4	8	4	4	8	12	12	24
Somali	A	—	—	—	2	2	4	—	3	3	2	5	7
	B	1	—	1	1	1	2	3	—	3	5	1	6
	C	3	4	7	1	1	2	1	1	2	5	6	11
	Total	4	4	8	4	4	8	4	4	8	12	12	24
Total	A	4	6	10	11	10	21	7	13	20	22	29	51
	B	11	6	17	9	9	18	10	5	15	30	20	50
	C	9	12	21	4	5	9	7	6	13	20	23	43
	Total	24	24	48	24	24	48	24	24	48	72	72	144

study using a similar test to Piaget's, Churchill (1961) connected the superior results of her experimental group with play periods involving a good deal of counting and manual matching activities. She was, by the use of a control group, thus able tentatively to distinguish between 'an enumeration which is a verbal accompaniment to an intuitive corres- pondence, and an enumeration which is a numerical correspondence.' Her Subjects were only five years old, which means that considerable learning may have taken place during the play periods. In this investigation, how- ever, all the children in the upper age groups must have had considerable experience in counting activities, so the ability to count up to six could not, by itself, be accepted as 'operational'. In this, as in other tests, a child who gave a numerical answer for a reason, was automatically asked, 'Is there any other reason?' Had numerical answers been accepted as examples of 'operational' reasoning, more than two-thirds of the Subjects would have been graded 'A'. They were, however, required to point out that the equivalence was due to the stability of the material.

Piaget regards the ability to make a one–one correspondence as basic to the understanding of mathematical reasoning. Children so frequently use this method in the interest of 'fair play' in their games, that it is surprising to find lack of conservation. Having shared out sweets, toys or 'turns' at handling the skipping rope, etc., they do not, typically, later complain of inequality, even in the case of sweets, which are eaten at an unequal rate. Beard (1963) reported that this was the typical method of solving a prob- lem by children of poor intelligence in her group.

Dodwell (1960, 1961), who repeated this test, using eggs and egg-cups, as part of a series of Piaget-type number tests, found Piaget's stages and confirmed that counting did not help the child. His most important ob- servation was:

> It appears that a child may be in Stage A for one type of material and situation, and in Stage B or even C for another. This of course does not mean that a theory of stages is untenable, but it does suggest that a child may acquire the set of operations necessary for dealing con- sistently with one type of material and situation without simultane- ously being able to deal consistently with all apparently similar situations.

Like many other investigators, he confirms the need for Lunzer's fourth stage to be added to Piaget's scheme.

This experiment was also repeated by Wallach and Sprott (1964), using dolls and beds instead of baths. As in Aden, when the dolls were taken out of the beds and placed close together, children at Piaget's first stage thought that the number had changed. However, experience with reversi- bility, i.e. returning the dolls to the beds, and also demonstrating that this could not take place if a doll or bed were taken away, helped the children to see the equality of the two sets. This knowledge was transferred when a new set of objects was used. Wallach, Wall and Anderson (Sigel and Hooper, 1968, chapter 5) devised training procedures to see whether conservation of number could be induced by training in (1) reversibility alone and (2) addition and subtraction alone. Details may be found in Sigel and Hooper (1968). Briefly, they found that doll reversibility training had a strong effect, only 2 out of 14 children adhering to non-conservation answers, while 12 out of 14 children who were given doll addition–subtraction training continued as non-conservers. An important finding was that reversibility training did not have an equally strong effect when a different material (in this case, liquid) and procedure were used. A discussion on concept training will be found in chapter 16. It will be seen that it poses similar problems to those encountered by researchers in concept formation.

Bath, Towel and Doll Test:
multiplication and the coordination of relations of equivalence

Introduction

These problems test the child's understanding of further basic principles in mathematics:

1. If a = A, and b = A, then a = b.
2. If B also = A, then any relationship between a, b, c, etc., and A (if the series is continued), will also be true of a, b, c, etc., and B.
3. The relationship between the series a, b, c, etc., and A or B can be ascertained by addition or, more economically, by multiplication.

To illustrate these problems Piaget extended his earlier experiments with vases and sets of flowers. Flowers could not be used in Aden, so an experiment was devised using the popular baths and dolls, and incorporating as much as practicable of Piaget's technique.

Description of the tests

MATERIALS

8 rubber baby dolls 2 inches in length
8 slightly bigger toy baths
At least 40 small pieces of paper cut up to represent towels

PROCEDURE

The eight baths were placed in front of the child, not in a row, and pointing in different directions. The investigator then started a story: 'We must get ready to bath all those dirty babies. Here are some towels (handing a pile). Put a towel for each bath. Have you got enough?'. In view of fans overhead, the towels were placed with the edges under the baths. After a suitable interval, the investigator continued the story: 'Those towels *are* dirty: I think we had better send them to the dhobie.' The child then gathered the towels together, gave them to the investigator who put them in a pile, placed a doll on top and said: 'He's the dhobie.'

Then the child was given another pile of towels, and told: 'Here are some more. Put one for each bath. Have you enough?' After a brief interval the investigator said: 'I think these towels are rather damp. Let us put them on the line to dry.' The towels were then spread out on an imaginary line. The child was asked to compare the number of the towels in the wash with those on the line (Question 1).

The tin of dolls was then brought out, and the child was instructed to put a baby into each bath. The pile of towels was taken from the dhobie and put by the side of the spread-out towels. 'Let us give these towels to the children,' said the investigator, 'all of them—those that were with the dhobie and those that were on the line. How many will each child have?'

Three more piles of towels were produced and placed beside the other towels, the question being asked each time: 'Suppose we give these as well? How many will they have each?' On the last occasion the child is asked to account for these answers (Question 2).

QUESTIONS

1. Are the towels in the wash the same number as the towels on the line?
2. And if they had these as well? (Last batch of towels.) How many? Why?

Comments on performance

This was a favourite test. Several of the children, both boys and girls, asked for water to bath the babies, a few of which disappeared in the course of the investigation. The first problem was an advance on the first Bath and Doll Test. In that, the numerical equivalence was between the same group of objects which had first been heaped and afterwards spread out. In this test two groups of objects were used, but the same reasoning was demanded. As in the first test, many children confused space with number (as some of Piaget's Subjects did in his tests). Some typical examples of this were:

No. 144 'The towels on the line are more because (pointing) that is one, and that is one, and that is one, etc.'

No. 121 'The towels on the line are more, because they are one and one and one, etc., and those are one on top of the other.'

There were, however, those who took the opposite point of view:

No. 106 'The towels with the dhobie are more because they are many put together.'

No. 115 'The towels with the dhobie are more because the others are one and one, and these are together.'

Among the 'odd' answers, No. 70 may have confused number with weight: 'Those with the dhobie are more because they are wet.' No. 17 showed a pile with his hands and said 'The towels with the dhobie are more because when he washes the towels he has a lot.'

In the second question most children got the sequence correct once they had started but quite a number started with one towel instead of two. If they did this, to prevent any irrelevant misunderstanding, the investigator repeated that all the towels were to be given to the children, those at the dhobie and those on the line, and that no towels were to be left. In spite of this they were apparently viewed by many as one group. No. 63, having answered the first question correctly, apparently abandoned arithmetical reasoning, entered into the spirit of the story and, in spite of repeated instructions that all the towels were to be given to the children, insisted that in all circumstances they should only have one! Her final justification was: 'She must have only one because the baby is one.'

Some children substituted a rule for a reason: 'You add one each time.' Several children who got the correct sequence could not explain how they had arrived at it:

No. 105 'because they are wet and you need a lot of towels.'

No. 14 'because they are children you put one underneath, one on top, one for the face, etc.'

Grading system

1. 'A' Equivalence with reason

No. 2 'the same because each bath had one and they were given to the dhobie, and each bath had one and they were put on the line.'

'B' Equivalence with inadequate or no reason

No. 9 'the same because these are a lot and these are a lot.'

'C' Non-equivalence

2. 'A' If it was expressed, however crudely, that if B = A, the relationship of a, b, c, etc., with B results from their relationship with A

Or if a clear rule of multiplication had been arrived at:

No. 66 'because the children are like the baths and have the same as the towels for the baths.'

No. 112 'In every lot there is one for each baby, then you add another lot for each baby.'

'B' Correct sequence but inadequate or wrong reason, or if the child started with one instead of two, but reasoned correctly

No. 4 'because each time you increase by one towel.'

No. 97   'because you add one each time, because they keep getting damp or dirty and you have to have another one.'
'C' Incorrect answer

Results (Tables 12 and 13)

EQUIVALENCE OF THE TOWELS ON THE LINE AND THOSE WITH THE DHOBIE (i)

On the whole, the trend for age was normal in this test, although the six-year group achieved more correct answers than the seven-year group, and

Table 12

Bath, Towel and Doll Test

Frequency distribution of results obtained with test no. 12(i)

Group	Rating	Age 6+ M	F	Total	Age 7+ M	F	Total	Age 8+ M	F	Total	Total M	F	Total
European	A	6	7	13	6	6	12	6	7	13	18	20	38
	B	2	1	3	2	1	3	2	—	2	6	2	8
	C	—	—	—	—	1	1	—	1	1	—	2	2
	Total	8	8	16	8	8	16	8	8	16	24	24	48
Arab	A	—	2	2	2	—	2	3	3	6	5	5	10
	B	1	—	1	5	2	7	2	3	5	8	5	13
	C	7	6	13	1	6	7	3	2	5	11	14	25
	Total	8	8	16	8	8	16	8	8	16	24	24	48
Indian	A	1	1	2	2	—	2	—	2	2	3	3	6
	B	—	1	1	1	2	3	1	1	2	2	4	6
	C	3	2	5	1	2	3	3	1	4	7	5	12
	Total	4	4	8	4	4	8	4	4	8	12	12	24
Somali	A	—	1	1	—	—	—	2	—	2	2	1	3
	B	—	1	1	2	—	2	2	2	4	4	3	7
	C	4	2	6	2	4	6	—	2	2	6	8	14
	Total	4	4	8	4	4	8	4	4	8	12	12	24
Total	A	7	11	18	10	6	16	11	12	23	28	29	57
	B	3	3	6	10	5	15	7	6	13	20	14	34
	C	14	10	24	4	13	17	6	6	12	24	29	53
	Total	24	24	48	24	24	48	24	24	48	72	72	144

in some groups there was very little difference. Nor was there much differ-ence according to sex. This was one of the easier tests, for only two Europeans failed to find equivalence. In the Arab and Indian communities half the Subjects failed, while the Somalis were least successful, with only three 'A' grade answers, and more than half 'C' grades.

EQUIVALENCE BETWEEN GROUPS: ARITHMETIC RULE (ii)

The trend for age was in the right direction for all groups. In this part of the test, girls were better in all communities except the Somali, where the

Table 13

Bath, Towel and Doll Test

Frequency distribution of results obtained with test no. 12(ii)

Group	Rating	Age 6+			Age 7+			Age 8+			Total		
		M	F	Total	M	F	Total	M	F	Total	M	F	Total
European	A	—	—	—	1	4	5	1	4	5	2	8	10
	B	6	7	13	5	3	8	6	4	10	17	14	31
	C	2	1	3	2	1	3	1	—	1	5	2	7
	Total	8	8	16	8	8	16	8	8	16	24	24	48
Arab	A	—	1	1	—	—	—	1	1	2	1	2	3
	B	1	1	2	4	2	6	1	4	5	6	7	13
	C	7	6	13	4	6	10	6	3	9	17	15	32
	Total	8	8	16	8	8	16	8	8	16	24	24	48
Indian	A	—	—	—	—	—	—	—	—	—	—	—	—
	B	—	1	1	1	2	3	3	2	5	4	5	9
	C	4	3	7	3	2	5	1	2	3	8	7	15
	Total	4	4	8	4	4	8	4	4	8	12	12	24
Somali	A	—	—	—	—	—	—	1	—	1	1	—	1
	B	—	—	—	1	—	1	2	2	4	3	2	5
	C	4	4	8	3	4	7	1	2	3	8	10	18
	Total	4	4	8	4	4	8	4	4	8	12	12	24
Total	A	—	1	1	1	4	5	3	5	8	4	10	14
	B	7	9	16	11	7	18	12	12	24	30	28	58
	C	17	14	31	12	13	25	9	7	16	38	34	72
	Total	24	24	48	24	24	48	24	24	48	72	72	144

boys were slightly better. This may have been due to an extra interest in dolls, but the numbers involved are not big enough to justify more than a tentative suggestion.

All the children had difficulty in expressing the reason for the progressive number of towels given to the dolls. Only ten appeared to appreciate the problem, although many found the rule.

Discussion

The first part of this test is a more complicated version of test 7. In the latter, equivalence is found between two series (baths and dolls), in which the second is rearranged twice (heaped and then spread out). It can be expressed as an equivalence between Series A and Series B_1, and Series A and Series B_2. In this test, the first set of towels is heaped, like the dolls, but a second set of towels is spread out, so the problem becomes that of finding equivalence between Series A and Series B, Series A and Series C, and then reasoning on this basis, that Series B must be equivalent to Series C. The results of these two tests can be compared by reference to tables 10, 11 and 12, or the combined tables at the end of the book. This appears to be a situation in which Piaget would claim that it would be 'logically necessary' for a child to recognize equivalence in test 7 before equivalence in test 12, which involves further reasoning. This is not borne out by the results, which are set out in the table below.

Age (years)	Test 7 'A' Grades		Test 12 'A' Grades
	Heaped (i)	Spread (ii)	Heaped and Spread (i)
6	12	10	18
7	22	21	16
8	20	20	23
Total	54	51	51

It appears that, to the child, the second problem is no more difficult, and may even be less difficult than the first. Is this because it is easier for him to see that the heaped and spread towels are equivalent than to remember that the spread dolls, which had been heaped, had originally been in the baths? This cannot be the answer, since the child's assertion in test 12 was not accepted unless he referred back to the baths in his answer.

In the second part of the problem, a number of children finally arrived at a correct arithmetic progression, although several of them made the initial mistake of giving one instead of two towels to each doll. These children appeared to have difficulty in adjusting themselves to the idea that each bath could be matched by more than one towel simultaneously. Some children clung to this one–one correspondence regardless of the number of towels at their disposal and the instructions that they were all to be used. It was quite obvious that for several of these children the problem was not a mathematical one at all, and that their reasoning was not following the pattern described by Piaget.

The methods by which children arrive at 'operational multiplication' have been explored recently by Willington (1967), who set up an experiment using flowers and vases, which is based on Piaget's original version but with differences in procedure. She appears to confirm Piaget's main stages, but includes some interesting sub-stages.

References

Beard, R. (1963). The order of concept studies in two fields. (i) Number concept in the infant school (ii) Conception of conservation of quantity among primary school children. *Educ. Rev.*, **XV**, Nos. 2, 3.

Churchill, E. M. (1961). *Counting and Measuring*. London: Routledge and Kegan Paul.

Dodwell, P. C. (1960). Children's understanding of number and related concepts. *Can. J. Psychol.*, **14**, 191–205.

Dodwell, P. C. (1961). Children's understanding of number concepts: characteristics of an individual and a group test. *Can. J. Psychol.*, **15**, 29–36.

Piaget, J. (1952). *The Child's Conception of Number*. London: Routledge and Kegan Paul.

Sigel, I. E., and F. H. Hooper, Eds. (1968). (7 occasions) *Logical Thinking in Children*. New York: Holt, Rinehart and Winston.

University of Leeds. (1958). (6 occasions) Inst. of Educ. Researches and Studies. No. 17, Jan.; No. 18, July.

Wallach, Lise, and R. L. Sprott. (1964). Inducing number conservation in children. *Child Dev.*, **35**, 1057–1071.

Willington, G. A. (1967). The development of mathematical understanding in primary school children. Unpublished M. Ed. Thesis: Manchester University (Experiment 3).

CHAPTER ELEVEN

House and Door Test: seriation, qualitative similarity and ordinal correspondence

House and Door Test

Introduction

In this test the child progresses from cardinal to ordinal correspondence.

To demonstrate this test Piaget used ten wooden dolls of the same thickness but of clearly different heights, the tallest being at least twice as big as the shortest, and ten sticks also varying in size but with less difference between them. In Aden such dolls were unobtainable and dolls of a different type were being used in two of the other tests, so it was decided to vary the material. Blocks, representing houses were used instead of the dolls, and small pieces of wood representing the doors replaced the sticks.

Description of the test

MATERIALS

10 wooden blocks 4 inches wide, 1 inch thick, ranging in height from 1 inch to $5\frac{1}{2}$ inches by $\frac{1}{2}$ inch intervals
10 pieces of 3 ply wood $\frac{1}{2}$ inch wide, ranging in height from $\frac{1}{4}$ inch to $5\frac{1}{4}$ inches, by $\frac{1}{4}$ inch intervals

PROCEDURE

The child was seated at a large table with space enough in front of him to take all the houses if arranged in a row. His attention was then drawn to the blocks standing in an unarranged group, right side up, on the table, and to the pile of 'doors' near by. The child was told: 'These are houses and these are their front doors. Arrange the houses and doors so that we can easily find the door that belongs to each house' (Problem 1).

A note was made if the child followed one of the two chief methods of attack described by Piaget. If he failed to seriate the houses and doors, the investigator said: 'Let us arrange them like this,' and put the three largest houses and their appropriate doors edge to edge, asking the child to finish the row. The child was then asked to make sure that all the houses had their right doors. If there were still mistakes in the seriation of the houses, further help was given.

The doors were then taken from the houses against which they had been propped, and spread out on the table in front of the houses so that the end doors were about four inches from the end houses and the others were unevenly spaced between. Opportunity was taken to correct any mistakes made in the seriation of the doors, without drawing the child's attention to the corrections. Pointing to the houses in random order the investigator said 'Which door will this one take?' (Problem 2).

Then the doors were placed in the same way, but the order was reversed. The same question was asked (Problem 3). The investigator then said: 'Let us make an estate of the houses (or put them like this)', and with the child, rearranged them, mixing the sizes. The child was then told: 'All the houses bigger than this (4th largest) are going to have their doors put in first. Can you find their doors?' (Problem 4).

Comments on performance

For the majority of the children this was a very difficult test. With the exception of one or two children who tried to make one house from all the blocks put together, they readily accepted the blocks as complete houses and the small pieces of wood as doors. In the cases referred to, the investigator said, pointing, 'This is a house and this is a house and this is a house, etc., each one is a house by itself.' Many children struggled to prop the doors against the houses as they stood in their original positions close together in a group at one end of the table, just in reach. To them the instruction to 'arrange' the houses was repeated very clearly, and the words added: 'You may move them' in case the child was too nervous to take the initiative.

Many children completely ignored the point about making it easy to find the door that belonged to each house, and arranged the houses in a group to form an estate. These children enjoyed the test. They talked about their arrangements: 'We'll put this little bungalow here, next to the big house.' Many of the children who failed to seriate, distinguished correctly between large and small houses and doors. They treated each house as a separate problem and put what they thought was a suitable door against it. If, when they reached the last two or three houses, they found themselves left, say, with a very large house and a tiny door, they re-arranged one or two until they were satisfied.

The children who managed the double seriation either seriated the houses and then looked for an appropriate door, or found the largest (or smallest) house first and then searched for the largest (or smallest) door. The tendency was to start with the extreme sizes and work up or down the series, although some children found the end members first and then worked from both ends. These methods of approach to the problem were found by Piaget among his Subjects. An exception among the successful children was No. 66 who, beginning with the largest house and door, successfully placed each door against its appropriate house without disturbing the original grouping of the houses.

Many children who failed to grasp that seriation was required, were capable of the exercise, and successfully completed the series after it had been begun by the investigator. These children usually spontaneously corrected their mistakes. Faced with a correct double seriation, some children whose original arrangement had been completely indiscriminate, managed to fit door with house even when the series was reversed. They usually counted from the ends. Many (as Piaget noted) were successful with the end members, but found the middle ones more difficult, and, like the failures, chose the nearest.

Seriation of houses or doors was used to solve the final problem, but no child made two complete series. Sometimes the larger houses were placed against the fourth for comparison and then the larger doors seriated, or the child, looking at the doors and estimating, handed the appropriate doors one at a time, perhaps measuring only the final door. No. 28 seriated all the larger doors and houses to prove that his estimate was correct, while No. 37, having estimated, said: 'To make sure you would make the doors and houses like steps.'

Many children whose efforts were otherwise successful could not solve the problem of what to do with the sample door. Should it be included or left out? If a mistake was made, the investigator said, as the doors were being handed to her: 'These are the doors of the houses *bigger* than that one,' so that if the child had not attended to the original instruction he had a chance to make a correction. One or two hastily replaced the last door, but most of them were satisfied with their responses.

Grading system

It was not practicable to devise a system of grading whereby all the above variations could be itemized, so the marking was limited to correct and incorrect responses, a note being made of the deviations significant for the comparison with Piaget's results.

PROBLEM 1

'A' Seriation
(i) simultaneous (direct correspondence)
(ii) separate and matching (simple seriation with correspondence)
'B' Seriation after preliminary help
'C' Incorrect

PROBLEMS 2 AND 3

'A' Both correct
'B' One correct
'C' Incorrect

PROBLEM 4

'A' Re-seriation and/or correct answer
'B' Correct except for sample being included
'C' Incorrect

Results (Tables 14, 15 and 16)

DOUBLE SERIATION (i)

The results in this test are rather erratic. In the European community, the six-year group did better than the seven-year group, while in the Arab and Indian community the seven-year groups did slightly better than the eight-year groups. The Somalis showed a normal trend for age. This was also seen in the totals of the 'A' grades, but not in the 'B' grades which showed an unusually high number at the six-year-old level.

The Europeans and Indians had better results for girls while the boys were better in the Arab and Somali groups. A great difference is seen in the results for the communities. About half of the Europeans were successful, with three eight-year olds failing even after initial help. However, only four out of 48 Arabs seriated spontaneously and the majority could not finish even after the process had been begun for them. Only one Subject in each of the Indian and Somali communities did not need help.

CORRESPONDENCE (ii)

In this part of the test, the age trend was normal for all groups, and there was very little difference between boys and girls except in the European community where the girls were slightly better.

A few more than half the European Subjects, including all the eight-year olds, achieved an 'A' grade, but most of the Arab children matched the house with the door nearest to it. About a quarter of them managed at least half the test. In the Indian and Somali communities about three-quarters of the Subjects failed completely, the Somalis having the better results.

Table 14
House and Door Test
Frequency distribution of results obtained with test no. 8(i)

Group	Rating	Age 6+			Age 7+			Age 8+			Total		
		M	F	Total	M	F	Total	M	F	Total	M	F	Total
European	A	2	4	6	2	3	5	4	7	11	8	14	22
	B	6	4	10	2	4	6	2	—	2	10	8	18
	C	—	—	—	4	1	5	2	1	3	6	2	8
	Total	8	8	16	8	8	16	8	8	16	24	24	48
Arab	A	—	—	—	1	1	2	1	1	2	2	2	4
	B	3	2	5	2	1	3	—	—	—	5	3	8
	C	5	6	11	5	6	11	7	7	14	17	19	36
	Total	8	8	16	8	8	16	8	8	16	24	24	48
Indian	A	—	—	—	—	1	1	—	—	—	—	1	1
	B	2	2	4	1	—	1	—	1	1	3	3	6
	C	2	2	4	3	3	6	4	3	7	9	8	17
	Total	4	4	8	4	4	8	4	4	8	12	12	24
Somali	A	—	—	—	—	—	—	1	—	1	1	—	1
	B	1	—	1	1	1	2	2	3	5	4	4	8
	C	3	4	7	3	3	6	1	1	2	7	8	15
	Total	4	4	8	4	4	8	4	4	8	12	12	24
Total	A	2	4	6	3	5	8	6	8	14	11	17	28
	B	12	8	20	6	6	12	4	4	8	22	18	40
	C	10	12	22	15	13	28	14	12	26	39	37	76
	Total	24	24	48	24	24	48	24	24	48	72	72	144

RANDOM SAMPLE (iii)

In all except the Arab community, and in the total, the trend for age was normal. In the Arab group, the eight-year olds did not do as well as the

Table 15

House and Door Test

Frequency distribution of results obtained with test no. 8(ii)

Group	Rating	Age 6+ M	Age 6+ F	Age 6+ Total	Age 7+ M	Age 7+ F	Age 7+ Total	Age 8+ M	Age 8+ F	Age 8+ Total	Total M	Total F	Total
	A	3	3	6	5	6	11	5	6	11	13	15	28
European	B	1	2	3	1	1	2	3	2	5	5	5	10
	C	4	3	7	2	1	3	—	—	—	6	4	10
	Total	8	8	16	8	8	16	8	8	16	24	24	48
	A	—	—	—	1	1	2	2	1	3	3	2	5
Arab	B	2	1	3	1	1	2	1	—	1	4	2	6
	C	6	7	13	6	6	12	5	7	12	17	20	37
	Total	8	8	16	8	8	16	8	8	16	24	24	48
	A	—	—	—	—	—	—	—	—	—	—	—	—
Indian	B	—	—	—	1	—	1	2	1	3	3	1	4
	C	4	4	8	3	4	7	2	3	5	9	11	20
	Total	4	4	8	4	4	8	4	4	8	12	12	24
	A	—	1	1	—	—	—	1	—	1	1	1	2
Somali	B	1	—	1	2	1	3	—	2	2	3	3	6
	C	3	3	6	2	3	5	3	2	5	8	8	16
	Total	4	4	8	4	4	8	4	4	8	12	12	24
	A	3	4	7	6	7	13	8	7	15	17	18	35
Total	B	4	3	7	5	3	8	6	5	11	15	11	26
	C	17	17	34	13	14	27	10	12	22	40	43	83
	Total	24	24	48	24	24	48	24	24	48	72	72	144

six- and seven-year olds. There was very little difference in results according to sex, since the superiority of the European and Indian girls was balanced by that of the boys in the other two communities. In the European community, about a third of the Subjects failed com-

Table 16

House and Door Test

Frequency distribution of results obtained with test no. 8(iii)

Group	Rating	Age 6+ M	F	Total	Age 7+ M	F	Total	Age 8+ M	F	Total	Total M	F	Total
European	A	3	2	5	5	5	10	5	6	11	13	13	26
	B	—	2	2	1	2	3	1	1	2	2	5	7
	C	5	4	9	2	1	3	2	1	3	9	6	15
	Total	8	8	16	8	8	16	8	8	16	24	24	48
Arab	A	1	1	2	2	—	2	—	—	—	3	1	4
	B	2	1	3	—	1	1	1	—	1	3	2	5
	C	5	6	11	6	7	13	7	8	15	18	21	39
	Total	8	8	16	8	8	16	8	8	16	24	24	48
Indian	A	—	—	—	—	—	—	—	1	1	—	1	1
	B	—	—	—	—	1	1	—	—	—	—	1	1
	C	4	4	8	4	3	7	4	3	7	12	10	22
	Total	4	4	8	4	4	8	4	4	8	12	12	24
Somali	A	—	—	—	2	—	2	1	1	2	3	1	4
	B	—	—	—	—	—	—	2	—	2	2	—	2
	C	4	4	8	2	4	6	1	3	4	7	11	18
	Total	4	4	8	4	4	8	4	4	8	12	12	24
Total	A	4	3	7	9	5	14	6	8	14	19	16	35
	B	2	3	5	1	4	5	4	1	5	7	8	15
	C	18	18	36	14	15	29	14	15	29	46	48	94
	Total	24	24	48	24	24	48	24	24	48	72	72	144

pletely, while in the Aden groups, the majority failed, the Indians achiev-ing the only two 'A' grades. Fifteen out of the 144 Subjects included the sample house, ignoring the instruction to find the doors for houses that were *bigger*.

Discussion

In the previous test, cardinal correspondence only was required. In this, the correspondence is between two series whose relationship rests on the ordinal position of corresponding members. Piaget, using dolls and balls, found two methods of attack used by his Subjects in solving this problem. Either the two series were made independently and then matched, or each member of Series A was matched with its corresponding member in Series B, the double series being gradually built up. Both of these methods were used in this investigation. Out of the 28 children who achieved the double seriation, twelve used the simultaneous, and fifteen the separate and match-ing procedures, while one used both, so it appears that there was no particular preference. Piaget's account tells us nothing about the devia-tions from these methods. One wonders whether any of his Subjects fol-lowed up their own ideas, as many of the Aden children did. The younger and the less able children, not understanding the nature of the problem, made arrangements that to them seemed sensible, such as groups of houses round a court yard, or streets in which the smaller houses were dis-cretely inserted between the more pretentious mansions. They grouped by theme rather than by logical transitivity. How does Piaget classify such approaches to the problems in his test? Are they discounted as irrelevant, as unworthy of record? It seems that a special category is required for such responses. Would it be creativity?

Piaget attributed failure in this test to lack of 'logical transitivity' which he considers necessary for arranging items in an ordinal series. Other in-vestigators suggest that experience may be a factor. Hendriks (1966), for example, comparing the results of tests given to urban Shona and European children in Southern Rhodesia, found that not only, as in Aden, were the Europeans generally better than the non-Europeans, but that both African and European nursery school groups tended to be more advanced than non-nursery groups. In an unpublished personal communication, Millie Almy describes a double seriation test included in an exploratory study with primary school children in Uganda. As this was a pilot study, the results are tentative and not regarded as of primary importance, but it is interesting to note that the Ugandan children not only found double seriation a much easier task than did Arab, Indian and Somali children of the same age, but that some of them found seriation tasks easier than conservation tasks. One wonders if this was partly due to the fact that six instead of ten items were used: in Aden the children found the double seriation not only difficult but a very slow task. Dodwell (1962) actually found that some children could deal operationally with tests involving ordinal and cardinal properties, as described in chapter 12, before they could deal with seriation separately. All Piaget's stages were found in his subjects, but not always in the same sequence.

References

Almy, Millie, E. Chittenden and P. Miller. (1966). *Young Children's Thinking: Studies of some Aspects of Piaget's Theory*. New York: Teachers College Press, Columbia University.

Dodwell, P. C. (1962). Relations between the understanding of the logic of classes and of cardinal number in children. *Can. J. Psychol.*, **16**, 152–160.

Hendriks, E. (1966). A cross-cultural investigation of the number concepts and level of number development in five-year old Urban Shona and European children in Southern Rhodesia. Unpublished M.A. Thesis: University of London.

Piaget, J. (1952). *The Child's Conception of Number*. London: Routledge and Kegan Paul.

Piaget, J. (1953). *Logic and Psychology*. Manchester: Manchester University Press.

CHAPTER TWELVE

Staircase Tests: ordination and cardination

Introduction

These tests are designed to confirm Piaget's hypothesis that ordination and cardination are interdependent, a fact already demonstrated in the previous test. Two of Piaget's three tests were selected, the materials and procedure being closely copied. At first it was intended to arrange for half of the Subjects in each group to do each test, but this plan was discarded for practical reasons. The stick test took so long that in order not to keep the following child waiting too long, a slow child was given the Card Test. Out of 144 children a quarter did the Stick Test and the rest the Card Test. As the same principle was being demonstrated in each of the tests, although they were graded separately, a parallel system was used.

Stick Test

Description of the test

MATERIALS

10 sticks of equal width and thickness and differing in length by 0·8 cm, the smallest stick being 9 cm in length
10 sticks exactly similar except in lengths, which ranged from 9·4 cm to 15·8 cm by intervals of 0·8 cm

PROCEDURE

The child was given the first set of sticks and instructed: 'Show me the smallest . . . Now show me the biggest . . . Now try to put the smallest first, then one a little bigger, then another a little bigger and so on.' (A demonstration with the first two sticks accompanied the instructions) (Problem 1).

After the child had completed the row, he was handed the second set of sticks and told: 'These have been forgotten: put them in their right places' (Problem 2).

At this point, if the top edges of the sticks formed roughly a staircase they were left for the next instruction, but if they were too inaccurately placed for further use, the investigator helped the child to make a correct series.

The child was told to count all the sticks, so that if he found difficulty, a number could be removed. Then a baby doll was shown climbing up from the bottom stair. It was placed on the stair about half-way in the series, and the child was asked: 'How many stairs will the baby have climbed when it reaches there?' (Problem 3). 'How many steps are behind the baby?' (Problem 4). 'How many stairs will it need to climb to reach the top of the stairs?' (Problem 5). After this the series was disarranged, the stairs not being in a row. A stair was selected, the doll placed at the top of it, and the child was asked again how many stairs were behind it, and how many it would need to climb to reach the top of the staircase (Problem 6).

Comments on performance

Most children made the first series very carefully and quickly. The usual method was to stand the sticks on end to compare with the next member of the series. No. 34 began seriating even before the instructions were finished. Some children, however, took the sticks indiscriminately and put them together, making stairs at the top edges, but completely ignoring the bottom edges. Some interesting deviations were made by other children. No. 49 selected sticks roughly in the right order, but arranged them so that the top edge made ascending stairs, and the bottom descending stairs. No. 23 made the first half of the stairs go up, and the second half go down. When told to make the staircase in one direction, he used the second half to continue the series by making the bottoms uneven (see figure 6).

The fitting in of the second series of sticks was, for most children a very slow and laborious task. The usual method was to take each stick in turn and measure it on top of each member of the first series until the correct position was found, after which the adjacent sticks were pushed to one side to make room for it. The series with the new member was then carefully arranged and bottom edges restraightened before the next stick was inserted and the whole process repeated. Some children who had been noticeably quick and accurate with the first series failed in this task. No. 34 for example, started to fit one stick in. When he found that it was not in the right place, he threw aside all the first series which he had built so carefully and started from scratch, this time making the bottom edges very uneven. No. 1 remarked that he would have to start all over again. He did not disarrange the whole pile, but pushed half to one side to make room for the others. No. 23 made a second detached staircase, then attached it to the first, making one continuous series by completely ignoring the bottom edges.

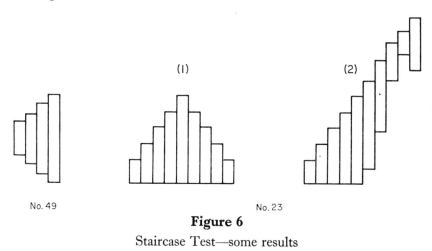

Figure 6

Staircase Test—some results

For the children who could manage the counting, the same difficulty presented itself as in the House and Door Test. Should the stair that the baby is standing on be included? No. 67, for example, failed to count this stair when calculating how many stairs the baby had climbed, but included it in the number of steps behind the baby.

Comparatively few children managed the re-seriating question. Some just counted all the stairs. No. 5 took the smallest stair and tried to estimate the number between that and the stair on which the baby stood by measuring the intervals. When asked if he could prove if his answer were right, he thought for a while, then seriated and counted, finding his mistakes. Some children made the whole series but a few having arranged the steps behind the baby just counted the remainder to answer the last question.

Grading system

In order not to make the marking too complicated, and to make possible a comparison between this test and the Card Test, the problems were grouped as follows:

PROBLEMS 1 AND 2

'A' Correct seriation
'B' Correct after initial help (first four sticks)
'C' Incorrect

PROBLEMS 3, 4 AND 5

'A' Relative position correct in each problem
'B' Two out of three problems correct
'C' Incorrect

PROBLEM 6

'A' Re-seriation and/or correct
'B' Corrected by seriation when asked for proof
'C' Incorrect

Results (Table 17)

N.B. Tables 19, 20, 21 give the combined results for the Stick and Card Tests.

In the Stick Test, 37 children took part, including 24 Europeans, nine Arabs and four Somalis, among whom twenty were boys and seventeen girls. The numbers are rather small for separate consideration, but the main points are as follows (see table 17).

SERIATION (i)

Half the children seriated correctly without help and a third failed even with help. Out of 24 Europeans two-thirds were successful and out of nine Arabs, one-third. The Somalis seriated with help, and the other two failed. The trend was in the right direction in the results for age groups, but owing to the uneven size of the groups, it is difficult to make a comparison.

RELATIVE POSITION (ii)

This was a more difficult task, for less than a third of the Subjects answered all three questions correctly. Half of them were correct for two out of three questions. A higher proportion of Arabs than Europeans were successful and the Somalis did even better, with three successes out of four. This may, however, have been due to sampling.

Table 17
Stick Test

Frequency distribution of results obtained with test no. 9a(i), (ii) and (iii)

	6+ M A	6+ M B	6+ M C	6+ F A	6+ F B	6+ F C	7+ M A	7+ M B	7+ M C	7+ F A	7+ F B	7+ F C	8+ M A	8+ M B	8+ M C	8+ F A	8+ F B	8+ F C	Total A	Total B	Total C
Part (i)																					
European	—	2	—	2	—	—	—	—	2	3	1	1	4	—	2	6	—	—	16	3	5
Arab	—	—	1	—	—	—	—	1	—	—	1	1	2	—	—	1	—	3	3	1	5
Somali	—	—	—	—	—	—	—	—	—	—	—	—	—	2	2	—	—	—	—	2	3
Total	—	2	1	2	—	—	—	1	2	3	2	2	6	2	4	7	—	3	19	6	12
Part (ii)																					
European	—	1	1	—	1	—	1	2	1	—	3	1	2	3	1	1	5	—	5	15	4
Arab	—	—	1	—	—	—	—	1	—	—	—	—	1	1	—	2	1	1	3	3	3
Somali	—	—	—	—	—	—	—	—	—	3	—	—	3	1	—	—	—	—	3	1	—
Total	—	1	2	—	1	—	1	3	1	3	3	—	6	5	1	3	6	1	11	19	7
Part (iii)																					
European	—	1	1	—	1	—	2	2	2	2	1	2	3	2	3	4	1	1	6	9	9
Arab	—	—	1	—	—	—	—	—	1	—	—	—	—	—	4	1	—	3	1	—	8
Somali	—	—	—	—	—	—	—	—	—	—	—	—	—	—	4	—	—	—	—	—	4
Total	—	1	2	—	1	—	2	3	1	2	2	3	3	2	9	5	1	4	7	9	21

RANDOM ORDER (iii)

This was the most difficult task of all, with seven out of 37 children successful, and 21 failures. Only six European children gave a correct answer immediately, but nine others corrected their own mistakes. Apart from one eight-year-old Arab girl, none of the Aden children gave a satisfactory answer.

These results are discussed in conjunction with the results of the Card Test.

Card Test

Description of test

MATERIALS

10 strips of cardboard 1 inch wide, the first 1 inch high, the second 2 inches, the third 3 inches, etc., so that each card represents one unit more than its predecessor.

PROCEDURE

The child was instructed: 'Put these cards in a row, beginning with the smallest, and then the next smallest, and so on, until you get to the biggest. Make a staircase of them' (Problem 1). (The first two of the series were used for demonstration.) If the series was completely inaccurate, the investigator then helped the child to rearrange it, in order that subsequent questions might be asked.

The child was then asked to count the cards so that if he found difficulty, a number could be removed. The investigator then pointed to the smallest card and to each of the series in turn asking: 'How many cards like this little one could we make with that?' (Problem 2).

Random cards were then selected, the child again being asked: 'How many cards like this (the smallest), could we make from that?' (Problem 3).

After the row had been disarranged so that the cards were pointing in all directions, a card was selected and the same question asked. If a child estimated without moving the cards, he was instructed: 'Show me what you could do to make sure' (Problem 4).

Comments on performance

Most of the children made the staircase quickly and accurately, great care being taken to keep the bottom edges level. The failures, as in the first seriation of sticks, were quite content provided that the top edges formed an uneven staircase. A few children could not do this, even after half the series had been completed for them. They just placed the cards indiscriminately along the top or put two small cards above each other to make a tall one.

Quite a number of children who had failed to seriate managed to say how many little cards would be needed to make a bigger one, even when a random card was selected. This may have been because the problem could be solved by counting, an operation which most of them automatically carried out every time they were faced with a collection of similar objects. Some children only counted correctly when the cards were kept in sequence (Problem 2).

Very few children re-seriated the cards spontaneously in order to solve the last problem. Some of them did so in response to the instructions: 'Show me what you could do to make sure', but most of them resorted to measuring. They either put the little card at the side of the bigger one and moved it up, keeping the place with a finger, or they put it on top and turned it over and over.

Grading system

The grading was brought into line with the grading for the Stick Test.

PROBLEM 1

'A' Correct seriation
'B' Correct after initial help (First 3 cards)
'C' Incorrect

PROBLEMS 2 AND 3

'A' Relative position correct in both problems
'B' Problem 2 or 3 correct
'C' Incorrect

PROBLEM 4

'A' Re-seriation and/or correct
'B' Corrected by seriation when asked for proof
'C' Incorrect

N.B. 'm' indicates that the child measured or estimated instead of seriating.

Results (Table 18)

Out of the 144 children in this investigation, 107 did this test, consisting of 24 Europeans, 39 Arabs, 24 Indians and 20 Somalis, of whom 55 were girls and 52 boys. Combined results for the Stick and Card Tests will be found at the end of the chapter

Table 18
Card Tests

Frequency distribution of results obtained with test no. 9b(i), (ii) and (iii)

Group	6+ M			6+ F			7+ M			7+ F			8+ M			8+ F			Total (107)		
	A	B	C	A	B	C	A	B	C	A	B	C	A	B	C	A	B	C	A	B	C
Part (i)																					
European	6	—	—	7	—	—	4	—	—	3	—	—	2	—	—	2	—	—	24	—	—
Arab	4	—	3	2	1	5	5	—	2	3	—	4	4	—	2	3	1	—	21	2	16
Indian	1	1	2	2	—	2	3	—	1	2	—	2	2	—	2	3	—	1	13	1	10
Somali	—	2	2	1	—	3	2	—	2	2	—	2	—	—	—	4	—	—	9	2	9
Total	11	3	7	12	1	10	14	—	5	10	—	8	8	—	4	12	1	1	67	5	35
Part (ii)																					
European	4	1	1	3	3	1	2	2	—	1	2	—	2	—	—	1	1	—	13	9	2
Arab	5	—	2	2	3	3	4	2	1	5	—	2	4	—	2	4	—	—	24	5	10
Indian	2	1	1	1	—	3	2	1	1	3	—	1	2	—	2	4	—	—	14	2	8
Somali	—	1	3	1	—	3	4	—	—	2	—	2	—	—	—	3	1	—	10	2	8
Total	11	3	7	7	6	10	12	5	2	11	2	5	8	—	4	12	2	—	61	18	28
Part (iii)																					
European	3	—	3	3	1	3	1	1	2	—	1	2	1	—	1	1	1	—	9	4	11
Arab	3	—	4	1	—	7	2	—	5	3	—	4	2	—	4	—	2	2	11	2	26
Indian	1	1	2	1	—	3	—	—	4	2	—	2	—	1	3	2	1	1	6	3	15
Somali	—	—	4	—	—	4	3	—	1	1	—	3	—	—	—	2	1	1	6	1	13
Total	7	1	13	5	1	17	6	1	12	6	1	11	3	1	8	5	5	4	32	10	65

SERIATION (i)

As in the Stick Test a third of the children failed, even with help, but more than half were successful. Out of the 24 Europeans, there were no failures at all, compared with one-third 'B' and 'C' grades in the previous test. More than half of the Arabs were successful (as compared with one-third in the Stick Test), and about half the Somalis.

RELATIVE POSITION (ii)

The most noticeable difference between difficulty of this and the Stick Test can be seen in the results of this part. It was slightly more difficult than the seriation, but whereas there was a difference of eight out of 37 'A' grades in the Stick Test, in this test the difference is only six out of 107. The proportion of 'C' grades, however, is in favour of the Stick Test. It is interesting to note that, in this section of the test, the Arabs were again more successful than the Europeans, who, like the Indians and Somalis, achieved about half 'A' grades.

RANDOM ORDER (iii)

This, as in the Stick Test, was the most difficult problem, but the proportion of successes was higher. The proportion of failures was, however, about the same. There was not a great difference between the percentages of 'A' results in the communities. They were approximately as follows: European 37½ per cent, Arab 28½ per cent, Indian 25 per cent, Somali 30 per cent.

Combined results of Stick and Card Test (Tables 19, 20 and 21)

SERIATION (i)

The trend for age is in the right direction, but there is not much difference in the six-year and seven-year groups. In the European, Indian and Somali groups the girls are better than the boys, but the totals show very little difference.

The difference in European and Aden communities is marked. The Europeans had only five failures, including none at six years, whereas only half of the Arabs and Indians were successful. Half the Somalis failed.

RELATIVE POSITION (ii)

The trend for age is normal on the whole but, as in the seriation task, the six-year group is slightly better than the seven-year group. There is little difference in results according to sex, although the boys are slightly better than the girls in the European group. Again it is interesting to note that the Aden groups, with more than half 'A' grades are more successful than the Europeans, with less than half.

Table 19

Stick and Card Tests: combined results

Frequency distribution of results obtained with test no. 9(i)

Group	Rating	Age 6+ M	F	Total	Age 7+ M	F	Total	Age 8+ M	F	Total	Total M	F	Total
European	A	6	8	14	6	6	12	6	8	14	18	22	40
	B	2	—	2	—	1	1	—	—	—	2	1	3
	C	—	—	—	2	1	3	2	—	2	4	1	5
	Total	8	8	16	8	8	16	8	8	16	24	24	48
Arab	A	4	2	6	5	3	8	6	4	10	15	9	24
	B	—	1	1	1	—	1	—	1	1	1	2	3
	C	4	5	9	2	5	7	2	3	5	8	13	21
	Total	8	8	16	8	8	16	8	8	16	24	24	48
Indian	A	1	2	3	3	2	5	2	3	5	6	7	13
	B	1	—	1	—	—	—	—	—	—	1	—	1
	C	2	2	4	1	2	3	2	1	3	5	5	10
	Total	4	4	8	4	4	8	4	4	8	12	12	24
Somali	A	—	1	1	2	1	3	—	4	4	2	6	8
	B	2	—	2	—	—	—	2	—	2	4	—	4
	C	2	3	5	2	3	5	2	—	2	6	6	12
	Total	4	4	8	4	4	8	4	4	8	12	12	24
Total	A	11	13	24	16	12	28	14	19	33	41	44	85
	B	5	1	6	1	1	2	2	1	3	8	3	11
	C	8	10	18	7	11	18	8	4	12	23	25	48
	Total	24	24	48	24	24	48	24	24	48	72	72	144

RANDOM ORDER (iii)

In the totals, the trend for age is normal, although in the European, Arab and Somali groups there is a tendency for some lower age ranges to be a

Table 20

Stick and Card Tests: combined results

Frequency distribution of results obtained with test no. 9(ii)

Group	Rating	Age 6+			Age 7+			Age 8+			Total		
		M	F	Total	M	F	Total	M	F	Total	M	F	Total
European	A	4	3	7	3	2	5	4	2	6	11	7	18
	B	2	4	6	4	5	9	3	6	9	9	15	24
	C	2	1	3	1	1	2	1	—	1	4	2	6
	Total	8	8	16	8	8	16	8	8	16	24	24	48
Arab	A	5	2	7	4	5	9	5	6	11	14	13	27
	B	—	3	3	3	—	3	1	1	2	4	4	8
	C	3	3	6	1	3	4	2	1	3	6	7	13
	Total	8	8	16	8	8	16	8	8	16	24	24	48
Indian	A	2	1	3	2	3	5	2	4	6	6	5	14
	B	1	—	1	1	—	1	—	—	—	2	—	2
	C	1	3	4	1	1	2	2	—	2	4	4	8
	Total	4	4	8	4	4	8	4	4	8	12	12	24
Somali	A	—	1	1	4	2	6	3	3	6	7	6	13
	B	1	—	1	—	—	—	1	1	2	2	1	3
	C	3	3	6	—	2	2	—	—	—	3	5	8
	Total	4	4	8	4	4	8	4	4	8	12	12	24
Total	A	11	7	18	13	12	25	14	15	29	38	34	72
	B	4	7	11	8	5	13	5	8	13	17	20	37
	C	9	10	19	3	7	10	5	1	6	17	18	35
	Total	24	24	48	24	24	48	24	24	48	72	72	144

little superior to higher ones. On the whole, girls are better than boys, although the opposite is true in the Arab group.

At the 'A' grade level there is not much difference between the communities, but the Europeans are a little better than the Aden children.

Table 21

Stick and Card Tests: combined results

Frequency distribution of results obtained with test no. 9(iii)

Group	Rating	Age 6+ M	F	Total	Age 7+ M	F	Total	Age 8+ M	F	Total	Total M	F	Total
European	A	3	3	6	1	1	2	2	5	7	6	9	15
	B	1	2	3	3	3	6	2	2	4	6	7	13
	C	4	3	7	4	4	8	4	1	5	12	8	20
	Total	8	8	16	8	8	16	8	8	16	24	24	48
Arab	A	3	1	4	2	3	5	2	1	3	7	5	12
	B	—	—	—	—	—	—	—	2	2	—	2	2
	C	5	7	12	6	5	11	6	5	11	17	17	34
	Total	8	8	16	8	8	16	8	8	16	24	24	48
Indian	A	1	1	2	—	2	2	—	2	2	1	5	6
	B	1	—	1	—	—	—	1	1	2	2	1	3
	C	2	3	5	4	2	6	3	1	4	9	6	15
	Total	4	4	8	4	4	8	4	4	8	12	12	24
Somali	A	—	—	—	3	1	4	—	2	2	3	3	6
	B	—	—	—	—	—	—	—	1	1	—	1	1
	C	4	4	8	1	3	4	4	1	5	9	8	17
	Total	4	4	8	4	4	8	4	4	8	12	12	24
Total	A	7	5	12	6	7	13	4	10	14	17	22	39
	B	2	2	4	3	5	6	3	6	9	8	11	19
	C	15	17	32	15	14	29	17	8	25	47	39	86
	Total	24	24	48	24	24	48	24	24	48	72	72	144

Discussion

The results of the Staircase Tests are interesting from so many points of view that it is only possible to draw attention to a few of them. The most obvious feature is the disparity between the results on the Stick and Card Tests. Why were these two tests, closely following Piaget's procedure and both used by him to demonstrate the peculiar relationships between ordination and cardination, so unequal in difficulty? Why did the European community, who showed superiority on most of the tests, get inferior grades on this one when compared with the Aden children? Answers to these questions underlie the importance of ensuring that tests selected to demonstrate a sequence of stages in intellectual growth are subgraded for shades of difference in procedure or material. Ideally a series would be built up in which similar material and procedure would be used. Each test demonstrating some small growth in the concept would add one additional feature or complication to the previous test, but no other variation.

Piaget is not interested in the order of difficulty of his tests, his purpose being to illustrate, with different types of material, used in problems essentially the same, but differently expressed, a principle basic to his theory. There is therefore no evidence to show how his little subjects who did the Stick Test fared in the Card Test, or even whether the same children were used. In this investigation it was originally intended to give the Stick and Card Tests to alternate subjects, but this was found to be impracticable, with results that the groups are uneven both with respect to age and community. In spite of this disadvantage, some comparison between results is possible.

There were 24 European children in each group, half male and half female, including three at six years, nine at seven years and twelve at eight years. None of the 24 in the 'Card Test' group failed to seriate correctly, although a third of their community failed to seriate the sticks. Similarly, the Aden groups found this operation easier with cards than with sticks. In this case the reason is not far to seek since the first seriation of the sticks is followed by the more difficult process of breaking up the series in order to insert a second series. Many children failed at this point. Once their original staircase pattern at the top of the sticks had been interrupted by the addition of one of the new series, the necessity to get it right again very often made them ignore the bottom edges which up till then had been kept straight, in order to concentrate on the intervals at the top edges. Alternatively, they refused to spoil their first series, preferring to append the new series.

A further analysis of the results of the second part of these two Staircase Tests was made to find what particular difficulty in the former test was lacking in the latter. Again an additional complication was found in the problem. In the Card Test, the answer to 'How many of the little cards would we need to make that one?' could be answered by a straightforward counting of the series. In the Stick Test, however, the investigator wanted to know not only how many steps were behind the baby, but also the number climbed and how many steps it was necessary to climb in order to reach the top. Out of 37 Subjects who did this test twenty gave a wrong answer because of failing to include or exclude the step on which the baby was standing. This failure is significant as Piaget designed the test to see at what stage the child could deal with problems of cardination and ordination simultaneously, operations which he considers to be interdependent.

As a greater proportion of European children than Aden children took the harder test it seemed possible that this might account for their inferior results in the combined total [(ii) Relative position]. This, however, would be difficult to prove without retesting, as the Arabs were superior in this part of both tests. The twenty children who were confused by the 'sample' step included four out of nine Arabs and fifteen out of 24 Europeans. In any further investigation it is obvious that either one of these tests must be selected, or both used for all subjects if the results are to be used for comparative purposes. Students may note that an unsatisfactory design for an experiment leaves questions unanswered when the results are studied!

In the Genevan tests, the strategies used by the children were very similar to those used by the Aden children. Most convincing for Piaget's theories are the similarities of their mistakes and the steps taken to rectify them. Whether one thinks in terms of Piaget's stages of mental structures or Bruner's strategies there must be *some* developmental pattern to account for the fact that, for example, Lil in Geneva and Mohamed in Aden both make a staircase by ignoring the bottoms of the sticks and making the tops project in a series. It must be emphasized that the Aden child lacked experience with building blocks and other toys available to most children in Europe and America. All the stages were demonstrated as in Geneva: the failure to seriate, trial and error seriation and seriation without hesitation; the arbitrary estimate for the position of the inserted stair, the reconstruction of the whole staircase to solve the problem relating to one small part of it and the immediate knowledge that the number of steps climbed or still to be climbed is determined by the position of the stick on which the doll is placed, implying, according to Piaget, a true understanding of the relationship between cardination and ordination. As in the conservation tests, the child at first attends to one perceptual element, in this case, the tops of the sticks, which he arranges in the form of a staircase, in the second stage he 'intuitively' grasps what is required but makes many mistakes when a new element is introduced and, in the final stage, he is capable of 'operational' thought, demonstrated by maintaining a stable grouping after the material has been disarranged and appreciating the interaction of cardinal and ordinal values.

The Staircase Tests have been repeated by Beard (1963), Dodwell (1962) and others, including Elkind (1964), who used standardized procedures and a satisfactory statistical design. One of Elkind's aims was to see whether the perceptibility of size differences in one-dimensional, two-dimensional and three-dimensional materials affects the ages at which the stages appear. Using size-graded blocks, slats and sticks, he tested the child for discrimination (smallest, largest), seriation (staircase), and number (doll climbing). His results support Piaget's findings in every particular, beginning with the order of difficulty of the three operations. In the seriation tests, however, he did construct a staircase first, making sure that the child was watching, and then, after it had been disarranged, asked the child to repeat the performance. This, in the author's opinion, introduced a factor which would make it difficult to know with certainty (based on this test alone) whether the child had really reached the third stage. However, carefully graded scoring was used on all the tests. Elkind also found that there was a significant difference in favour of increase in size differences of the material, which also agrees with Piaget's comments on perception.

As Elkind indicates, infinite variations are possible with these tests, to demonstrate the significance of different variables. Most interesting, perhaps at this stage, would be standardized tests using Piaget's three varieties of materials and procedures, randomized with the same group of subjects. It is very much regretted that this was not done in the Aden investigation.

References

Beard, R. (1963). The order of concept studies in two fields (i) Number concept in the infant school (ii) Conception of conservation of quantity among primary school children. *Educ. Rev.*, **XV**, Nos. 2, 3.

Dodwell, P. C. (1962). Relations between the understanding of the logic of classes and of cardinal number in children. *Can. J. Psychol.*, **16**, 152–160.

Elkind, D. (1964). Discrimination, seriation and numeration of size and dimensional differences in young children: Piaget replication study VI. *J. genet. Psychol.*, **104**, 275–296. (Reprinted in I. E. Sigel and F. H. Hooper (Eds.), *Logical Thinking in Children*. New York: Holt, Rinehart and Winston, 1968.)

Piaget, J. (1952). *The Child's Conception of Number*. London: Routledge and Kegan Paul.

Piaget, J. (1953). *Logic and Psychology*. Manchester: Manchester University Press.

CHAPTER THIRTEEN

Bead Test: relationship between class and number

Bead Test

Introduction

This test is concerned with the problem of the relationship of part to whole, of a partial class which is included in a total class. The adult takes for granted the distinction between 'some' and 'all', but for the child it can present difficulties if the part attracts his attention sufficiently to block out, as it were, his concept of 'whole', encouraging him to think in terms of the two parts.

In Piaget's tests wooden beads of different colours and shapes were used. Because of the time factor, only coloured beads were used in this investigation, but the procedure and questions followed those of Piaget. For the sake of the local children, who were being tested by a foreigner, some slight changes in the instructions were made. The details are noted below.

Description of the test

MATERIALS

16 wooden beads, the size of small marbles, the round type used for bead threading in nursery schools, 14 of them painted a pillar-box red, and 2 painted a bright blue
1 small tray (the lid of a tin box was used)
1 container

PROCEDURE

The tray containing the sixteen beads was placed in front of the child who was asked if they were made of wood and if there were more wooden ones or red ones and why he thought so (Question 1). Then, instead of, as in

Piaget's test, being asked to imagine how many beads would be left if the red and the blue were put into two empty boxes by the side of the box of beads, one box only was used, and the child was asked to put in it first the red beads, noting how many were left on the tray (Question 3), and then the wooden beads (Question 3), after the red had again been restored to the tray. This variation produced some interesting results. It was possible to note the order used for the beads in the second instruction and to ensure that a child who had been inattentive to the first question had a chance to make a correction. If a child put only the blue beads into the box, the investigator said: 'What about the rest? Aren't they made of wood too?' and repeated that all the beads were made of wood. After this reassurance, any mistakes in the following questions could reasonably be attributed to faulty thinking and not to the influence of set.

The child was then asked, as in Piaget's test, which of two necklaces would be longer, one made with the wooden beads or one made with the red beads (Question 4). It was decided that, as only one box had been used, the question in the original form might be misleading. The child might think of the making of the two necklaces as one process, so that if he made the red necklace first only two would be left for the second necklace, making it shorter. To make quite sure that the child mentally took the first necklace to pieces before constructing the second, each step was described in the form of a story. This change was made after the pilot study had been completed.

Finally the child was asked the original question to see whether his experiences with the beads had modified his judgment (Question 5).

QUESTIONS

1. Are all these beads made of wood, or not? Are there more wooden ones or red ones? Why?
2. Put the red beads in that empty box. Are there any left?
3. Put them back on the tray. Now put all the wooden beads in that empty box. Are there any left?
4. Now we are gonig to make some necklaces. Let's make one of the wooden beads first (mimed). Now let's take that to pieces and make another one, this time of the red beads (mimed). Which was the longer necklace, the wooden one or the red one?
5. Are all the beads made of wood? Are there more wooden ones or more red ones?

Comments on performance

The question of whether the beads were all made of wood was taken very seriously by almost all the children, and usually entailed a detailed examination of the interior of each as well as tapping. Some children appeared to think that there might be a catch in the question, so if they concentrated on a certain bead and seemed rather doubtful, the investigator remarked that they *should* all be made of wood, or that she thought they were, which reassured the child and made it possible for the test to be continued. No. 11 insisted on giving details of the process of making them.

Typical correct answers to the second half of the question were:

No. 22   'Wooden, there are two blue and they are all wood.'
No. 2   'Wooden, because the red and the blue are made of wood.'
No. 28   'Wooden, because they are all wood, and they aren't all red.'

The children who failed in this question were substituting for it: 'Are there more red than blue beads?' In some cases it was a question of anticipation rather than a genuine confusion of part with whole. No. 64 for instance, said: 'More *blue* ones?' No. 50 asked: 'Did you say blue?' while No. 88, expressing the matter very clearly said: 'I thought for the moment that you said "wood"'. He was most astounded when he received the reply: 'I did'.

Typical answers were:

No. 20   'Red, because there are a lot of them.'
No. 21   'Red, there are 14 and I can only see two blue.'
No. 35   'Red, because there are two blue ones and a lot more red.'
No. 19   struck a note of originality: 'Red, because I suppose that if you had a necklace you would have two blue ones at the front.'

When the children put the beads into the box, a note was made of the ones who, for the wooden beads, put the two blue ones only, as this confirmed that they had not understood the original question. Either it was a genuine confusion of classes or just a matter of careless listening. If the latter, one would expect a correction made in Question 4. This appeared to be the case with No. 35, who having originally stated that the red were more because there were two blue ones and a lot of red, chose the wooden necklace, 'Because it had the blue ones in as well.' Similarly No. 21, who had stated that the red were more 'Because there are 14 and I can only see 2 blues,' thought the wooden necklace was longer 'Because there are 14 wood and 12 red.' Many children, however, clung to their original impression regardless of the correction mid-way.

A surprising result was that children who had answered the necklace question very satisfactorily still asserted that the red were more in Question 5. These included the following:

No. 75   'The wooden necklace is longer because you'll use them all.'
No. 30   'The wooden is longer because there are red and blue.'
No.   'The wooden is longer because there aren't so many of the others.'

The conflict between wood and blue was neatly solved by No. 120, who in the final question answered: 'The red wooden ones are more.'

Grading system

'A' Wooden beads more throughout the test
'B' Inconsistent answers
'C' Red beads more throughout

N.B. If in Question 3 the wooden beads were identified with blue it was noted thus: (b).

Results (Table 22)

The trend for age was normal in this test, but although the Arab community was actually a little better at the six-year level than at the eight-year level, there was very little difference in the scores. The sexes also had almost equal results with the males enjoying a slight advantage in the total.

The difference in the scores of the European and Arab communities was not as marked as in most of the other tests. More than a third of the Europeans were successful as compared with a quarter of the Arabs, while nearly half the Europeans and rather more than half the Arabs failed. The Indians and Somalis had less good results, with 19 out of 24 failing in each group.

Discussion

It was felt at the time of testing that although, undoubtedly this *is* a test on the relationship of part to whole, and although, as such, it fits into Piaget's general scheme of the development of the child's conception of number, there remains doubt as to whether the child views it this way. The impression left, after giving this test to many children outside this particular investigation, is that in spite of the precautions described above, the problem is essentially one of set or expectation. The moment the child sees the beads he appears to make a mental note that there are two blue ones among many red. To the less wary child this must be the heart of the problem: what has the talk about their being made of wood got to do with it? In order to test this theory it would be necessary to devise other part–whole problems in which the expectation factor could be minimized.

This has, in fact, been done by other investigators during the last ten years. The most important confirmation of the author's theory was made by Wohlwill (1968) who reports a series of studies comparing children's responses to class-inclusion questions when the items are presented in a pictorial, as opposed to a purely verbal, form. There was a consistent, highly significant superiority under the verbal conditions, which Wohlwill attributes to 'the weakening of sub-class comparison set engendered by perception of majority and minority sub-classes in the standard pictorial condition'. His results convinced him that, when class-conclusion items are presented in a pictorial form, perceptual sets are elicited by the stimuli. He concludes that 'factors other than reasoning capacity must be taken into account in studying the question of class inclusion'. However, he also

Table 22

Bead Test

Frequency distribution of results obtained with test no. 10

Group	Rating	Age 6+ M	F	Total	Age 7+ M	F	Total	Age 8+ M	F	Total	Total M	F	Total
European	A	—	—	—	3	4	7	4	3	7	7	7	14
	B	2	3	5	2	1	3	4	2	6	8	6	14
	C	6	5	11	3	3	6	—	3	3	9	11	20
	Total	8	8	16	8	8	16	8	8	16	24	24	48
Arab	A	2	2	4	3	—	3	1	3	4	6	5	11
	B	2	2	4	1	2	3	1	1	2	4	5	9
	C	4	4	8	4	6	10	6	4	10	14	14	28
	Total	8	8	16	8	8	16	8	8	16	24	24	48
Indian	A	—	—	—	—	—	—	—	1	1	—	1	1
	B	1	1	2	2	—	2	—	—	—	3	1	4
	C	3	3	6	2	4	6	4	3	7	9	10	19
	Total	4	4	8	4	4	8	4	4	8	12	12	24
Somali	A	—	—	—	—	1	1	1	—	1	1	1	2
	B	1	—	1	1	—	1	—	1	1	2	1	3
	C	3	4	7	3	3	6	3	3	6	9	10	19
	Total	4	4	8	4	4	8	4	4	8	12	12	24
Total	A	2	2	4	6	5	11	6	7	13	14	14	28
	B	6	6	12	6	3	9	5	4	9	17	13	30
	C	16	16	32	12	16	28	13	13	26	41	45	86
	Total	24	24	48	24	24	48	24	24	48	72	72	144

found indications that 'the effects of a perceptual set are superimposed on factors of a more intrinsic nature, relating to the child's level of cognitive development'.

Inhelder and Piaget (1964) themselves report further experiments in which the materials include pictures of flowers, with blue primulas as the sub-class, and pictures of animals. The children found the bead and the flower problems less difficult than the animal problems, although the same procedure was used. Inhelder explains this as an example of *décalage verticale*, one of the most difficult concepts in Piagetian theory. A full explanation is given by Flavell, the gist of which is that the child, in this instance, is only *apparently* at two different stages of cognitive development for the two tests: 'vertical décalages express a hidden uniformity within the apparent differences between one stage and another' (Flavell, 1963). This problem, referred to in chapter 3 and discussed more fully in chapter 6 which illustrates décalage horizontale, presents the greatest difficulty in validating the sequence of Piaget's stages.

Other investigators interested in the inclusion problem include Morf (1959), Dodwell (1968), Kohnstamm (1967) and Lasry and Laurendean (1969). Among these, Dodwell, exploring the influence of 'set', not from the point of view of colour, but from the type of instruction, confirms Piaget's original results. Feeling that the form of the question 'Are there more wooden beads or more red beads' suggests that they are mutually exclusive categories, he attempts to minimize this drawback. He uses toy garden tools (rakes and shovels), toy cars (yellow and red), and dolls (boys and girls), and each child is given all the tests, the crucial question always being asked about the larger sub-group. The numbers in the sub-groups are varied to test for this effect. The results give no evidence of décalage: they show the typical stages of global comparison, intuitive judgment and operational judgment, with no significant differences arising from the kind of test material used.

Morf (a colleague of Piaget) had already tried, unsuccessfully, to get children to understand the correct answer by rearranging the materials and giving some specific training in skills related to the problem. His aim was to test how far success could be attributed to environmental as distinct from maturational factors. To summarize very briefly indeed Piaget and Morf's conclusions from these experiments, learning plays a very minor role in the development of logical structures.

Kohnstamm (1967), repeating Morf's experiments with modifications in materials and learning methods, has challenged the whole basis of the inclusion problem in a comprehensive series of studies. His book covers an analysis of the problem, correspondence with Piaget's colleagues and learning studies used with French-Canadian and Dutch children. He accused Morf of equating 'learning' with 'bringing the child into contact with 'various kinds of material which he could manipulate freely', whereas 'only experience whereby the child takes an active part can lead to partially new structure within a short space of time'. His main aim was to show that learning possibilities had not been exhausted by Morf and that 'the quantification of inclusion relations (as shown by correct answers to questions like: Are there more A or more B? and the reverse) is of doubtful value if a criterion is sought for a certain stage in general thought development supposed to be independent of chance environmental variables.' Choosing twenty-five versions of the question, 'in the whole world are there more . . . or more . . .?' he not only told his Group 1 the answers but drilled them rote-fashion. Group 2 were trained with picture problems and Group 3 with Lego blocks of various colours and sizes. In half an hour of individual teaching, eighteen of the twenty children of five years were able to learn to solve the problems designed by Piaget and Morf. Kohnstamm interpreted his results thus: 'Presumably we taught the child an active restructuring of the phenomenal field; a restructuring which rapidly became a principle and then a routine for solving certain sorts of problems.' He then challenged Piaget's complicated explanation of the process. The stimulating dialogue between Kohnstamm and Piaget's colleagues which followed is worth reading for its reformulation of basic Piagetian theory. The main conclusion in Geneva was that what the children in Kohnstamm's experiment acquired 'forms an isolated schema and thus cannot be termed operational'. The explanation of problem solving as the result of the composition of the perceptual field is rejected on the grounds that figural cues can be very misleading: in fact, release from 'the bonds of perception' is a basic part of Piaget's theory of development. The accusation that Kohnstamm established a 'learning set' leading to the right answers is interesting in view of the difficulty found by both Dodwell and the present author in dissociating the factor of 'set' with the original experiment using beads.

An account of Lasry's experiments with French-Canadian children received in a personal communication, can also be found in Kohnstamm's book (1967). He criticizes Kohnstamm for failing in his scoring to take into account the justifications given by the children for their answers and for the lack of a control group, which would enable 'operational' answers to be distinguished from those arising from the use of a simple strategem. Lasry suggests, for example, that a pre-operational child might answer contrary to what he perceives because of the training he has received. Lasry's control groups, consisting of sixteen operational children aged seven to nine years and sixteen pre-operational children of five to six years, were selected, as well as the experimental group, by means of a pre-test standardized on French-Canadian children. The control tests included pre-tests and post-tests of transfer, classical inclusion items, tests on 'all' and 'some', transitivity and conservation. Children of the experimental group went through two learning sessions and three control sessions: the first right after learning, the second a month after and the last six months after. Both control groups went through the second and the third control session. Lasry sums up his results thus: 'The children of the learning group are significantly better than control pre-operational children of the same age, and quite similar, in their handling of concrete as well as verbal inclusion problems, to children two years older, who have spontaneously reached the operational notion of inclusion. An empirical teaching seems to have accelerated the spontaneous development of a logical notion.' So, scoring only right answers and operational justification, his results were identical with those of Kohnstamm who scored only answers.

Kohnstamm's most interesting comment on Lasry's study is the fact of spontaneous improvement between two sessions a month apart, when no training was given, interpreted by Lasry as an argument in favour of a gradual process of assimilation and integration. Kohnstamm made the same observation with reference to his own studies but has no evidence at present to support the interpretation. The question arises whether an improvement which is achieved after only one month can be regarded as the result of a 'gradual process', unless this means that, coincidentally, the children concerned had, by the time of the first session, almost reached the stage when improvement would be measurable.

Kohnstamm's second attempt to teach Dutch children the inclusion problem was designed to deal with the various problems unresolved by previous investigations, such as the relative effects of using 'discovery' and teaching programmes and the part played by language and language environment in cognitive growth. He observed the differences between four groups: immediate discovery, discovery after a series of related problems, success after some teaching, success only after intensive training. He then compared his own sets of conclusions with those in line with Piaget's theories. Kohnstamm is here raising very important learning issues which have far-reaching implications for education. The subject is more appropriately discussed under concept training in the final chapter. From his experiments Kohnstamm concludes that there is no apparent difference in the final level of understanding between those who 'discover' a solution after a series of related problems and those who were not taught; between those who need some help and those who need more; and that it is improbable that the processes by which they reached their conclusions are different.

Piaget stresses the importance of the whole–part relation as an important element in the whole process of classification. The child, according to his theory, does not reach cognitive maturity until he is able to form a hierarchical system of classes based on the notions of 'some' and 'all', so that for example all the beads form a larger class than some of the beads. Any challenge resulting from investigations of the 'inclusion' problem must therefore be treated very seriously. To the Genevan school success in this operation is the best criterion for diagnosing the presence or absence of the stage of concrete logical operations in development.

References

Dodwell, P. C. (1968). Relations between the understanding of the logic of classes and cardinal number in children. (In I. E. Sigel and F. H. Hooper. (Eds.), *Logical Thinking in Children.* New York: Holt, Rinehart and Winston.

Flavell, J. H. (1963). *The Developmental Psychology of Jean Piaget.* New York: Van Nostrand.

Inhelder, B., and J. Piaget. (1964). *The Early Growth of Logic in the Child: Classification and Seriation.* London: Routledge and Kegan Paul.

Kohnstamm, G. A. (1967). *Piaget's Analysis of Class Inclusion: Right or Wrong?* The Hague: Monton. (See also Sigel and Hooper, 1968.)

Lasry, Jean-Claude, and Monique Laurendean. (1969). To be published in *Hum. Dev.*, 1969).

Morf, A. (1959). Apprentissage d'une structure logique concrète (inclusion): effets et limites. In J. Piaget (Ed.), *Etudes d'Epistémologie génétique,* vol. 9. Paris: Presses Universitaires.

Piaget, J. (1952). *The Child's Conception of Number.* London: Routledge and Kegan Paul.

Wohlwill, J. F. (1968). *Child Dev.*

CHAPTER FOURTEEN

Shell Tests: additive composition of number

Shell Tests

Introduction

These tests are concerned with the manipulation of the members of a set. In the first problem the set is split so that the number of members in the two sub-sets is unequal, and the task is to rearrange these sections to equalize them. In the second problem the set must be divided into two sub-sets with the same number of members in each. Piaget used these two tests among others to trace the stages by which children grasp the additive composition of number and the arithmetical relation of part to whole. An important factor is the dependence or otherwise on ability to count. In the original tests counters were used. The local Aden children are not as familiar with these as European children, so local shells of the same shape and approximately the same size were used.

Description of the tests

MATERIALS

A tin of local shells of the same shape and approximately the same size

PROCEDURE

Test 1

Two piles of shells, one containing eight and the other fourteen were placed in front of the child, who was then instructed: 'Make this pile of shells and that pile of shells the same number.' The child was allowed to continue the adjustment until he was satisfied with the result.

Test 2

The tin of shells was emptied on the table in front of the child who was then instructed: 'Divide these shells into two parts, one for you and one for me, so that we both have the same amount.'

Comments on Performance

In this investigation the children found test 2 very much easier than test 1 although a much larger group of shells was used. This may have been because straightforward sharing problems form part of the normal existence of most children. Sweets must be shared among members of the family and eager eyes detect the slightest inaccuracy. In the first test the sweets have, so to speak, been distributed unfairly, and much trial and error and re-counting may take place before the child is convinced that the error has been rectified.

TEST 1

Successful children either adjusted the piles or put them together, counted the whole number and then divided by two. The usual method of adjustment was to make the larger pile the size of the smaller, and then share the remainder one at a time. There were some interesting deviations:

Nos. 131 and 143 made the larger pile the size of the smaller, pushed the remainder to one side and announced that they had made the two piles the same.

No. 83 after a period of puzzled staring made the small pile large and the large small.

No. 43 took a handful from the larger pile, put it on the smaller and said that they were now the same.

No. 120 made both piles into pairs and then separated the pairs to make two groups.

The children who could not manage this test either spread the shells out aimlessly, completely bewildered, or made one pile of them and left them.

TEST 2

Again two main methods were used: sharing out in ones or small groups, or adding up the number of shells and dividing by two. No. 23, who used the first method, kept stopping the process to make sure that he had not made a mistake, but most children who could count did so at the end to check their results. Other variations included:

No. 135 put 7 in each pile and then discarded the Test.

No. 118 shared out in fives (which he tried to check by weighing), but did not know what to do with the two remaining, so put them back into the tin.
No. 120 used the same method as in the first test.
No. 5 tried counting first, found that the division sum was too hard for him, so shared them out 1–1.
No. 3 gave 1–1, 2–2, 3–3, 4–4 until he was left with 2.
So many children divided the pile by pushing the shells with both hands, that a note was made to see whether this was a characteristic of age or community.

Grading system

If a different method was used in the two tests they were marked separately.
'Aa' Correct: sharing 1–1, 2–2, etc.
'Ab' Correct: counting all the shells and dividing or adjusting the piles
'B' Rough Estimate: checked or correct
'C' Incorrect
N.B. If both hands were used to push the shells into piles, this was indicated by 'h'.

Results (Tables 23 and 24)

READJUSTING PILES (i)

In the Aden groups the trend was normal in this test, except that among the Arabs, there were one or two more 'A' grades in the six- and seven-year groups than in the eight-year group. In the European community the only child who failed was a seven-year old. The girls were slightly better than the boys, but only by two 'A' grades. The European community obviously found this an easy task. In the Somali group less than a quarter failed, all being in the two lower age groups, while among the Arabs there were slightly more failures and less 'A' grades. The Indians were the least successful, with two-thirds of the group failing.

SHARING SHELLS (ii)

The age trend was normal in all the Aden groups, while in the European community one child failed at each age level. All three were boys, but the Arab boys were slightly better than the girls. In the overall results, the Indians and Somalis tipped the balance in favour of the girls. The European group again found this a very easy test. More than half the Arabs and Somalis were successful, but less than a third of the Indians.

Discussion

There is not much difference in the overall results of these two tests, but the investigator notes with surprise, that the second task was found to be

Table 23
Shell Tests

Frequency distribution of results obtained with test no. 11(i)

Group	Rating	Age 6+ M	F	Total	Age 7+ M	F	Total	Age 8+ M	F	Total	Total M	F	Total
European	A	8	8	16	7	8	15	8	8	16	23	24	47
	B	—	—	—	—	—	—	—	—	—	—	—	—
	C	—	—	—	1	—	1	—	—	—	1	—	1
	Total	8	8	16	8	8	16	8	8	16	24	24	48
Arab	A	5	4	9	5	5	10	4	4	8	14	13	27
	B	—	—	—	—	2	2	3	2	5	3	4	7
	C	3	4	7	3	1	4	1	2	3	7	7	14
	Total	8	8	16	8	8	16	8	8	16	24	24	48
Indian	A	—	—	—	1	1	2	2	3	5	3	4	7
	B	—	—	—	—	—	—	1	—	1	1	—	1
	C	4	4	8	3	3	6	1	1	2	8	8	16
	Total	4	4	8	4	4	8	4	4	8	12	12	24
Somali	A	1	1	2	2	3	5	4	4	8	7	8	15
	B	—	—	—	2	1	3	—	—	—	2	1	3
	C	3	3	6	—	—	—	—	—	—	3	3	6
	Total	4	4	8	4	4	8	4	4	8	12	12	24
Total	A	14	13	27	15	17	32	18	19	37	47	49	96
	B	—	—	—	2	3	5	4	2	6	6	5	11
	C	10	11	21	7	4	11	2	3	5	19	18	37
	Total	24	24	48	24	24	48	24	24	48	72	72	144

slightly more difficult than the first. The numbers involved, however, are small, since the two extra European failures in the second test account for the difference in the 'A' grade finals totals. It is not surprising that the European children found the sharing easy, as it is a practical experience

Table 24

Shell Tests

Frequency distribution of results obtained from test no. 11(ii)

Group	Rating	Age 6+			Age 7+			Age 8+			Total		
		M	F	Total	M	F	Total	M	F	Total	M	F	Total
European	A	7	8	15	7	8	15	7	8	15	21	24	45
	B	—	—	—	—	—	—	—	—	—	—	—	—
	C	1	—	1	1	—	1	1	—	1	3	—	3
	Total	8	8	16	8	8	16	8	8	16	24	24	48
Arab	A	3	3	6	6	4	10	7	6	13	16	13	29
	B	3	1	4	—	2	2	1	1	2	4	4	8
	C	2	4	6	2	2	4	—	1	1	4	7	11
	Total	8	8	16	8	8	16	8	8	16	24	24	48
Somali	A	—	1	1	3	2	5	3	4	7	6	7	13
	B	1	1	2	—	2	2	1	—	1	2	3	5
	C	3	2	5	1	—	1	—	—	—	4	2	6
	Total	4	4	8	4	4	8	4	4	8	12	12	24
Indian	A	—	—	—	—	3	3	2	2	4	2	5	7
	B	2	—	2	1	—	1	—	1	1	3	1	4
	C	2	4	6	3	1	4	2	1	3	7	6	13
	Total	4	4	8	4	4	8	4	4	8	12	12	24
Total	A	10	12	22	16	17	33	19	20	39	45	49	94
	B	6	2	8	1	4	5	2	2	4	9	8	17
	C	8	10	18	7	3	10	3	2	5	18	15	33
	Total	24	24	48	24	24	48	24	24	48	72	72	144

with which they are familiar in home and school. One wonders whether social factors are partly responsible for less accuracy among the Aden children. They have even more experience of sharing than many of the European children, since families are larger and incomes lower. Their methods, however, appear to be different, as, for example, in the sharing of food. When the European mother of a large family confronts her hungry children round the dinner table, she usually dishes out the available food, portion by portion on the plates, so that each member gets his share. The Arab child, however, takes his share from a common dish, and, no doubt, has to learn to curb his appetite and estimate his fair portion, in order to leave enough for the other members of the family. This custom too, may account for the method used by a large number of the Aden children in sharing the shells. They just separated the pile into two portions with their hands, sometimes with surprising accuracy. This method was used by fifteen out of 48 Arabs, sixteen out of 24 Indians and thirteen out of 24 Somalis, but only one out of 48 Europeans.

Among Piaget's tests this one appears to have been omitted in replication studies. Another test on the additive composition of number in which children are asked to compare 'sweets' grouped as $4 + 4$ and $7 + 1$ was repeated by Beard (1957). Her finding that children used many methods of comparing the groups may be due to the use of number apparatus and number games which have been available to infant classes for many years.

References

Beard, R. (1957). An investigation of concept formation among infant school children. Unpublished Ph.D. Thesis: University of London.

Piaget, J. (1952). *The Child's Conception of Number*. London: Routledge and Kegan Paul.

CHAPTER FIFTEEN

Non-verbal intelligence tests

Introduction

Various reasons prompted the inclusion in this investigation of four non-verbal tests of intelligence. Ideally the Subjects from different communities should have been matched for intelligence but this was impossible, as, apart from the fact that they were self-selected volunteers, there are no intelligence tests standardized on an Aden population. It was felt desirable that, in addition to the Piaget tests, some other type of test should be given to the children for a basis of comparison between the groups, tests not depending on language or verbal ability, so that, at least from one point of view, each child would have an equal chance of success. Even though no absolute comparison could be made between the groups on the basis of the results, the distribution might provide a rough guide.

'Might' is the operative word, for this was essentially an 'I wonder what will happen' situation. These tests, were, in fact, being tried out on the Aden children and some or all of them might prove unsuitable for detecting ability. As a further check teachers were asked to rate the Subjects on a five-point scale. It is realized that such ratings are not reliable but, at this stage of research in Aden, something might be learned from them. For example, if all the bright Arab boys, the potential Aden College scholars, failed the non-verbal intelligence tests completely, their usefulness even as a ranking device within the group would be questionable. Alternatively, the distribution might indicate that this particular type of test would be suitable for inclusion in a standardized batch at some future date.

From the same point of view, it would be interesting to compare the range of results in these tests and in the Piaget tests. Would the latter provide a more sensitive guide to potentiality in the local population than other types of intelligence test? Of course this investigation does not answer such questions, but it might give a pointer to further research.

In the giving of these tests the investigator was assisted by the Arab Education Officer who had so kindly checked her Arabic. After being present at many demonstrations and becoming thoroughly acquainted with the procedure he took over the testing of the Arab-speaking children. This was a very happy arrangement, since the Subjects could be tested while waiting their turn for the Piaget tests, thus saving valuable time, the investigator could refer to him if the odd rare word was produced in a child's response, and he could refer to her in any doubtful case. In view of the fact that the Subjects were not only Arabs using their own language but Indians and Somalis using a second language, no word for word translation was made of the instructions given to the child in the four tests. They were used as a guide, the main consideration being that the Subject should understand exactly what he had to do. The instructions with regard to procedure were however carried out. Because of the circumstances of the testing, only raw scores could be used in the results.

Progressive Matrices

Introduction

In this investigation the coloured Progressive Matrices (Raven, 1947) sets A, Ab, B were used. To the European children, educated in Infant, Nursery and Kindergarten schools the task was novel but, in the solving of it, they could bring a valuable background of experience in the form of colour and form matching, pattern making, etc. For the Aden child it was just one of the new and strange experiences with which he was coping in rather quick succession.

Comments on performance

Sometimes it was possible to follow the child's methods and anticipate his choice, but at other times it appeared to be a random selection. In the group as a whole wrong answers mainly showed the following tendencies:

1. *Fixations*
Having chosen No. 2, for example, about five times successively, the child seemed to have a great difficulty in changing his choice. It may have been that finding the task too difficult, keeping to one number saved effort.

2. *'Gestalt' responses*
Where the choice of patterns included a complete figure some Subjects systematically chose it in preference to one of its sections enlarged.

3. *Complicated patterns*
In the harder tests children who failed chose either the pattern left of the blank or the one above it for a straight matching.

The colours appeared to give pleasure to most of the Subjects, some children taking a great interest in the designs. The outstanding example was an Irish six-year-old girl who greeted each turn of the page with an ecstatic, 'Isn't that a pretty pattern! Isn't that *lovely.*' Every time she met the investigator she spoke about her favourite puzzle and begged for another session.

Results and discussion (Tables 25, 26, 27 and 28)

There is very little difference between the means for each age group in this test, although in the overall result a progression can be seen. The Arab boys, for example, at the six-, seven- and eight-year levels have means of 14, 13½, 13½ while the Somali means for boys are 13½, 12½, 14½ and for girls, 13½, 13½, 13½. It appears that age of Subject had very little to do with success on this test. There was, however, a great deal of difference between the individual scores as seen by the range of scores, though not as much as in some of the other tests. The range was greatest among the Europeans who, although they had superior scores on the whole, were not consistently better than the other communities.

In the Indian community the girls were consistently better than the boys, although the difference was not great. It hardly existed in the other groups. It is interesting to note that the difference between the results of the European communities and the Aden communities becomes more marked as age increases. At the six-year level, for instance, the mean for the European community is eighteen, while for all groups it is fourteen, whereas at eight years the figures are 23½ and 16½. This suggests that school experience may be an important factor in this test. The gap between educational experience widens at the eight-year level, as most of the Europeans have had three years at school compared to the Aden child's year.

On the basis of his wide experience of testing, Vernon (1969) considers Matrices as a fairly pure test of general ability (Spearman's 'g' factor). In his own investigations he usually used his own version, which is 'similar to Raven's though designed to get across rather more readily to unsophisticated and duller boys' (Vernon, 1969). Vernon has noted from other investigations the doubtful value of Raven's Progressive Matrices in non-Western cultures. Even in our own country young immigrant children, according to Vernon 'just don't get the hang of what they are supposed to do.'

Porteus Maze Test

Introduction

Not one of the Aden Subjects had had experiences of mazes so this test (see Porteus, 1947) was particularly interesting. For the British children it was such a familiar experience that it could hardly be termed a test at all. All Subjects started the series at the five-year level and were credited with four years.

Comments on performance

The British children enjoyed the mazes, but not as a novelty. They made such comments as: 'Oh, mazes. I do one every week in my comic' or 'I did one just like this last week'. The investigator felt very strongly that the time is past when norms for this test can be taken seriously at least for British Subjects. Familiarity made some of these children careless, but even so, only three were below average and most had 'test ages' well above their chronological age. The most interesting feature of the Aden children's performance was the quickness with which they 'caught on' to the test, compared with, for example, the Koh's Blocks Test. Two or three children who needed two trials for 'Year 5' tests or other earlier ones needed only one trial for later tests and reached 'Year 14'. A few younger children made no progress at all but the general impression was that this type of test was suitable for Aden children.

Results and discussion (Tables 25, 26, 27 and 28)

Only quantitative results were noted in this test. It can be seen from the means that the trend for age is normal in all communities, but there is more difference between the seven- and eight-year groups than between the six and seven. On the whole, the boys' results are slightly better than the girls', but it is not invariably so. The difference between the results of the Arab, Indian and Somali communities is very slight, their means at six, seven and eight years being respectively $5\frac{3}{4}$, $5\frac{3}{4}$, $4\frac{3}{4}$; 6, $6\frac{1}{4}$, 6; 7, 8, $7\frac{3}{4}$. None of these children had seen a maze problem before, so far as the investigator could ascertain. The European group, however, were very experienced in this type of problem, and this is reflected in the mean scores which are about three years above the scores of the other communities at all age levels. The impression, as will be seen in the comments made on the performance, is that the mental ages for the European group were artificially high in this test, and that, with a little practice in this type of exercise, the Aden children might achieve comparable success.

Vernon (1969) relates success on this test to a prominent spatial factor and a broad perceptual-practical factor. Ugandan boys did very well on it, by working slowly and carefully and lifting their pencils which is against the instructions. His most notable results were from Eskimos and Red Indians, whose scores were only a little below the average for his white subjects. Vernon suggests that 'cultural experience in finding one's way in woods, waterways and snows may have contributed to this result.' In Aden the Porteus Maze Tests certainly differentiated between the ethnic and age groups no more precisely than Koh's Blocks, Coloured Matrices and the Piaget Conservation Tests, but the most interesting factor, not investigated, was its relationship with a spatial factor. Arab Yemini servants showed the same inability to hang pictures straight or even to put them the right way up, as reported by Biesheuval of African domestic servants. Experience in some form or other appears to be an important factor in the results of this test when used with non-European subjects, but whether it is determined by cultural experience or practice on mazes or a combination of both is still unclear. Vernon (1969), who discusses this question in detail in his chapter on 'Sensory-motor and Perceptual Factors', thinks that deficit in spatial orientation may be due to lack of experience in constructional tasks in later childhood, a deficiency which needs to be made up in the schools.

Cube Imitation Test

Introduction

In this test the investigator taps cubes of wood in prearranged series and the child is simply told to watch and then do the same. In this practical test it really seemed that the children in all communities had equal advantage. Success depended on attention and memorizing ability displayed at the time of the testing rather than on previous experience in similar situations. The type of mistake made by the European Subjects was the same as that made by the local children.

Comments on performance

This was a very simple test and the results followed a simple pattern. The children who failed outright completely ignored the changes in the investigator's performance and tapped '1, 2, 3, 4' or '4, 3, 2, 1' on every occasion. The majority of the children tapped correctly until tappings increased beyond their memory span. [It would incidentally, be interesting to compare results on this and the Digit Span Test in the Terman–Merrill (1937) batch.] One Arab girl had a very low score because she consistently made just one mistake nearly every time, failing four tap tests, but getting five taps correct on the six tap tests, but this was exceptional. The main mistake apart from the above was the reversal of the taps. A number of the children reversed the order of the first line, which was a plain sequence of four taps, but got the order right as soon as a fifth tapping drew their attention to the correct order. Several however continued reversing although it added to the difficulty of the task. An extreme example was

No. 22 who reversed (correctly) nine rows. She was one of the highest scorers in all the other tests, so this illustrated the danger of basing judgment on any one test.

Results and discussion (Tables 25, 26, 27 and 28)

In this test, the scores for the different groups and communities show least variation. If the age means are looked at first, it will be seen that the Europeans have the same means at seven and eight years and the Arabs at all age levels. The Indians show a progression with age, and a slight progression is seen in the total means, but on the whole, age was not an important factor in this test.

The results also show no clear sex difference, the girls being slightly better in the younger European groups, while the boys are better in most of the Aden groups.

On the whole, the Arabs did better than the other Aden groups. It is interesting to note, that, as in the Progressive Matrices, the gap between the European and Arab community results, which hardly exists at the six-year level, widens with age.

This visual memory test appears to be suitable for all communities. The most interesting use of it has been made by I. G. Ord (in Vernon, 1969), whom Vernon reports as having given it, as part of a battery of performance tests, to subjects in Papua and New Guinea, where hundreds of different dialects are spoken. Ord adapted these tests to be given through mime as well as using an interpreter.

Koh's Blocks Test

Some children in all communities found this test difficult, but for the Aden children it was almost impossible. One or two even failed to copy the example after it had been demonstrated and explained several times. Many more managed the first card after wrong attempts and encouragement far beyond the normal limits allowed. The investigator tried to find out what made the task so difficult and came to a tentative conclusion that, in the absence of experience in the use of such material, the child was searching, not for four blocks to make the required pattern, but for one block displaying the pattern on a single side. This conclusion was reinforced by the complaints of one or two children that they had looked at all the blocks and that there was not one like the picture.

Most of the children who got beyond the first card forgot that they had seen for themselves that each block was alike, and wasted valuable time rejecting blocks in favour of those with the right colour facing them. There were, however, one or two who, having selected four blocks, used them all the time and were very puzzled indeed when further blocks were needed. They still ignored the rest. Others failed the more difficult cards because of the time limit. The real test came when, to make the pattern, it was necessary to use half colours. Many children tried to arrange the squares instead of the triangles to form the pattern, losing the square contour of the pattern completely. Others tried the triangles but, having found them wrong in one position, failed to twist them round to try another, or twisted them so rapidly that the correct position was not noticed.

Results and discussion (Tables 25, 26, 27 and 28)

In this test, the trend for age, as shown by the mean results, is in the right direction for all groups, but the Arabs are practically the same at the six- and seven-year levels, and the Indians the same at the seven- and eight-year levels. On the whole, the boys are better than the girls in all communities.

The most striking feature of these results is the exceptional difference between the European and Aden scores, and the enormous range within the European scores themselves. The difficulty of this test for the Aden children has already been remarked in the comments on their performance. A comparison of the means of the results confirms the fact that for most of these children it was an almost impossible task. If the scores themselves are scrutinized, it will be seen that eleven Arab children, including four seven-year olds, eleven Indians, including two eight-year olds, and thirteen Somalis, including two eight-year olds failed to score at all. Some of them even failed the demonstration card. Suggestions have already been made to account for this quite startling result. It is perhaps necessary to say that every care was taken to see that the Subjects had understood what was required of them. The Arab who assisted was very pleased when the local children were successful, although he was conscientious in carrying out the instruction, which he gave in Arabic. It is inconceivable that these results represent the level of intelligence of so many of the Aden Subjects, even allowing for unsatisfactory sampling. The only conclusion appears to be that this is not a satisfactory test for children in these communities.

The very great range in the European results is also difficult to account for. At the eight-year level it was 103 in the girls' group, one child getting a score of 105 and another only 2. Two seven-year-old European children only scored one each and a six-year-old girl made no score at all. The subjects concerned did not get high scores on the other intelligence tests, but they were all about average on the Progressive Matrices. They were all rated as weak or very weak by their teachers. It seems possible that this test was the most discriminative for the European Subjects, and that their

P.C.D.—7**

range of intelligence was wider than the other tests would lead one to expect.

Koh's Blocks Test, which is regarded as a good test of general intelligence (i.e. Spearman's 'g' factor), has been widely used in cross-cultural studies and in undeveloped countries. It was the best single test in Ord's battery, (mentioned in the discussion on Cube Imitation), which was used for selection of the army and public services, as well as educational selection of children, in Papua and New Guinea. Its suitability for occupational testing was confirmed by J. L. Dawson (1963) who, using it in his battery given to groups of mine employees in Sierra Leone, found it to be one of his two best tests when compared with work assessments. McConnell (in Vernon, 1969) used it with Indians in Mexico, Dawson with Africans in Sierra Leone, Berry (1966) with Scots, Eskimos and the Temne tribe in Sierra Leone and Vernon himself with Jamaicans, Ugandans, Red Indians and Eskimos.

Results of the tests above appear to be wide ranging, with, roughly, Europeans having the greater success, peoples in close contact with Europeans, such as urbanized Eskimos and Mexican Indians, being in some cases only a little less successful, while Jamaicans in rural schools, like the local Aden children, give poor results. It seems that, as with Progressive Matrices, there is a deprivation factor partly responsible for failure with Koh's Blocks. To quote Vernon, 'Even with repeated demonstration some English boys and many more West Indians and Africans completely fail to break down the printed designs and reproduce them with the painted blocks; they can only copy the block models.' As reported above, the Aden children attended to the tops of the blocks and disregarded the sides, a difficulty removed by Ord, who substituted flat pieces used with pictures the same size as the squares. Performance greatly improved. In short, a test like Koh's Blocks needs to be standardized on a population before its usefulness as a test of intelligence can be assessed.

General discussion

Non-verbal and performance tests have long been a feature of individually administered comprehensive tests of intelligence, such as the Stanford–Binet and the Wechsler tests. In the latter they are scored separately. Usually non-verbal tests, among which the four used in Aden are only a small sample, are included as part of a battery in investigations not necessarily aimed at testing intelligence as such, but to provide a yardstick for sorting out the subjects into groups, or to assess the part played by intelligence in the main investigation. Intelligence being an important factor in all human behaviour, it must be controlled in many experimental situations. Verbal tests are often very unsatisfactory for this purpose. The importance of language in conceptual development was discussed in chapter 3, but intelligent behaviour also occurs in practical situations, without the mediation of language. In comparative studies, there is not only the problem of interpretation when verbal tests are used, but the risk of mis-

Table 25
Individual raw scores on intelligence tests: 6-year olds

		Subject No.	Terms at School	Prog. Matrices	Porteus Maze	Cube Imit.	Koh's Blocks
European							
	Boys	135	2	14	6	4	15
		57	$2\frac{1}{2}$	15	$9\frac{1}{2}$	5	2
		45	3	20	$9\frac{1}{2}$	7	54
		68	3	23	$9\frac{1}{2}$	3	8
		133	$4\frac{1}{2}$	24	13	7	46
		67	5	17	9	6	3
		132	$6\frac{1}{2}$	16	$10\frac{1}{2}$	6	5
		16	8	11	8	0	15
	Girls	69	$2\frac{1}{2}$	17	$9\frac{1}{2}$	7	3
		66	$3\frac{1}{2}$	17	11	3	25
		77	$3\frac{1}{2}$	17	7	8	3
		82	$3\frac{1}{2}$	18	7	4	11
		27	4	11	11	7	23
		93	$4\frac{1}{2}$	26	12	7	37
		75	5	16	4	7	0
		134	5	23	$6\frac{1}{2}$	6	13
Arab							
	Boys	58	0	10	6	6	8
		59	0	13	$5\frac{1}{2}$	3	0
		60	0	15	7	6	4
		117	1	14	$4\frac{1}{2}$	8	1
		118	1	9	$5\frac{1}{2}$	4	1
		126	1	16	$5\frac{1}{2}$	7	1
		129	1	17	$5\frac{1}{2}$	5	0
		47	$2\frac{1}{2}$	16	$5\frac{1}{2}$	5	1
	Girls	62	0	18	8	7	8
		86	0	8	$4\frac{1}{2}$	3	0
		136	0	14	$4\frac{1}{2}$	1	0
		10	1	15	$6\frac{1}{2}$	5	3
		46	1	16	$4\frac{1}{2}$	9	1
		81	1	9	4	4	0
		88	1	14	7	7	0
		51	$1\frac{1}{2}$	4	$7\frac{1}{2}$	4	1
Indian							
	Boys	18	0	8	$4\frac{1}{2}$	6	0
		140	0	13	6	3	0
		142	0	10	5	0	0
		78	$3\frac{1}{2}$	10	$6\frac{1}{2}$	5	4
	Girls	73	$\frac{1}{2}$	15	$4\frac{1}{2}$	3	0
		99	1	14	$7\frac{1}{2}$	5	1
		83	$2\frac{1}{2}$	12	$7\frac{1}{2}$	0	0
		79	$5\frac{1}{2}$	12	4	2	0
Somali							
	Boys	91	0	16	$4\frac{1}{2}$	8	0
		139	0	15	$4\frac{1}{2}$	3	0
		144	0	11	5	5	0
		127	1	11	5	3	0
	Girls	141	0	11	$4\frac{1}{2}$	1	0
		103	1	18	5	4	0
		143	1	12	4	5	1
		124	4	12	5	4	1

interpreting results because language is more important in one society than in another, or, as Bernstein's (1961) work shows, it may have different functions and expression within the same society. It is to meet such problems that non-verbal and performance tests have

Table 26
Individual raw scores on intelligence tests: 7-year olds

		Subject No.	Terms at School	Prog. Matrices	Porteus Maze	Cube Imit.	Koh's Blocks
European		21	4	20	9½	9	28
		131	4	13	6½	4	9
		2	5	30	10	8	72
		64	6	12	11	6	7
	Boys	50	7	23	10	5	40
		34	7½	21	9	7	1
		112	7½	31	10	7	66
		114	10	21	12	6	21
		38	5	13	9½	7	33
		94	5½	16	13½	7	3
		25	6	16	9½	6	2
	Girls	56	6	15	7½	6	5
		1	6½	17	7½	7	38
		19	7	30	9	8	24
		24	7	14	13	9	29
		130	7	12	6	6	1
Arab		61	½	13	5½	4	0
		63	½	12	7	7	1
		48	1	14	7	4	1
		53	1	14	8	6	1
	Boys	54	1	10	5	0	0
		55	1	15	6½	3	1
		39	1½	15	5½	5	1
		52	4	14	7½	9	2
		29	1	12	7	5	0
		43	1	13	6	5	1
		87	1	12	4½	4	0
		105	1	17	5½	7	0
	Girls	85	2	9	4½	5	3
		89	4	11	4½	5	1
		100	4	15	5	6	1
		14	7	14	7½	6	0
Indian		76	0	12	6½	0	0
	Boys	95	½	9	5½	4	1
		96	1½	9	8½	6	0
		30	6½	14	7	9	14
		72	3½	13	4½	6	1
	Girls	101	4	12	5½	6	5
		102	4	18	6½	6	6
		36	4½	9	5	0	0
Somali		92	½	16	4½	8	0
	Boys	115	1	11	6	3	4
		116	1	11	10½	2	0
		128	1	12	7½	3	1
		106	4	8	5	3	0
	Girls	107	4	10	5½	5	1
		125	4	20	5½	3	0
		123	7	15	4½	0	0

been devised. At first it was assumed that they would be 'culture free' because they would reveal skills unrelated to educational training. This has not proved to be the case: as demonstrated (see tables 26, 27 and 28), performance on them can differentiate ethnic groups. This does not mean

Table 27

Individual raw scores on intelligence tests: 8-year olds

		Subject No.	Terms at School	Prog. Matrices	Porteus Maze	Cube Imit.	Koh's Blocks
European		5	5	17	12	8	23
		49	7	23	10½	6	50
		28	8	35	13	9	67
		90	9½	20	14	7	17
	Boys	23	10	26	11½	8	32
		35	10	18	11	7	59
		113	11	19	8	7	48
		119	11	27	12½	7	108
		65	6	23	11½	8	47
		15	7	25	10	8	39
		22	9	31	12½	0	105
		37	9	23	11	7	41
	Girls	98	9½	14	14	7	13
		97	10½	25	16½	8	83
		3	11½	17	7½	4	2
		26	11½	30	13	9	50
Arab		11	1	10	6½	5	1
		20	1	12	4	5	1
		31	1	10	6½	7	1
		6	3½	14	9½	7	16
	Boys	12	3½	16	8½	7	5
		8	4	16	6½	7	3
		13	4	16	7	6	6
		70	4	14	10	8	11
		32	1½	15	8	6	8
		33	1½	7	6½	1	1
		4	4	10	4½	3	1
		7	4	5	6½	6	4
	Girls	42	4	13	7½	4	1
		44	4	13	6	6	13
		41	4½	10	5	4	1
		40	7½	15	7	5	1
Indian		9	4	16	11	6	0
	Boys	17	4½	17	5½	8	5
		71	5½	12	5½	2	1
		84	6	11	9½	7	11
		74	3½	19	11½	5	3
	Girls	80	5½	16	5	4	2
		122	7	13	5½	6	4
		138	7½	15	10½	7	0
Somali		108	1	13	8½	5	1
	Boys	109	4	17	10	1	11
		110	4	14	10	4	0
		111	5	13	7	6	1
		120	4	14	5½	6	1
	Girls	104	7	14	6	4	0
		121	7	13	6	6	1
		137	7	12	8	8	1

that they are useless. Vernon has correlated the results of many of these tests with tests of special factors, such as spatial ability, perceptual and practical ability. If used with discrimination, they can provide important information to corroborate what has been surmised from other sources. For example, the results of Piaget-type tests of spatial concepts can be correlated with non-verbal tests showing a high spatial factor. As intelligence

Table 28

Intelligence test scores: summary

Terms at school

	Age 6+						Age 7+						Age 8+					
Group	Boys		Girls		Total		Boys		Girls		Total		Boys		Girls		Total	
	M	R	M	R	M	R	M	R	M	R	M	R	M	R	M	R	M	R
European	4½	6	4	2½	4½	6	6½	6	5½	2	6½	7	9	6	9½	5½	9½	6
Arab	1	2½	½	1½	1	2	1½	3½	2½	5	2	5	3	3	4	6	3½	6
Indian	1	3½	3½	5	2	5	2	6½	4	1	3	6	5	2	6	4	5½	5
Somali	½	1	1½	4	1	4	1	3½	5	3	3	6	3½	4	6½	3	5	5
Mean	2½	3½	2	3½	2	4½	3	4½	4½	2½	4	6	5	4	6½	4	6	5½
Progressive Matrices																		
European	17½	13	18	15	18	15	21½	19	16½	18	19	19	23	18	23½	17	23½	21
Arab	14	7	12	14	13	14	13½	5	13	8	13½	8	13½	6	11	10	12½	11
Indian	10½	5	13½	3	12	7	12	5	13	9	12	9	14	6	16	6	15	8
Somali	13½	5	13½	7	13½	7	12½	5	13½	12	13	12	14½	4	13½	2	14	5
Mean	14	7½	14	10	14	11	14½	8½	14	12	14½	12	16½	8½	16	9	16½	11½
Porteus Maze																		
European	9½	7	8½	8	9	7½	10	5½	9½	7	9¾	6¼	11½	6	12	9	11¾	7½
Arab	5½	2½	6	4	5¾	3¼	6½	3	5½	2½	6	2¾	7½	6	6½	3½	7	4¾
Indian	5½	2	6	3½	5¾	2¾	7	3	5½	2	6¼	2½	8	5½	8	6½	8	6
Somali	5	½	4½	1	4¾	¾	7	6	5	1	6	3½	9	3	6½	2½	7¾	2¾
Mean	6¼	3	6¼	4	6¼	3½	7½	4¼	6¼	3	7	3¾	9	5	8¼	5½	8½	5
Cube Imitation																		
European	5	7	6	5	5½	6	6½	5	7	3	6¾	4	7½	3	6½	9	7	6
Arab	5½	5	5	8	5¼	6½	5	9	5½	3	5¼	6	6½	3	4½	5	5½	4
Indian	3½	6	2½	5	3	5½	5	9	4½	6	4¾	7½	6	6	5½	3	5¾	4½
Somali	5	5	3½	4	4¼	4½	4	6	3	5	3½	5½	4	5	6	4	5	4½
Mean	5	5¾	4¼	5½	4½	5½	5	7¼	5	4¼	5	5¾	6	4¼	5½	5¼	5¾	4¾
Koh's Blocks																		
European	18½	52	14½	37	16½	44½	30½	71	17	37	24	54	50½	91	47½	103	49	97
Arab	2	8	1½	8	1¾	8	1	2	2	9	1½	5½	5½	15	4	12	4¾	13½
Indian	1	4	½	1	¾	2½	4	14	3	6	3½	10	4½	11	2½	3	3½	7
Somali	0	0	½	1	¼	½	1½	4	½	1	2	2½	3½	11	1	1	2¼	6
Mean	5¼	16	4¼	11¾	4¾	13¾	9¼	22¾	5½	13¼	3	18	16	32	13¾	29¾	14¾	30¾

M = Mean; R = Range.

tests they are inadequate if administered alone, but can add to a 'profile' if administered in a battery.

Bearing in mind that education is largely concerned with verbal skills, Vernon (1969) warns that, for educational predictions, it is preferable to sample an educational skill rather than give a non-verbal test. For example, he found in Jamaica that a group of tests, including Matrices, Porteus Mazes and Koh's Blocks, yielded an average correlation of ·59 with the school achievement in English and Arithmetic of ten- to eleven-year boys, whereas the rote learning of a list of monosyllables gave a correlation of ·83. Among the Ugandans he found the non-verbal tests even less predictive.

We are also indebted to Vernon for accumulating a mass of data on the dependence of test scores on such variables as nutrition, linguistic ability, home and educational conditions. It is a warning against lightly referring to a child's IQ arrived at by a teacher's use of one of the many group 'intelligence' tests available to schools. Hebb's 'Intelligence B' expressed in American and European society has characteristics not found in all other societies. To quote Vernon once more,

> It is a kind of intelligence which is specially well adapted for scientific analysis, for control and exploitation of the physical world, for large-scale and long-term planning and carrying out of materialistic objectives. It has also led to the growth of complex social institutions such as nations, armies, industrial firms, school systems and universities. But it has been notably less successful than have the intelligences of some more primitive cultures in promoting harmonious personal adjustment or reducing group rivalries. Other groups have evolved intelligences which are better adapted than ours for coping with problems of agricultural and tribal living.

In sum, non-verbal tests have been successfully applied to non-Western groups, for example, in the selection of employees, but they must be used with caution. They are more successful in societies whose culture or educational system or employment pattern has been influenced by Western standards.

References

Bernstein, B. (1961). Social class and linguistic development: a theory of social learning. In A. H. Halsey (Ed.), *Education, Economy and Society.* Glencoe, Ill.: Free Press.

Berry, J. W. (1966). Temne and Eskimo perceptual skills. *Int. J. Psychol.,* **1**, 207–229.

Dawson, J. L. (1963). Psychological effects of social change in a West African community. Unpublished Ph.D. Thesis: University of Oxford. (Reprinted in Vernon, 1969.)

Porteus, S. D. (1947). *The Porteus Test Manual.* London: Harrap.
Raven, J. C. (1947). *Progressive Matrices.* London: Harrap.
Terman, L. M., and M. A. Merrill. (1937). *Measuring Intelligence.* Boston: Houghton Mifflin.
Vernon, P. E. (1969). *Intelligence and Cultural Environment.* London: Methuen.

CHAPTER SIXTEEN

General discussion

Results of Aden tests*

In summing up the results of this investigation, it is proposed to begin by looking at the main questions in the investigator's mind when the work was first undertaken.

1. Do the Aden children, the Arabs, Indians and Somalis, and European children living in Aden, faced with the same type of problem as the Genevan children, exhibit characteristics analysable in terms of Piaget's 'stages'?

The answer to this is undoubtedly that they do. During the investigation, it was a common experience to hear a small Arab, Somali or Indian child give in Arabic almost a word for word translation of an answer given to the same question by a Swiss child. When the answers were analysed, it was found possible to use Piaget's categories as a basis for distinguishing between them. Not only verbal answers, but the types of mistakes they made in the practical problems followed those of the Swiss subjects very closely.

A careful scrutiny of the answers, however, especially those in category 'B', characterized by inadequate or incomplete reasoning, suggests that children do not always reason in the way that Piaget describes. In other words there is no 'logical necessity' for them to arrive at a correct solution by a given route, since childish logic is not necessarily an incomplete version of adult logic. It appears to have its own characteristics. The clearest examples of this are seen in the Bath, Towel and Doll Test. This test, which aroused the maximum interest, was treated as a serious practical problem. Facing the child was a veritable creche of babies in baths, need-

---

* Tables indicating the statistical bases of the results can be found in the Statistical Appendix.

ing towels, one lot of which were already at the laundry and another lot hanging on the line. Fortunately, the investigator had a good supply, so the babies' needs could be satisfied. Why, when these were distributed, did the babies each have two (from the laundry and the line), and, in due course, three, four, five, etc.? This, of course, is a central problem in the care of babies. The answers included the following:

'When one got wet, they wanted to have another bath.'

'They are children, so you must put one underneath, one on top, one for the face, etc.'

'They are all dirty.'

'They keep getting damp or dirty and you have to have another one.'

Children who gave this type of answer had grasped the idea of progression and found the rule, but they appeared to be reasoning from different premises.

2. Are the 'stages' applicable to each test independently, or do the tests represent a definite progression in the child's conception of number?

According to Piaget's theories of the development of the concept of number, apart from some overlapping at the intermediate stage, one would expect to find consistency in results. However, it will be seen in the summary of individual overall results at the end of the book, that many children with 'A' grades on some tests were at the 'C' stage on others (left blank in the overall summary). Piaget makes it quite clear that he has not ranked his tests in order of difficulty, but he insists that some of the later ones, such as those on one–one correspondence, are no more difficult than earlier ones, such as seriation, because the same processes are used. It will be seen from the summary of his book on number (chapter 4) that he does, however, give the impression that the mathematical principles he is demonstrating represent an orderly progression, an understanding at each stage depending on insight at a previous one. Lack of standardization of the tests, and the theoretical difficulties involved in a mental 'stage' system depending on 'content to be structured' (discussed in chapters 3 and 4), rule out any satisfactory answer to the above question. In this investigation, the overall rankings of the tests in terms of difficulty, judged by the number of 'A' graded responses, were as follows:

Test	1	2	3	4(i)	4(ii)	5	6	7(i)
Ranking	13	17	16	7	9	20	19	6
Test	7(ii)	8(i)	8(ii)	8(iii)	9(i)	9(ii)	9(iii)	10
Ranking	8	14	11	12	3	4	10	15
Test	11(i)	11(ii)	12(i)	12(ii)	13			
Ranking	1	2	5	18	21			

If the tests are grouped according to Piaget's scheme in *The Child's Conception of Number* it is found that, although the correlation between difficulty of tests and the order of mathematical concepts selected by Piaget for demonstrating the child's progression is not significant, there is substantial agreement if two anomalies are removed. The first are the 'conservation' tests, whose rank order of difficulty (including sub-sections), range from seventh to nineteenth; second is the Shell Test which was found to be one of the easiest tests by children in all the communities except the younger Indians, who had so few 'A' scores that the rankings are unsatisfactory. The implications of these discrepancies are discussed in connection with the Staircase Tests.

3. Is there any significant difference in the results obtained from children of different communities in Aden with respect to:
   (a) characteristic responses,
   (b) average age at which these appear.
   How do they compare with Piaget's norms?

In answer to the first part of the question, the responses of the children in the different Aden communities were qualitatively very similar. In all except test 13, somebody in each community gave an 'A' grade answer as well as answers graded 'B' and 'C'. When the results were analysed (see Statistical Appendix table A1) according to difficulty, using Kendall's W Test for concordance of m rankings, it was found that the order of difficulty was the same for all communities within each age range, and between the age ranges in each community.

The results, however, are quite different when comparisons are made between the quantitative results of the different communities. An analysis of variance test was made on the Piaget-type tests, each individual score consisting of the total number of 'A' grades obtained by that individual over the 21 tests and sub-tests. The results (tables A2 and A3) show that sex was not an important variable and that there were no significant interactions. The rate of progress was not significantly different for the different communities. The main variance was attributed to age and community. With regard to community it can be seen from the summary that the European scores, as anticipated from the raw data, were significantly higher than those in the other communities.

When age is considered, the variance between the three groups is significant. This confirms the progression of Piaget's 'stages': the eight-year-old children were significantly better than the seven-year olds, and the seven-year olds than the youngest group. From the combined table, however (table A9, p. 220), it can be seen that there are many 'C' grade answers at the eight-year level. It appears that the age at which responses characteristic of Piaget's 'stages' appear, varies between communities.

Many of the eight-year-old children in this investigation gave responses comparable to those reported by Piaget from children under six years.

In view of the marked difference between the grades of the European and Aden communities, association was sought between success on the tests and the amount of formal schooling enjoyed by each Subject (table A7). Ranking tests carried out for each group at each age, however, did not confirm that there was any significant association. Only the European eight-year group showed a one per cent level of significance.

In previous chapters, reference has already been made to the growing belief among investigators that the relationship between mental age and success in the Piaget-type tests is stronger than the relationship between chronological age and these tests. As Piaget himself fits in his theories of concept formation with his theories concerning the growth of intelligence, one would expect to find a positive relationship between the two. It is a little strange that Piaget does not make use of the available tests himself, to strengthen his assumptions, instead of which, he continues to modify his chronological age groups to embrace results of later investigations. As already mentioned Inhelder includes intelligence test scores in her data, but admits that they are unsatisfactory as the Subjects were tested by a number of people using various tests. In this investigation, the position was also unsatisfactory, the best that could be achieved being raw scores on four non-verbal intelligence tests. A full account of the tests was given in the previous chapter, so mention here will only be made of the overall results.

First of all the results for the different tests were compared (tables A4 and A5). An analysis of concordance was made between the rank orders to indicate whether or not these tests ranked the children in the same order. No trend was easily discernible in the results, but it was decided to carry out an analysis of variance. As in the Piaget-type tests, the major sources of variance are age and community. There is also a significant age and community interaction, indicating that increase of score is not a simple function of the absolute score size. Scrutiny of the means indicates that Arabs do not improve as they might be expected to with increasing age, and there are discrepancies in the scores for Indians and Somalis.

An analysis was then made of the association of each intelligence test score with the overall 'A' scores in the Piaget-type tests (table A6). Pi's were computed for each sub-group, and, where necessary, corrected pi's were computed. In the results no trend is easily discernible. No single IQ test always produced positive correlations for all groups, age and race. This is not, of course, an indication that there is no positive connection between Piaget's tests and the measured intelligence of the Subjects. The particular tests chosen to test intelligence were selected on account of their non-verbal character. A larger battery, with more variety, might have produced clearer-cut results.

A further analysis was made of the association of the overall intelligence test scores with number of terms of schooling (table A7). The results indicate that the intelligence test scores are more associated with schooling for Indians and Somalis than for Europeans and Arabs. It is difficult to account for this unless it is a function of the main difference between the communities concerned, that, whereas the Arabs and Europeans were using their own languages in the investigation, the Indians and Somalis were using a second language. As most of them use their own language at home, but begin their education in Arabic, it is reasonable to surmise that terms of schooling would affect favourably success on intelligence tests in which the instructions were given in Arabic, even if the tests themselves are non-verbal.

This investigation shows all the defects inherent in a pilot study carried out in unfavourable conditions. Unfortunately, political events prevented the carrying out of follow-up studies which had been planned and set in train.

Cross-cultural studies

Introduction

Comparative studies have become increasingly important in all fields of knowledge, partly due to the work of UNESCO which finances and encourages cultural cooperation. Most scientific organizations, such as the International Union of Scientific Psychology, hold periodic international congresses providing a platform for the cross-fertilization of ideas.

In psychology the comparative approach has traditionally meant the study of the behaviour of lower forms of animal life, ranging from the amoeba to the ape, to throw light on human development. One was introduced to the subject by lectures on the sexual behaviour of naive rats. It was not only philogenetic interest that prompted this approach, but the possibility of studying behaviour under controlled conditions. Setting aside the controversy aroused by the use of animals for experimental purposes, it is obvious that the experimental frustration of children, for example, raises ethical problems not encountered when the subjects are cats.

Confinement to the laboratory situation in the interest of scientific respectability is obviously limiting if the final object of the study is man. Students of abnormal psychology have developed techniques for studying 'natural' materials. Tests, especially relating to intelligence and personality have been given to patients suffering from brain lesions, diseases, deprivations, neurotic and psychotic illnesses, severe anti-social symptoms, birth-injury, etc., to establish the effects of such disorders on the quality and functions of intelligence and personality. Such studies have been particularly valuable where records of the patients have been available, making possible a 'before' and 'after' comparison.

The 'cultural' element which has been added to the comprative study raises a host of problems partly because, representing man's contribution to his environment, it embraces such a variety of concepts that precision is difficult. The Aden project, for example, was planned as a 'cross-cultural' study, using four ethnic groups. An attempt was made to isolate the 'cultural' element. The children lived in the same town, were attending the same type of school (if they had reached school age) and were matched for age and sex. The difference between them lay not in the sights and sounds which greeted them on their way to school, but in their distinctive home backgrounds, roughly covering such variables as child-rearing practices, religion, social custom and standard of living. It will be seen immediately that great caution is necessary in interpreting results: if the three local groups showed a uniform result distinct from the European, it might be the result of under-privilege rather than other 'cultural' factors, since this was, with a few exceptions, common to all three groups. But 'privilege' or more exactly in this case, 'low income', is a relative term, not defining exactly the same conditions in all communities.

What makes a study 'cross-cultural'? At present the term appears to be loosely applied to, among others:

1. Investigations such as those of Price-Williams (1961) in which he studied the occurrence of abstract and concrete modes of classification among the Tiv tribe. (One tribe, but two classes, literate and illiterate);
2. Studies like those of Jahoda (1956) who tested Piaget's predictions about the age norms of moral concepts among primitive tribes. (The only subjects were West African natives);
3. Innumerable replication studies in which an experiment carried out in one country is repeated in another, by a different experimenter using different materials and different procedure, after which the results are compared;
4. Studies carried out in more than one country, in which an agreed concept, e.g. social distance, is the common factor, each investigator devising appropriate techniques for measuring it in his own culture.

(A reply to a question put to Harry C. Triandis at a lecture at the International Congress of Psychology, 1969.)

Anthropologists have devised techniques for studying primitive peoples and sociologists for studying categories of people according to class, occupation, etc. The 'field' psychologist, trained in the rigorous procedures of the laboratory, is still in the process of working out a methodology that will satisfy the scientific nature of his discipline and yet be flexible enough for use in the 'field' situation. A few of the major problems are discussed below.

Language

This problem is minimized in the kind of research carried out by Triandis (1964), because the experts in each country, having made a joint plan, carry it out in the idiom of their respective populations. If the cooperation is between countries like U.S.A. and Greece (e.g. Triandis and Vassiliou studying the concept of justice), the situation is further eased by the fact that there are trained psychologists in Greece, many of whom have received their higher education in America.

Language becomes a real problem when experiments are carried out in a population lacking members who are bilingual psychologists. Ideally, to reduce the variables in a situation in which control is limited, all the tests should be given by the experimenter himself. This was done in Aden (except for the non-verbal tests), because it so happened that the experimenter was at the time living there permanently, a familiar figure, working among the population and using Arabic daily as a means of communication. Even so, it was felt necessary to get the help of a bilingual educationist of high standing, who would sit in and confirm that linguistic misunderstandings were not occurring. The situation is not so acute in non-verbal tests, since it is only necessary to make sure that the subjects understand the instructions. Even miming can be used instead of translation. In the Piaget-type tests, the crucial questions can be standardized, but the crucial answer which justifies the child's interpretation of his actions *must* be interpreted. This involves a wider knowledge of the language than can be obtained by learning a translation.

Investigators have used various methods to overcome the language problem, Almy (in Almy *et al.*, 1966), for instance, trained her Ugandan interviewers after having instructions translated into Lugandan. They were not only re-translated to make sure that equivalent terms were used, but several interviewers observed and checked the instructions. Price-Williams (1969) mastered a sufficient knowledge of the language to conduct the questioning without the assistance of translators, after enlisting the help of teachers, but, he says, 'it has to be admitted that a thorough mastery of the language was not sufficient to allow follow-up questions of the type which Piaget asks, other than the question "why?"'. De Lemos (personal communication) applied her tests in English to Aboriginal children because they were attending an English-medium mission school, and apparently had no difficulty with communication. She had, in fact, used an Aboriginal interpreter in her pilot study, but abandoned this procedure when inaccuracies of translation and prompting by the interpreter were suspected. Philip de Lacy, who is currently administering classificatory tests to remote Aboriginal children, has taken note of her experience. In the introduction of his Ph.D. Thesis (to be submitted in 1969 and kindly forwarded in a personal communication), he writes:

> De Lemos' practice of using translations of some of the questions for younger subjects was not followed on the advice of the teachers at Aurukun and Weipa, who considered that such an attempt to converse with the children in their own language by an unskilled European might induce in them distracting mirth.

To the difficulties above must be added that small children speak elliptically, so that to get them to enlarge their explanations without making suggestions is a skill not necessarily possessed by the interpreter. The 'promptings' may also have a motivational origin. In communities where the only known tests are the kind administered in schools, the experiment is inevitably a part-competitive situation in which everyone is on the side of the child. In Aden it was thought necessary to deceive even the European parents about the object of the investigation and to make a secrecy pact with the children, who were, of course allowed to take home a general account of their activities.

Materials

Wallace (1965) has stressed the importance of using indigenous materials in cross-cultural studies. Reference has already been made to the cultural bias of some non-verbal tests. Piaget's tests of number and quantity have the advantage that he uses very simple material, such as clay, water and sugar, common to most communities. It is therefore possible to make a straightforward replication with 'culture' as the experimental variable or to vary the material to test a theory, for example, décalage, within any one cultural group. Comparison of results becomes difficult when a study is both cross-cultural and 'cross-material', unless the experiment is deliberately designed to find an interaction between these variables.

Importance

Piaget himself (1966) has said that comparative studies are indispensable in the field of genetic psychology both for general psychology and for sociology 'because only such studies allow us to separate the effects of biological or mental factors from those of social and cultural influences on the formation and socialization of individuals.' The influences which Piaget says can be separated by comparative (in this case cross-cultural) studies are:

1. Biological depending on the maturation of the nervous system, etc.
2. Equilibration or autoregulation factors, determining behaviour and thought in their various specific activities. (For details see chapter 2.)
3. General socialization factors, which are identical for all societies: cooperations–discussions–oppositions–exchanges, etc., between children or adults, or children and children.
4. Factors related to educational and cultural transmission, which differ from one society to another, usually termed 'social factors'.

Piaget believes that it is the biological factors under (1) (above) which probably explain the sequential aspects (constant and necessary order) of the stages of development of operative intelligence. Not only does he think that cross-cultural studies are interesting for sorting out the various cultural influences, such as education, language transmission, a stimulating environment, etc., at work when children perform operative tasks, but he acknowledges that for his theories of sequence such studies are crucial. Will the stages of logical-mathematical operations be found everywhere? So far, from the meagre data discussed in this book, they are if one can accept the limitations discussed above and the need for closer cooperation between investigators to minimize the factors that make a scientific comparison difficult. Piaget concludes: 'The kind of psychology we develop in our social environments remains conjectural as long as comparative extensive and systematical research is not available; a great effort is still to be made in this direction.'

The importance of cross-cultural studies not only for genetic but for social psychology is gaining recognition in the universities. For example, two American universities, Syracuse and Columbia, have established centres in Africa with reciprocal arrangements with the governments concerned for exchange of personnel and facilities. A Cross-cultural Social Psychology Newsletter was proposed by Segall as the result of a conference on the social psychological problems of developing countries, held in Ibadan, Nigeria, 1966/7. The interest stimulated has made possible the circulation of up-to-date information of current research and the participation in studies taking place in almost any part of the world.

The necessity is no longer to stimulate enthusiasm or defend this type of investigation but to come to agreements with reference to terminology, methodology and policy with reference to the interchange of communication. Basic principles are already being clarified by Goodnow (1968, 1969), Price-Williams (1969) and Sigel (in Sigel and Hooper, 1968). Triandis (1969) has suggested that the time has come when a set of norms should be developed which scholars could employ in conducting cross-cultural research. In this, the first of a series of articles, he is mainly concerned with ethical problems. He believes that some weight should be given to scientifically irrelevant considerations, and suggests that rules might be adopted by individuals and groups when making a decision to operate in any particular country. Ethical questions, he believes, also arise, for example, in connection with the use of research funds, the choice of problems to be studied, research methods, publication and interpersonal relationships among the investigators. Not every psychologist will agree with Triandis' suggestions about what is ethical, but many would consider that the time has come when scientifically relevant norms should be discussed and agreed and that the matter is becoming so urgent that they should take priority over scientifically irrelevant considerations, which, indeed, they might influence.

Concept training

The belief that the mind can be trained is not new. For a long period cognitive psychology was based on the assumption that the mind consists of distinct powers or faculties such as reasoning, observation and memory, which can be strengthened by the discipline of training and practice. This doctrine of 'formal discipline' was linked with the then current view of transfer of training. For example, it was believed that a training in mathematics would not only toughen the mind, as if it were a muscle, but would help the pupil to solve problems encountered in adult life.

Since Thorndike's and Woodworth's classic experiments on the transfer of training (1901) challenged the assumptions underlying the doctrine of formal discipline, the nature of transfer and the conditions under which it operates have been explored by many investigators, perhaps the most famous being Harlow, whose experiments suggested to him that, more important than the transfer of specific skills, is the transfer of 'learning how to learn'. Piaget's theories of conceptual development have stimulated an old controversy which is being presented in a new guise, relevant to modern educational problems. Experiments are being devised to answer the following questions:

1. Is it possible by training procedures to intervene in the maturational processes of the mind so that, for example, the child who has achieved Stage 1 in Piaget's scheme of structural development can be eased into Stage 2 in advance of his normal rate of progress?
2. Does transfer of training occur in concept formation? For example, if the child is trained to understand the concept of conservation in one or more situations, will he then apply the principle generally?
3. What is the relevance for educational practice?

For decades the education of children has been dominated by maturational concepts. From twin studies by McGraw (1951) and Gesell (in Gesell and Ilg, 1946) we learned that, while Twin A gained temporary supremacy over Twin B through intensive training, maturational factors made possible accelerated progress in Twin B at a later period. Likewise the restriction of behavioural activity among Hopi Indian babies, who spent most of the day tied up into tight bundles for the first three months of their lives, did not prevent them from developing at the same pace as white children. Studies of twins who had been fostered in totally different environments (notably those of Newman, Freeman and Holzinger, 1937) favoured maturational as against environmental factors in growth. Ethologists, particularly Spalding (1890) and Lorenz (1956), with their fascinating accounts of 'imprinting' (i.e. the adoption of human beings as 'mother' by baby ducks and chicks at an early stage in their development), added the concept of 'critical periods' in development, a concept which forms the basis of Bowlby's studies (1953) of the relationship of mother-separation in the first two years of life with later delinquency. In educational practice the importance attached to maturational factors in growth led to such concepts as 'reading readiness' and 'number readiness' and a general fear of 'hot house' practices in the primary school.

Bruner (1966), linking his psychological theories to educational practice, believes that 'There is a way of communicating ideas to children that is appropriate to a particular age and it is futile educationally simply to wait passively for the child to grow in readiness.' Piaget believes that the 'concrete' mental operations of children are, through the processes of development, rendered unnecessary, Bruner is, in effect, saying, 'Why wait for development? Find out what the obstacles are to concept attainment and remove them by giving the children practical and verbal training.' Piaget's theories are based on the interaction of heredity and environment, implied in his description of child development as a process of accommodation and assimilation, but Bruner is suggesting calculated and active intervention in the process.

Such thinking is very much in line with modern educational thinking. In the schools, no less than the laboratory, experiments to accelerate achievement are in progress. Technological advance and competition have highlighted the seriousness of under-achievement in the general population, while social problems resulting from material deprivation, and, in particular, the special problems attendant to large-scale immigration, have all created a climate favourable to what is now established as 'compensatory education'. For the exceptionally intelligent child, 'acceleration' can mean, in Russia and America, education in special schools, in America and England, education in a higher stream and in Russia the improvement of instruction making possible the reduction of the primary courses by one year. Other schemes, like the Headstart Programme in America, include 'enrichment' courses and early admission. For the deprived it can mean a nursery school experience designed to compensate for deficiencies in the home, special language courses for infants and, ideally, all the audio-visual aids that technology can provide in addition to the very best teachers available. Typically, both in England and America, 'acceleration' schemes in education are socially acceptable for the deprived child, because of the compensatory element, but adversely criticised for gifted children. Evaluation in both the psychological laboratory and the school situation is in its infancy.

Most of the above activity is directed towards improved methodology and increasing the input of knowledge. Most educators would probably accept the former but look askance at the latter, preferring changes in selection, rather than increase. If it really were possible to teach basic concepts so that the acceleration took place as a result of the growth of the child's reasoning powers, educationists would have no cause for complaint and, incidentally, science fiction could increase the scope of its activities!

Educationists have always been interested in the application of Piaget's theories to educational practice. Lunzer (1968) has stated that 'The psycho-logical processes involved in the elaboration of concepts need to be ex-amined separately. Not infrequently, education plays a considerable part in their development.' Churchill (1958), who was one of the first to repeat Piaget's number tests, matched two groups of five years for their under-standing of them and then gave one of the groups a special programme of number experience, designed to help them discover for themselves the in-variance of number relations. At the end of the period, another battery of tests given to both groups showed that the experimental group had made a significant improvement, judged by the number of 'operational' answers, an improvement which was maintained when they were tested three months afterwards.

Concept training programmes have become an important feature in studies of conceptual development, especially among psychologists in sympathy with Bruner's theories. Reference has been made not only to Bruner's own experiments but to those of Kohnstamm (1967), Lasry and Laurendean (1969) and others. The major reference books recommended in the Acknowledgements all contain details of such programmes. The Geneva school has met the challenge. Morf (1959) gave his subjects ex-perience (but not instruction) designed to accelerate the process of under-standing the problem of inclusion (see chapter 13). Inhelder and col-leagues (1966) used learning procedures, some of them akin to Bruner's in the Water Tests (chapter 7). Unlike the procedure in Bruner's masking experiment, at no time did their procedures mask those aspects of the situation that tend to create obstacles to the correct solution. In a novel experiment six glasses were fixed to a vertical board in three rows, the top and bottom rows being of the same size and shape. By using outlet taps which could be controlled, it was possible to show, by slow motion, the transformations in the shape of the liquid, to ask anticipatory questions and demonstrate reversibility. Pre-tests and post-tests followed the classic pattern. The results were not clear cut. Apparent progress was observed in some cases, but, in her detailed analysis, Inhelder shows that evaluation was difficult and that the children's gain was limited to a fragmentary understanding. Piaget and his colleagues have not been successful in training experiments, because what they are investigating is not subject to training, although they do not deny that changes take place.

Concept formation must be regarded as a complex process which is not only linked with other cognitive abilities, such as perception and language, but which can be retarded by unfavourable conditions and, to a limited degree, aided by training and experience. In the last chapter, reference was made to Vernon's data (1969) concerning the effects of nutrition, linguistic ability and home and educational conditions on test scores. Without equating test scores with concept formation, it is a reasonable assumption that efficient reasoning is no less affected by the conditions mentioned. A broad term used to cover these and other conditions contributed by man to his society is 'culture'. It is the culture of a society which decides what form Hebb's 'Intelligence B' (1949) will take, that is, the intelligence which is the result of the interaction of innate potentiality and the environment in which it is nurtured.

The fundamental difference between Piaget and Bruner appears to be their approach, a difference which goes far to justify Wohlwill's criticism (1968) that, in spite of his theory of stages, Bruner is not primarily interested in the development of cognition. Whereas Piaget began his studies with the infant, tracing his mental development from his first random movements to the stage where he is capable of formal reasoning, Bruner began with a detailed study of an adult's strategies of thought, and then looked back, so to speak, to see what influences had been at work to produce those modes of thought. His latest work (1969) has involved studying babies. For Bruner, unlike Piaget, these influences had been external, rather than internal, environmental rather than maturational. He believes that, in the course of evolution, certain capacities have been slowly acquired, but that the development of them is a function of education in its widest sense: 'Cognitive growth in all its manifestations occurs as much from the outside as from the inside.'

Piaget believes that logical structure develops as a function of an *internal* process, equilibration. Equilibration is one of Piaget's most difficult concepts, but a very important one, since it distinguishes his theory from learning theory. Whereas learning results from external reinforcement, equilibration is a kind of self-regulating function which enables the child to organize his thinking on the basis of his activity and experience. Piaget sometimes appears to be in search of that elusive genetic factor, Hebb's

'Intelligence A', the inherited potentiality. In fact, he, like Bruner, is concerned with 'Intelligence B' which results from the accommodation and assimilation of an individual to his environment. However, he is searching for a common thought structure which is genetically determined, for basic laws of thinking which apply universally.

Piaget and Inhelder stress that they are not in opposition to the Harvard school, their work and that of Bruner is complementary. They believe that the information-processing techniques, which Bruner investigates, are very important, but that they should not be confused with structures of thought which coordinate information. To trace the whole course of intellectual development from birth to maturity, is a formidable task even for a scientist of Piaget's stature: it necessitates a broad theory of development within which details can be explored, elaborated and defined by subsequent studies. Piaget's interdisciplinary approach has enabled him to provide this framework. It is not possible to assess or evaluate his work at this stage: one can only admire him for the breadth and depth of his interests and expertise in many fields of knowledge. As pointed out by Hooper (Sigel and Hooper, 1968), Piaget's work has, in fact, three very significant points of contact with educational practice: '(1) when a certain content or subject area should be taught, (2) what content-subject matter is most important, and (3) how it may be best presented to the pupil.' The gaps in his investigations are a stimulus and challenge to specialists in many areas of child development. There is scope for all: the clinician can study the abnormal functionings of the structure, the educationist the effects of environmental factors, others the modifications due to individual differences, while the cross-cultural psychologist can try to show how far the overall theory of development is independent of cultural factors. The body of knowledge that may eventually result from Piaget's work is incalculable.

References

Almy, Millie, E. Chittenden and P. Miller. (1966). *Young Children's Thinking: Studies of some Aspects of Piaget's Theory.* New York: Teachers College Press, Columbia University.

Bowlby, J. (1953). *J. ment. Sci.*, **99**, 265.

Bruner, J. S. (1966). *Toward a Theory of Instruction.* Cambridge, Mass.: Harvard University Press.

Bruner, J. S. (1969). Eye, hand and mind. In D. Elkind and J. H. Flavell (Eds.), *Studies in Cognitive Development.* New York: Oxford University Press.

Churchill, E. M. (1958). *The Number Concepts of the Young Child.* Parts I and II. Researches and Studies, 17, 18. Leeds University.

Cross-Cultural Social Psychology Newsletter. Circulated to private subscribers. Present Editor: Yasumasa Tanaka, Dept. Political Science, Gakashuin (Peers') University, Mejiro, Tashima-Ku, Tokyo, Japan.

Gesell, A., and F. Ilg. (1946). *The Child from Five to Ten*. London: Hamish Hamilton.

Goodnow, J. J. (1968). Cultural variations in cognitive skill. *Cognitive Studies*, vol. 1.

Goodnow, J. J. (1969). Problems in research on culture and thought. In D. Elkind and J. H. Flavell (Eds.), *Studies of Cognitive Development*. New York: Oxford University Press.

Hebb, D. O. (1949). *The Organization of Behavior*. New York: Wiley.

Inhelder, B., M. Bovet, H. Sinclair and C. Smock. (1966). Comments on Bruner's course of cognitive development. *Am. Psychol.*, **21**, 160–164.

Jahoda, G. (1956). Assessment of abstract behavior in a non-Western culture. *J. abnorm. soc. Psychol.*, **53**, 237–243.

Kohnstamm, G. A. (1967). *Piaget's Analysis of Class Inclusion: Right or Wrong?* The Hague: Monton. (See also Sigel and Hooper, 1968.)

de Lacy, P. R. Personal Communication.

Lasry, Jean-Claude, and Monique Laurendean. (1969). (To be published in *Hum. Dev.*, 1969.)

de Lemos, M. Personal Communication.

Lorenz, K. Z. (1956). In J. M. Tanner and B. Inhelder (Eds.), *Discussions on Child Development*. London: Tavistock. (See also *King Solomon's Ring*. London: Methuen.)

Lunzer, E. A. (1968). Children's thinking. In H. J. Butcher (Ed.), *Educational Research in Britain*. London: University of London Press.

McGraw, M. B. (1951). Maturation of behaviour. In L. Carmichael (Ed.), *Manual of Child Psychology*. New York: Wiley.

Morf, A. (1959). Apprentissage d'une structure logique concrète (inclusion): effets et limites. In J. Piaget (Ed.), *Etudes d'Epistémologie génétique*, vol. 9. Paris: Presses Universitaires.

Newman, H. H., F. N. Freeman and K. J. Holzinger. (1937). *Twins: A Study of Heredity and Environment*. Chicago: University of Chicago Press.

Piaget, J. (1952). *The Child's Conception of Number*. London: Routledge and Kegan Paul.

Piaget, J. (1966). Nécessité et signification des recherches comparatives en psychologie génétique. *Int. J. Psychol.*, **1**, No. 1, 3–13.

Price-Williams, D. R. A. (1961). A study concerning concept of quantities among primitive children. *Acta Psychol.*, **18**, 293–305. (Reprinted in Price-Williams, 1969.)

Price-Williams, D. R. A., Ed. (1969). *Cross-Cultural Studies*. Harmondsworth, Mddx.: Penguin.

Sigel, I. E., and F. H. Hooper, Eds. (1968). *Logical Thinking in Children*. New York: Holt, Rinehart and Winston.

Spalding, D. A. (1890). In W. James (Ed.), *Principles of Psychology*, vol. 2. New York: Holt.

Thorndike, E. L., and R. S. Woodworth. (1901). The influence of improvement in one mental function upon efficiency of other functions. *Psychol. Rev.*, **8**, 247–261, 384–395, 553–564.

Triandis, H. C. (1964). Culture and cognition. In L. Berkowitz (Ed.), *Advances in Experimental Social Psychology*, vol. 1. New York: Academic.

Triandis, H. C. (1969). *Cross-Cultural soc. Psychol. Newsletter*, **3**, No. 1, Issue 18.

Vernon, P. E. (1969). *Intelligence and Cultural Environment*. London: Methuen.

Wallace, J. G. (1965). *Concept Growth and the Education of the Child*. Slough, Bucks.: National Foundation for Educational Research.

Wohlwill, J. F. (1968). In I. E. Sigel and F. H. Hooper (Eds.), *Logical Thinking in Children*. New York: Holt, Rinehart and Winston.

Statistical Appendix

Table A1

Piaget-type tests—summary of analysis of concordance

Communities ($m = 4$)

6 year	7 year	8 year
$W_6 = 0.6243$	$W_7 = 0.6834$	$W_8 = 0.7945$
$\pi < 0.001$	$\pi < 0.001$	$\pi < 0.001$
$= 0.4990$	$= 0.5778$	$= 0.7113$
	$W = 0.6245$	
	$\pi < 0.001$	
	$= 0.4993$	

Ages ($m = 3$)

European	Arab	Indian	Somali
$W = 0.8395$	$W = 0.8150$	$W = 0.8591$	$W = 0.7180$
$\pi < 0.001$	$\pi < 0.001$	$\pi < 0.001$	$\pi < 0.005$
$= 0.7594$	$= 0.7225$	$= 0.7886$	$= 0.5770$
		$W = 0.9402$	
		$\pi < 0.001$	
		$= 0.9103$	

Table A2

Analysis of variance—Piaget test scores

Each entry in the table below is the sum of the individual scores for that group. Each individual score consists of the total number of A's obtained by that individual over the 21 Piaget tests.

n = number in group

u = mean

		6 years	7 years	8 years
European	Boys	$u = 7 \cdot 67$ $n = 8$	$u = 9 \cdot 50$ $n = 8$	$u = 11 \cdot 25$ $n = 8$
	Girls	$u = 8 \cdot 01$ $n = 8$	$u = 11 \cdot 00$ $n = 8$	$u = 11 \cdot 50$ $n = 8$
Arab	Boys	$u = 3 \cdot 50$ $n = 8$	$u = 5 \cdot 25$ $n = 8$	$u = 6 \cdot 67$ $n = 8$
	Girls	$u = 3 \cdot 62$ $n = 8$	$u = 3 \cdot 62$ $n = 8$	$u = 5 \cdot 87$ $n = 8$
Indian	Boys	$u = 1 \cdot 25$ $n = 4$	$u = 3 \cdot 50$ $n = 4$	$u = 2 \cdot 50$ $n = 4$
	Girls	$u = 1 \cdot 5$ $n = 4$	$u = 4 \cdot 25$ $n = 4$	$u = 7 \cdot 75$ $n = 4$
Somali	Boys	$u = 0 \cdot 25$ $n = 4$	$u = 4 \cdot 50$ $n = 4$	$u = 5 \cdot 75$ $n = 4$
	Girls	$u = 1 \cdot 50$ $n = 4$	$u = 3 \cdot 75$ $n = 4$	$u = 8 \cdot 25$ $n = 4$

Table A3
Piaget-type tests—analysis of variance

Source	Sum of squares	df	Mean square	F-Ratio
Age	346·43	2	173·21	16·96ᵃ
				(2120)
Community	1002·77	3	334·26	32·74ᵃ
				(3120)
Sex	5·06	1	5·06	0·49
				(1120)
Age × Community	50·08	6	8·34	0·82
				(6120)
Sex × Community	35·32	3	11·77	1·15
				(3120)
Age × Sex	7·63	2	3·81	0·37
				(2120)
Age × Sex × Community	45·62	6	7·63	0·75
				(6120)
Error	1225·75	120	10·21	
Total	2718·66	143		

$^{a}\pi < 0\cdot001$

Table A4
Intelligence test scores—analysis of variance

Source	Sum of squares	df	Mean square	F-Ratio
Age	8279·28	2	4139·64	17·71ᵃ
Community	50,895·15	3	16,968·38	72·59ᵃ
Sex	655·21	1	665·21	2·85
Age × Community	7569·09	6	1261·51	5·40ᵃ
Sex × Community	373·21	3	124·40	0·53
Age × Sex	155·59	2	77·79	0·33
Age × Sex × Community	561·00	6	93·50	0·40
Error	28,049·60	120	233·75	
Total	96,548·13	143		

$^{a}\pi < 0\cdot001$

Table A5

Analysis of variance—intelligence test scores

Each entry in the table below is the sum of the individual scores making up the group. Each individual score is obtained by summing the scores obtained by that individual over the four intelligence tests which he took.

$(u = \text{mean})$

		6 year	7 year	8 year
European	Boys	$u = 50 \cdot 12$ $n = 8$	$u = 68 \cdot 12$ $n = 8$	$u = 92 \cdot 55$ $n = 8$
	Girls	$u = 47 \cdot 12$ $n = 8$	$u = 49 \cdot 93$ $n = 8$	$u = 88 \cdot 12$ $n = 8$
Arab	Boys	$u = 26 \cdot 87$ $n = 8$	$u = 25 \cdot 50$ $n = 8$	$u = 32 \cdot 81$ $n = 8$
	Girls	$u = 24 \cdot 68$ $n = 8$	$u = 25 \cdot 68$ $n = 8$	$u = 25 \cdot 50$ $n = 8$
Indian	Boys	$u = 20 \cdot 22$ $n = 4$	$u = 26 \cdot 37$ $n = 4$	$u = 31 \cdot 87$ $n = 4$
	Girls	$u = 21 \cdot 87$ $n = 4$	$u = 25 \cdot 87$ $n = 4$	$u = 31 \cdot 62$ $n = 4$
Somali	Boys	$u = 22 \cdot 75$ $n = 4$	$u = 24 \cdot 87$ $n = 4$	$u = 30 \cdot 37$ $n = 4$
	Girls	$u = 21 \cdot 87$ $n = 4$	$u = 21 \cdot 37$ $n = 4$	$u = 26 \cdot 37$ $n = 4$

Table A6

Association of intelligence and Piaget tests

		6 year	7 year	8 year
	W_{IQ} =	0·3910	0·4422	0·3642
	π =	0·05	0·05	0·1
	Prog. =	0·5430	0·4386	0·1660
	Port. =	0·4258	0·3265	0·0693
European	Cube =	−0·2557	0·5448	0·1509
$n = 16$	Koh's =	0·2403	0·6198	0·1863
$x = 680$	Overall =	0·4615	0·6363	0·1420
	W_{IQ} =	0·4662	0·5176	0·6709
	π =	0·025	0·01	0·001
	Prog. =	0·3745	0·6108	0·5748
	Port. =	0·7398	0·5073	0·4323
Arab	Cube =	0·3190	0·5095	0·3663
$n = 16$	Koh's =	0·6588	0·2108	−0·0008
$x = 680$	Overall =	0·6805	0·7908	0·2530
	W_{IQ} =	0·3650	0·5863	0·3136
	π =	0·1	0·025	0·1
	Prog. =	0·3098	0·4586	0·0005
	Port. =	0·8453	−0·2946	−0·3409
Indian	Cube =	0·0773	0·4524	0·4288
$n = 8$	Koh's =	0·7296	0·6073	−0·0354
$x = 84$	Overall =	0·6728	0·4943	−0·1671
	W_{IQ} =	0·2946	0·2233	0·1226
	π =	0·1	0·1	0·1
	Prog. =	0·1633	−0·5621	−0·995
	Port. =	0·2774	0·5835	−0·0116
Somali	Cube =	0·1670	0·520	0·2948
$n = 8$	Koh's =	0·2958	0·2453	0·4901
$x = 84$	Overall =	0·6133	0·0613	0·3860

Table A7

Association of Piaget battery score with number of terms at school

Summary of values

	6 year	7 year	8 year
European	0·1715	0·2175	−0·6204[a]
Arab	0·1096	−0·0520	0·3972
Indian	0·2209	0·2410	0·6467
Somali	0·1830	−0·3333	0·6500

[a] Significant at 1%

Table A8

Association of average intelligence test score with number of terms at school

Summary of values

	6 year	7 year	8 year
European	−0·1350	0·1413	0·1087
Arab	−0·0607	0·2809	0·0555
Indian	0·4024	0·4910	−0·3615
Somali	0·0000	−0·6203	0·4000

Table A9 (overleaf)

Overall results for individual subjects

	Subject		Results on test no.																					Subject								
Community	No.	Terms at school	1	2	3	4^i	4^{ii}	5	6	7^i	7^{ii}	8^i	8^{ii}	8^{iii}	9^i	9^{ii}	9^{iii}	10	11^i	11^{ii}	12^i	12^{ii}	13	No.	Terms at school	1	2	3	4^i	4^{ii}	5	6
European	135	2	A		A	B	B	B		A	A	B			A		A	B						21	4	A	A				B	B
	57	$2\frac{1}{2}$					B	B	B		A	A			A	A	B	B						131	4	A						B
	45	3	A				B	B	B	B	B	A.		B	B	B		A	A	B	B	B		2	5	A	A	A	A	A	A	B
	68	3	A		A	A	A	B	B	B	B	A	A	A	A	A	A	B	A	A	A	B	B	64	6						B	B
	133	$4\frac{1}{2}$	A		A	A	A		B		B	B	B		A	A	A	B	A	A	A	B		50	7	A	A					B
	67	5		A	A	A	B	B	A	A	B			B			A	A	A	B	B			34	$7\frac{1}{2}$	B	B	B	A	A	B	
	132	$6\frac{1}{2}$		A	A		B	B	A	A	B	A	A	A	A	A		A	A	A		B		112	$7\frac{1}{2}$	A	A	A	A	A	B	B
	16	8					B	B	B	A		A				A	A	A						114	10	A		A	A	A	B	B
	69	$2\frac{1}{2}$				B		A		A	A	B	A	A	A		A	A	A		B			38	5	A	A		A	A	B	B
	66	$3\frac{1}{2}$	A		A	A	A	B	B	A	A	B	A		A	A			A	A	A	B		94	$5\frac{1}{2}$	A	A	A	A	A	B	B
	77	$3\frac{1}{2}$					B	B		A	B		A	B		A	A	A	B					25	6							B
	82	$3\frac{1}{2}$		A			B	B	A	B	B	A		A		A	A	A	B	B				56	6	A	B	A	A	A		B
	27	4				B		B	B	A	B	A	A	B	B		A	A	B	B				1	$6\frac{1}{2}$	A	A	A	A	A	B	B
	93	$4\frac{1}{2}$	A		A	A	B	B	A	A	A	A	A	A	B	B		A	A	A	B	B		19	7	A					B	B
	75	5						A		B		A	B		B	A	A	A	B					24	7		A	A	A	B	A	
	134	5	A	B	A	A	B	B	A	A	B		A	A	A	B	A	A	A	B				130	7			A			B	B
Arab	58	0					A	A		A	A		A											61	$\frac{1}{2}$							B
	59	0			B						B							B						63	$\frac{1}{2}$				B	A	B	
	60	0			B	B		B	B	B	A	A	A	A	A	B								48	1	A		B		B	A	
	117	1			B		B	B		A			A	A										53	1		A	A	B	B		
	118	1	A		B	B	B	B		A	A	A	B		B		B							54	1							
	126	1			B			A	A		B													55	1				B	B		
	129	1			B	A	A	B		B	A	A		A	A									39	$1\frac{1}{2}$						B	
	47	$2\frac{1}{2}$			B	B	B	B	B		A	A	A	B										52	4						B	
	62	0			B	B	A	A	B	B		A	A	A	B	A	A							29	1						B	
	86	0		B		B	B		B	B				B										43	1						B	
	136	0					A	A										B						87	1							B
	10	1	A	A		A	A	A	B	B	B		A			A	A	A				B		105	1						B	B
	46	1		A			B	B	B	B		B	B					A						55	2							B
	81	1											B											89	4							B
	88	1				B	B	B	B		B	A	A		A	A	B							100	4			A	A	B.		
	51	$1\frac{1}{2}$	A			B	B					B	A	A	A	A								14	7						B	A
Indian	18	0							B				B											76	0			B		B	B	
	140	0			B		B	B		B	A	A												95	$\frac{1}{2}$		A				B	B
	142	0			B		B	B	B					B										96	$1\frac{1}{2}$			B		B	B	
	78	$3\frac{1}{2}$			B			B		A	A	B	B		A									30	$6\frac{1}{2}$							B
	73	$\frac{1}{2}$			B	B									B									72	$3\frac{1}{2}$	A	A		A	A	B	B
	99	1		B		B	B	A	A	B		A	A	A			A	B						101	4							
	83	$2\frac{1}{2}$				B		B		A														102	4						B	
	79	$5\frac{1}{2}$		B		B							B											36	$4\frac{1}{2}$						A	B
Somali	91	0							B		B	B		A	B									92	$\frac{1}{2}$							B
	139	0				B	B	B	B															115	1			B	A			
	144	0				B			B		B													116	1			B	A	B	B	
	127	1											B											128	1							B
	141	0				B		B																106	4						B	B
	103	1				B	B							A	A	A								107	4	A		B			B	B
	143	1				B																		125	4			B		B		
	124	4		B			B	B		A		A	A				B	B						123	7						B	B
Age												6+																					

Results on test no.	Subject		Results on test no.	Sex
$7^i\ 7^{ii}\ 8^i\ 8^{ii}\ 8^{iii}\ 9^i\ 9^{ii}\ 9^{iii}\ 10\ 11^i\ 11^{ii}\ 12^i\ 12^{ii}\ 13$	No.	Terms at school	$1\ 2\ 3\ 4^i\ 4^{ii}\ 5\ 6\ 7^i\ 7^{ii}\ 8^i\ 8^{ii}\ 8^{iii}\ 9^i\ 9^{ii}\ 9^{iii}\ 10\ 11^i\ 11^{ii}\ 12^i\ 12^{ii}\ 13$	
A A · A A A · B B A A B A	5	5	A A · A A B B B B A A A A A B B A A A B A	
A A · A A · A · B	49	7	A · A A · B B B A · A A A B · B	
B B A A A A B B A A A A B B	28	8	A A A A A A A B B A A A A B B A A A A A A	
B B · A A B · A A B	90	9½	A · A A B · A A A B A A B · A A A A B B	
B B B B A · A · A A A A B	23	10	A · B · B B · B B · A · B A A B B B	Boys
B B · A B · B · A A A B	35	10	B · A A B A B B · A · A A · B A A A B B	
A A A A A A B B A A A A B B	113	11	A A A A B B A A A A A A B A A A A A B	
A A B A · A A A B A A A B B	119	11	A A · A A A B A A B A · A A A B A · A B	
A A A A B A B · A A · B	65	6	B · A A A B A A A A B A A B A · A A A A B	
A A B B A A A A A A A A B	15	7	A A A A A B B B B A A A A A A A A A A B	
B B · A · B · A A B B B	22	9	A · A A A A A A A B A A B A A B A A A A B	
A A A A · B B · A A A A A	37	9	B A A A · A A A B A · A A A A B	
A A B A A A B · A A A A A	98	9½	A · A A B B A A A A A A B A B A A A B	Girls
A A B A A A B B A A A A A	97	10½	A A B B · B A A A A B · A A A · B B	
A A A A A A A B · A A A A B	3	11½	· B B B B B B A B · A B A · A A A B B	
B B B A B A B · B A A A B	26	11½	B · B B · A A A A B B B A A A B B	
· A A A B B	11	1	· B · A · B B B	
A A B · A A A · A A A	20	1	B · A A A	
B B B A A A A B · B B	31	1	A · A A · B A A · A A A · A B	
B B · A A A · A A A B B	6	3½	B B A A A B · B B · A A · B A B	
B	12	3½	A A B A A B · A A A A B A B · B A A B	Boys
A A · A B B	8	4	A · A A B B A A · B · A A · A A A A	
A A A B · B B · A A A B	13	4	A · A A B B B B · A A · A A	
B B · A B · A A A B	70	4	B · A A A A A A	
A A · B B	32	1½	· B B · A A A · A A B B	
B B · A A	33	1½	B · A A · A · A	
· A B	4	4	A · B A A · B · B A A B	
A A B · B A A · A A · B	7	4	B · A A B A B B A A	Girls
B B · B · B	42	4	A A · A B B · A A · A A A	
B · B A A A · A A	44	4	B · B B · A · A · A B B	
A A A B A A B B	41	4½	A A · A A · A · B A A B	
A A · A · B A A	40	7½	A · A A B · A A A · B A B · A A A B B	
A · A B · B	9	4	A · B · A B · A A	
A A · A A · A	17	4½	B B A A · B · A A · B · B	
B B B B · A	71	5½	B · B	Boys
A A · A A · B A B B B	84	6	B · B · A · A A B B	
B B · A · A	74	3½	B · A	
A · B A A A · A B B	80	5½	A · A A B · A A A · A A A	
B B · A A A · A A	122	7	A · B B A A · A A B A A A B B	Girls
B B · B B	138	7½	A A A A A B · A A B · A A A A · A B A B	
· B A A A · B · B B	108	1	A A B · B A A A B	
A A · A A A B A A	109	4	A A B A B B A A A B A · A A A B	
A A B B A · A A · A A B	110	4	A A B · B B B B · B A · A A B B	Boys
B B · A A · B A	111	5	A A · A B · B B B B · B B A · A B A A	
A A · A A A	120	4	A · B · A A B B · A B · B A A B B	
A A B B · A · A A	104	7	A A · A · A A B · A A B	
· A A A · A B	121	7	A A B B A A A · A A	Girls
B B · B B	137	7	A A A A A B B A A B · A A A · A A · B B	
7+			**8+**	

Bibliography

Adler, A. (1930). Individual psychology. In C. Murchison (Ed.), *Psychologies of 1930*. Mass.: Clark University Press.

Almy, Millie, E. Chittenden and P. Miller. (1966). *Young Children's Thinking: Studies of some Aspects of Piaget's Theory*. New York: Teachers College Press, Columbia University.

Anastasi, A., and J. P. Foley. (1949). *Differential Psychology*. New York: Collier-Macmillan.

A.T.C.D.E. (1963). Report on Primary Mathematics.

Baldwin, A. L. (1967). *Theories of Child Development*. New York: Wiley.

Ballard, P. B. (1928). *Teaching the Essentials of Arithmetic*. London: University of London Press.

Beard, R. (1957). An investigation of concept formation among infant school children. Unpublished Ph.D. Thesis: University of London.

Beard, R. (1963). The order of concept studies in two fields. (i) Number concept in the infant school (ii) Conception of conservation of quantity among primary school children. *Educ. Rev.*, **XV**, Nos. 2, 3.

Bernstein, B. (1961). Social class and linguistic development: a theory of social learning. In A. H. Halsey (Ed.), *Education, Economy and Society*. Glencoe, Ill.: Free Press.

Berry, J. W. (1966). Temne and Eskimo perceptual skills. *Int. J. Psychol.*, **1**, 207–299.

Binet, A. (1937). In L. M. Terman and M. A. Merrill (Eds.), *Measuring Intelligence*. Boston: Houghton Mifflin.

Bowlby, J. (1953). *J. ment. Sci.*, **99**, 265.

Bruner, J. S. (1966). *Toward a Theory of Instruction*. Cambridge, Mass.: Harvard University Press.

Bruner, J. S. (1969). Eye, hand and mind. In D. Elkind and J. H. Flavell

(Eds.), *Studies in Cognitive Development*. New York: Oxford University Press.

Bruner, J. S., J. J. Goodnow and G. A. Austin. (1956). *A Study of Thinking*. New York: Wiley. (London: Chapman and Hall, 1957.)

Bruner, J. S., R. R. Olver and P. M. Greenfield, Eds. (1966). *Studies in Cognitive Growth*. New York: Wiley.

Bühler, C. (1930). *The First Years of Life*. New York: Day.

Bunt, L. N. H. (1950). *The Development of the Ideas of Number and Quantity According to Piaget*. Groningen: Djakarta.

Cameron, N. (1963). *Personality Development and Psychopathology*. Boston: Houghton Mifflin.

Carmichael, L. (1926). *Psychol. Rev.*, **33**, 51–58; **34**, 34–47 (1927); **35**, 253–260 (1928).

Carmichael, L., Ed. (1951). *Manual of Child Psychology*. New York: Wiley.

Carpenter, T. E. (1955). A pilot study for a quantitative investigation of Jean Piaget's original work on concept formation. *Educ. Rev.*, **7**, 142–149.

Churchill, E. M. (1958). *The Number Concepts of the Young Child*. Parts I and II. Researches and Studies, 17, 18. Leeds University.

Churchill, E. M. (1961). *Counting and Measuring*. London: Routledge and Kegan Paul.

Cross-Cultural Social Psychology Newsletter. Circulated to private subscribers. Present Editor: Yasumasa Tanaka, Dept. Political Science, Gakashuin (Peers') University, Mejiro, Tashima-Ku, Tokyo, Japan.

Cuisenaire, G., and C. Cattegno. (1955). *Numbers in Colour*. London: Heinemann.

Dawson, J. L. (1963). Psychological effects of social change in a West African community. Unpublished Ph.D. Thesis: University of Oxford. (Reprinted in Vernon, 1969.)

Dennis, W. (1935). *J. genet. Psychol.*, **47**, 17–32; **53**, 149–158 (1938); *J. soc. Psychol.*, **12**, 305–317.

Dienes, Z. P. (1959). *Concept Formation and Personality*. Leicester: Leicester University Press.

Dodwell, P. C. (1960). Children's understanding of number and related concepts. *Can. J. Psychol.*, **4**, 191–205.

Dodwell, P. C. (1961). Children's understanding of number concepts: characteristics of an individual and a group test. *Can. J. Psychol.*, **15**, 29–36.

Dodwell, P. C. (1962). Relations between the understanding of the logic of classes and of cardinal number in children. *Can. J. Psychol.*, **16**, 152–160.

Dodwell, P. C. (1968). Relations between the understanding of the logic of classes and cardinal number in children. In I. E. Sigel and F. H.

Hooper (Eds.), *Logical Thinking in Children*. New York: Holt, Rinehart and Winston.

Duncker, K. (1926). *J. genet. Psychol.*, **33**, 642–708.

Elkind, D. (1961). Children's discovery of the conservation of mass, weight and volume. *J. genet. Psychol.*, **98**, 219–227. (Reprinted in I. E. Sigel and F. H. Hooper (Eds.), *Logical Thinking in Children*. New York: Holt, Rinehart and Winston, 1968.)

Elkind, D. (1964). Discrimination, seriation and numeration of size and dimensional differences in young children: Piaget replication study VI. *J. genet. Psychol.*, **104**, 275–296. (Reprinted in I. E. Sigel and F. H. Hooper (Eds.), *Logical Thinking in Children*. New York: Holt, Rinehart and Winston, 1968.)

Erikson, E. H. (1965). *Childhood and Society*. Harmondsworth, Mddx.: Penguin.

Fields, P. E. (1932). Studies in concept formation. *Comp. Psychol. Monogr.*, **9**. (Also in *J. Comp. Psychol.*, **21**, 341–355 (1936).)

Flavell, J. H. (1963). *The Developmental Psychology of Jean Piaget*. New York: Van Nostrand.

Freud, Sigmund. (1900 ed.). *The Interpretation of Dreams*. London: Allen and Unwin.

Freud, Sigmund. (1922 ed.). *Introductory Lectures on Psycho-Analysis*. London: Allen and Unwin.

Gardner, D. E. M. (1950). *Long Term Results of Infant School Methods*. London: Methuen.

Garrett, H. E. (1951). *Great Experiments in Psychology*. New York: Appleton-Century-Crofts.

Gates, A. L., and G. A. Taylor. (1925). *J. educ. Psychol.*, **16**, 583–592.

Gesell, A., and F. Ilg. (1946). *The Child from Five to Ten*. London: Hamish Hamilton.

Goldschmid, M. L. (1958). *Child Dev.*, 579–589.

Goldstein, K., and A. Gelb. (1918). *Z. ges. Neurol. Psychiat.*, **41**, 1–142.

Goldstein, K., and M. Scheerer. (1941). Abstract and concrete behaviour. *Psychol. Monogr.*, **53**, No. 2.

Goodenough, F. L., and K. M. Maurer. (1942). *The Mental Growth of Children from Age 2 to 14 Years*. Minn.: University of Minnesota Press.

Goodnow, J. J. (1962). A test for milieu effects with some of Piaget's tests. *Psychol. Monogr.*, **76**, Whole No. 555.

Goodnow, J. J. (1968). Cultural variations in cognitive skill. *Cognitive Studies*, vol. 1.

Goodnow, J. J. (1969). Problems in research on culture and thought. In D. Elkind and J. H. Flavell (Eds.), *Studies of Cognitive Development*. New York: Oxford University Press.

Greenfield, P. M. (1966). On culture and conservation. In J. S. Bruner,

R. R. Olver and P. M. Greenfield (Eds.), *Studies in Cognitive Growth.* New York: Wiley. pp. 225–256.

Guyler, K. R. (1966). The effects of variations in task content and materials on conservation and transitivity. Unpublished M.Ed. Thesis: Manchester University.

Hanfmann, E., and J. Kasanin. (1937). *J. Psychol.*, 3, 521–540.

Hazlitt, V. (1930). Children's thinking. *Br. J. Psychol.*, 20, 354–361.

Hebb, D. O. (1949). *The Organization of Behavior.* New York: Wiley.

Heidbreder, E. The attainment of concepts. A series of articles in: *J. gen. Psychol.*, 35, 173–223 (1946); *J. Psychol.*, 24, 93–138 (1947); 25, 299–329 (1948); 26, 45–69, 193–216 (1948); 27, 3–39, 263–309 (1949).

Hendriks, E. (1966). A cross-cultural investigation of the number concepts and level of number development in five-year old Urban Shona and European children in Southern Rhodesia. Unpublished M.A. Thesis: University of London.

Hilgard, E. R. (1956). *Theories of Learning*, 2nd ed. New York: Appleton-Century-Crofts.

Hilgard, J. R. (1932). *J. genet. Psychol.*, 41, 35–56; *Genet. Psychol. Monogr.*, 14, 493–567.

Hood, H. B. (1962). An experimental study of Piaget's theory of the development of number in children. *Br. J. Psychol.*, 53, 273–286.

Hull, C. L. (1920). Quantitative aspects of the evolution of concepts. *Psychol. Monogr.*, 28, Whole No. 123.

Humphrey, G. (1951). *Thinking.* London: Methuen.

Inhelder, B. (1943). *Le Diagnostic du Raisonnement chez les Débiles mentaux.* Neuchâtel: Delachaux et Niestlé.

Inhelder, B., M. Bovet, H. Sinclair and C. Smock. (1966). Comments on Bruner's course of cognitive development. *Am. Psychol.*, 21, 160–164.

Inhelder, B., and J. Piaget. (1964). *The Early Growth of Logic in the Child: Classification and Seriation.* London: Routledge and Kegan Paul.

Isaacs, Susan. (1930). *Intellectual Growth in Young Children.* London: Routledge and Kegan Paul. (New York: Harcourt, 1930.)

Jahoda, G. (1956). Assessment of abstract behavior in a non-Western culture. *J. abnorm. soc. Psychol.*, 53, 237–243.

Jung, C. (1939). *The Integration of Personality.* New York: Farrar and Rinehart.

Köhler, W. (1925). *The Mentality of Apes.* Harmondsworth, Mddx.: Penguin.

Kohnstamm, G. A. (1967). *Piaget's Analysis of Class Inclusion: Right or Wrong?* The Hague: Monton. (See also Sigel and Hooper, 1968.)

Kuo, Z. Y. (1923). *J. exp. Psychol.*, 6, 247–293.

de Lacy, P. R. Personal Communication.

Lashley, K. S. (1938). The mechanism of vision. *XV J. gen. Psychol.*, **18**, 123–193.

Lasry, Jean-Claude, and Monique Laurendean. (1969). (To be published in *Hum. Dev.*, 1969.)

Lewin, K. (1935). *A Dynamic Theory of Personality.* New York: McGraw-Hill.

Lewin, K., R. Lippitt and R. K. White. (1939). Patterns of aggressive behaviour in experimentally created 'social climates'. *J. soc. Psychol.*, **10**, 271–299.

de Lemos, M. Personal Communication.

Lorenz, K. Z. (1956). In J. M. Tanner and B. Inhelder (Eds.), *Discussions on Child Development.* London: Tavistock. (See also *King Solomon's Ring.* London: Methuen.)

Lovell, K. (1965). *The Growth of Basic Mathematical Concepts in Children.* London: University of London Press.

Lovell, K. (1969). *An Introduction to Human Development*, 2nd ed. London: Macmillan.

Lovell, K., and E. Ogilvie. (1960). A Study of the conservation of substance in the junior school child. *Br. J. educ. Psychol.*, **30**, 109–118.

Lovell, K., and E. Ogilvie. (1961). A study of the conservation of weight in the junior school child. *Br. J. educ. Psychol.*, **31**, 138–144.

Lovell, K., and E. Ogilvie. (1961). The growth of the concept of volume in junior school children. *J. Child Psychol. Psychiat.*, **2**, 118–126.

Lunzer, E. A. (1968). Children's thinking. In H. J. Butcher (Ed.), *Educational Research in Britain.* London: University of London Press.

Luria, A. R., and F. I. Yodovich. (1960). *Speech and the Development of Mental Processes in the Child.* (Trans. J. Simon, 1960) London: Staples Press.

McCarthy, D. (1951). Language development in children. In L. Carmichael (Ed.), *Manual of Child Psychology.* New York: Wiley.

McGraw, M. B. (1951). *Maturation of Behaviour.* In L. Carmichael (Ed.), *Manual of Child Psychology.* New York: Wiley.

Maier, H. W. (1966). *Three Theories of Child Development.* New York: Harper and Row.

Miller, G. A. (1962). *Psychology.* Harmondsworth, Mddx.: Penguin.

Mohseni, N. (1966). La comparaison des réactions aux épreuves d'intelligence en Iran et en Europe. Thèse d'université: University of Paris.

Morf, A. (1959). Apprentissage d'une structure logique concrète (inclusion): effets et limites. In J. Piaget (Ed.), *Etudes d'Epistémologie génétique*, vol. 9. Paris: Presses Universitaires.

Munn, N. L. (1950). *Handbook of Psychological Research on the Rat.* Boston: Houghton Mifflin.

Newman, H. H., F. N. Freeman and K. J. Holzinger. (1937). *Twins: A*

Study of Heredity and Environment. Chicago: University of Chicago Press.

N.F.E.R. (1960). National Survey of Attainments: Number Concepts Test (7 plus).

Norsworthy, M. (1906). *Psychology of Mentally Deficient Children.* New York.

Pavlov, I. P. (1964 ed.) *Lectures on Conditioned Reflexes.* London: Lawrence and Wishart. (Also in N. L. Munn (1956). *Psychology,* 5th ed. Boston: Houghton Mifflin.)

Petrie, A. (1952). *Personality and the Frontal Lobes.* London.

Piaget, J. (1950). *The Psychology of Intelligence.* London: Routledge and Kegan Paul.

Piaget, J. (1951). *Judgment and Reasoning in the Child.* London: Routledge and Kegan Paul.

Piaget, J. (1951). *Play, Dreams and Imitation in Childhood.* London: Routledge and Kegan Paul.

Piaget, J. (1952). *The Language and Thought of the Child.* London: Routledge and Kegan Paul.

Piaget, J. (1952). *The Child's Conception of Number.* London: Routledge and Kegan Paul.

Piaget, J. (1953). *Logic and Psychology.* Manchester: Manchester University Press.

Piaget, J. (1953). *The Origin of Intelligence in the Child.* London: Routledge and Kegan Paul.

Piaget, J. (1966). Nécessité et signification des recherches comparatives en psychologie génétique. *Int. J. Psychol.,* **1,** No. 1, 3–13.

Piaget, J. (1969). *Six Psychological Studies.* (Ed. David Elkind.) London: University of London Press.

Piaget, J. (1969). *The Mechanisms of Perception.* London: Routledge and Kegan Paul.

Piaget, J., and B. Inhelder. (1941). *Le Développement des Quantités chez l'Enfant.* Neuchâtel: Delachaux et Niestlé.

Piaget, J., and B. Inhelder. (1969). *The Psychology of the Child.* London: Routledge and Kegan Paul.

Pinard, A., and M. Laurendean. (1969). 'Stage' in Piaget's cognitive-developmental theory: exegesis of a concept. In D. Elkind and J. H. Flavell (Eds.), *Studies in Cognitive Development.* New York: Oxford University Press.

Porteus, S. D. (1947). *The Porteus Test Manual.* London: Harrap.

Price-Williams, D. R. A. (1961). A study concerning concepts of quantities among primitive children. *Acta Psychol.,* **18,** 293–305.

Price-Williams, D. R. A., Ed. (1969). *Cross-Cultural Studies.* Harmondsworth, Mddx.: Penguin.

Raven, J. C. (1947). *Progressive Matrices*. London: Harrap.

Reed, H. B. (1946). *J. exp. Psychol.*, **36**, 71–87, 252–261.

Robertson, J., and J. Bowlby. (1952). Quoted in Yarrow (1961).

Schonell, F. J., and F. E. Schonell. (1958). *Diagnostic and Remedial Teaching in Arithmetic*. Edinburgh: Oliver and Boyd.

Shirley, M. M. (1951). In L. Carmichael (Ed.), *Manual of Child Psychology*. New York: Wiley.

Sigel, I. E., and F. H. Hooper, Eds. (1968). *Logical Thinking in Children*. New York: Holt, Rinehart and Winston.

Sinclair-de-Zwart. (1969). In D. Elkind and J. H. Flavell (Eds.), *Studies in Cognitive Development*. New York: Oxford University Press.

Skard, A. G. (1968). Personal Communication.

Smedslund, J. (1959). Apprentissage des notions de la conservation et de la transivité du poids. In J. Piaget (Ed.), *Etudes d'Epistémologie génétique*, vol. 9. Paris: Presses Universitaires, pp. 85–124.

Smedslund, J. (1961). The acquisition of conservation of substance and weight in children. *Scand. J. Psychol.*, **2**, 203–210.

Smoke, K. L. (1932). An objective study of concept formation. *Psychol. Monogr.*

Spalding, D. A. (1890). In W. James (Ed.), *Principles of Psychology*, vol. 2. New York: Holt.

Spitz, R. A., and K. Wolf. (1946). Quoted in Yarrow (1961).

Stafford-Clark, D. (1965). *What Freud Really Said*. Harmondsworth, Mddx.: Penguin.

Stern, C. (1949). *Children Discover Arithmetic*. New York. (London: Harrap, 1953.)

Strauss, A. A., and L. E. Lehtinen. (1947). *Psychopathology and Education of the Brain-injured Child*. New York: Grune and Stratton.

Tanner, J. M., and B. Inhelder, Eds. (1956). *Discussions on Child Development*. London: Tavistock.

Terman, L. M., and M. A. Merrill. (1937). *Measuring Intelligence*. Boston: Houghton Mifflin.

Thomson, R. (1958). *The Psychology of Thinking*. Harmondsworth, Mddx.: Penguin.

Thorndike, E. L. (1922). *The Psychology of Arithmetic*. New York.

Thorndike, E. L. (1924). Mental discipline in high school studies. *J. educ. Psychol.*, **15**, 1–22, 83–98.

Thorndike, E. L., and R. S. Woodworth. (1901). The influence of improvement in one mental function upon efficiency of other functions. *Psychol. Rev.*, **8**, 247–261, 384–395, 553–564.

Triandis, H. C. (1964). Culture and cognition. In L. Berkowitz (Ed.), *Advances in Experimental Social Psychology*, vol. 1. New York: Academic.

Triandis, H. C. (1969). *Cross-Cultural soc. Psychol. Newsletter*, **3**, No. 1, Issue 18.

University of Leeds (1958). Inst. of Educ. Researches and Studies. No. 17, Jan.; No. 18, July.

University of Birmingham Educational Review (1955). Vol. 7, No. 2.

University of Birmingham Educational Review (1955). Vol. 8, No. 3.

Valentine, C. W. (1946). *The Psychology of Early Childhood*, 3rd ed. London: Methuen.

Valentine, C. W. (1956). *The Normal Child*. Harmondsworth, Mddx.: Penguin.

Vernon, P. E. (1965). *The Measurement of Abilities*, 2nd ed. London: University of London Press.

Vernon, P. E. (1969). *Intelligence and Cultural Environment*. London: Methuen.

Vernon, P., and T. Husen. (1951). *Theoria*, **17**, 61–68.

Vygotsky, L. S. (1962). *Thought and Language*. (Trans. E. Haufmann and G. Vaker, 1962) Mass.: M.I.T. Press.

Wallace, J. G. (1965). *Concept Growth and the Education of the Child*. Slough, Bucks.: National Foundation for Educational Research.

Wallach, Lise, and R. L. Sprott. (1960). Inducing number conservation in children. *Child Dev.*, **35**, 1057–1071.

Watson, J. B. (1930). *Behaviourism*. New York: Norton. (Also in N. L. Munn (Ed.), *Psychology*, 5th ed. Boston: Houghton Mifflin, 1956.)

Wechsler, D. (1944). *The Measurement of Adult Intelligence*. Baltimore: Williams and Wilkins.

Weigh, E. Z. Quoted in Humphrey (1951).

Welch, L., and L. Long. *J. Psychol.*, **9**, 59–95.

Williams, A. A. (1958). Number readiness. *Educ. Rev.*, **11**, 31–45.

Willington, G. A. (1967). The development of mathematical understanding in primary school children. Unpublished M.Ed. Thesis: Manchester University (Experiment 3).

Wohlwill, J. F. (1968). *Child Dev.*

Wohlwill, J. F. (1968). In I. E. Sigel and F. H. Hooper (Eds.), *Logical Thinking in Children*. New York: Holt, Rinehart and Winston.

Woodworth, R. S. (1950). *Experimental Psychology*. London: Methuen.

Yarrow, L. J. (1961). Maternal deprivation: toward an empirical and conceptual revaluation. *Psychol. Bull.*, **58**, 459–490.

Yerks, R. M., and L. Bloomfield. *Psychol. Bull.*, **7**, 253–263.

List of books by Piaget

The dates given throughout the text are the publication dates of the English translations of these works.

Inhelder, B., and J. Piaget. (1958). *The Growth of Logical Thinking from Childhood to Adolescence*. London: Routledge and Kegan Paul. (New York: Basic Books, 1958.)

Inhelder, B., and J. Piaget. (1964). *The Early Growth of Logic in the Child: Classification and Seriation*. London: Routledge and Kegan Paul.

Piaget, J. (1932). *The Moral Judgment of the Child*. London: Routledge and Kegan Paul. (Glencoe, Ill.: Free Press, 1948.)

Piaget, J. (1950). *The Psychology of Intelligence*, London: Routledge and Kegan Paul. (New York: Harcourt, Brace and World, 1950.)

Piaget, J. (1951). *The Child's Conception of the World*. London: Routledge and Kegan Paul.

Piaget, J. (1951). *Judgment and Reasoning in the Child*. London: Routledge and Kegan Paul.

Piaget, J. (1951). *Play, Dreams and Imitation in Childhood*. London: Routledge and Kegan Paul. (New York: Norton, 1951.)

Piaget, J. (1952). *The Child's Conception of Number*. London: Routledge and Kegan Paul. (New York: Humanities Press, 1952.)

Piaget, J. (1952). *The Language and Thought of the Child*. London: Routledge and Kegan Paul.

Piaget, J. (1953). *The Origin of Intelligence in the Child*. London: Routledge and Kegan Paul. (New York: International Universities Press, 1952.)

Piaget, J. (1953). *Logic and Psychology*. Manchester: Manchester University Press. (New York: Basic Books, 1957.)

Piaget, J. (1955). *The Construction of Reality in the Child*. London: Routledge and Kegan Paul. (New York: Basic Books, 1954.)

Piaget, J. (1969). *Six Psychological Studies*. London: University of London Press. (New York: Random House, 1968.)

Piaget, J. (1969). *The Child's Conception of Movement and Speed.* London: Routledge and Kegan Paul. (New York: Basic Books, 1969.)

Piaget, J. (1969). *The Mechanisms of Perception.* London: Routledge and Kegan Paul. (New York: Basic Books, 1969.)

Piaget, J., and B. Inhelder. (1941). *Le Développement des Quantités chez l'Enfant.* Neuchâtel: Delachaux et Niestlé (2nd ed. 1962).

Piaget, J., and B. Inhelder. (1951). *La Genèse de l'Idée de Regard chez l'Enfant.* Paris: Presses Universitaires.

Piaget, J., and B. Inhelder. (1956). *The Child's Conception of Space.* London: Routledge and Kegan Paul.

Piaget, J., and B. Inhelder. (1966). *L'Image mentale chez l'Enfant.* Paris: Presses Universitaires.

Piaget, J., and B. Inhelder. (1969). *The Psychology of the Child.* London: Routledge and Kegan Paul.

Author index

Numbers in italics indicate pages on which full bibliographic details can be found.

Subject index